COMPLETE BOOK OF BASKETBALL POST PLAY

Complete Book of Basketball Post Play

Terry D. Battenberg

Parker Publishing Company, Inc. West Nyack, N.Y.

Library of Congress Cataloging in Publication Data

Battenberg, Terry D
Complete book of basketball post play.

Includes index.
1. Basketball coaching. 2. Basketball--Offense.
I. Title.
GV885.3.B37 796.32'32 78-7704
ISBN 0-13-155960-5

Printed in the United States of America

HOW THIS BOOK WILL HELP YOU

During my coaching career, I have found the "post position" to be the most important part of any basketball team. Whether the post man is used as a screener, rebounder, defensive intimidator, or scorer, he is the backbone of many attacks.

Good post play is often ignored by coaches simply because they do not understand the position. Many basketball coaches were guards or forwards in their playing days, so their philosophy centers around the position they understand best. This book is for coaches who want to develop a stronger post position. It is for coaches who want to develop a recently acquired tall player, and for coaches who want to expand their guard-oriented offense to include more front line scoring. In short, it is intended for every coach from elementary level up to college and even professional basketball.

Regardless of the size of your players, you can have effective post play. This also applies to the guards and forwards who should utilize the principles of my post philosophy. In essence, I try to develop a whole team of "effective post players." While height is very much desired in the post area, knowing what to do in that area is more desirable.

This book will help you develop all of your players. I do not believe in waiting for tall talent to come to me, but rather, develop what talent I have to its fullest potential. I picked up a saying a while back that typifies my theory of basketball. It is: "PUT PRESSURE ON THE HOOP." This can be done by any player, at any time, against any opponent. You do not need a tall player to put pressure on the basket, the defense, and the opponent.

Many coaches are looking for an offense that will allow them to score inside. Later chapters explain single, double, and triple post offenses. However, I want to stress that the theories presented are good for any offense, defense, or system of play. Most defenses rely on protection of the post area, so the defensive theories in this book will be helpful to all coaches. Just about every offense looks to score around the basket, therefore, my post theory will also be helpful. My ideas are presented in such a way that you can take whatever you want from this book, and incorporate it into your style of play.

There is truth to the idea that "a strong post man is the backbone of a team," so much of this book will be geared to the center position. Chapters are included on extra tall centers and the posting of any player. This covers post play for every type of player, but keep in mind the key is the use of the post man.

Terry D. Battenberg

Table of Contents

Acknowledgments

I wish to express my thanks to the many coaches with whom I have worked in my coaching career.

Credit must especially go to my former assistants Jeff Kester, Len Stevens, and Gary Weber. Each helped to initiate my interest in the POST POSITION.

Special thanks go to Sharon Kramarich for correcting and typing the manuscript. Without her help, this book would never have been finished.

To Skip Shuman, I express my gratitude for photographing and developing the pictures in this text. Also, a special acknowledgment to the subjects in the photos: Ken O'Brien, Tim Ridge, Oscar Bugarin, and Marvin Penner.

T.B.

KEY TO DIAGRAMS

Offensive player	Ⓟ OR P
Defensive player	5 (in square) OR □
Player with ball	Ⓖ• OR G•
Path of dribble	(wavy line with arrow)
Path of player	(solid line with arrow)
Pass	(line with cross ticks and arrow)
Screen	(line ending in bracket)
Potential path of pass	- - - - - →

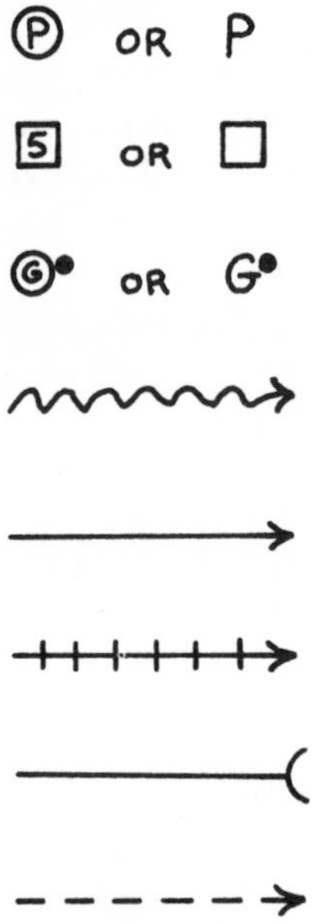

1

EIGHT REASONS WHY POST PLAY IS IMPORTANT

There are essentially eight important ways that strong post play will help you.

1. Post Men Shoot Higher Percentage Shots

Post men play nearer the basket, so they shoot easier shots. Given a choice between a shot at twenty feet or one at five feet, most players would choose the closer. No matter how tall they are, post men usually shoot inside bank shots, easy lay ups, and short hooks. All of these goal attempts are better percentage shots than guards or forwards generally get. Check the statistics in any college or pro league. Who has the highest field goal percentages? More often than not, post men dominate this statistical area.

2. Post Men Can Draw More Fouls

Trying to stop an opponent underneath the basket can be quite a test. It requires a lot of physical contact to limit a player going to the hoop. Often, the choice is between giving up an easy shot or fouling. A player who is constantly going to the goal will draw more than his fair share of free throws. Fouling a guard shooting a twenty foot shot is ridiculous, but it is very hard to restrain one's self from fouling around the basket.

The more fouls your team draws, the sooner you will be in the "one and one" bonus situation. Every coach knows the importance of this extra advantage, so drawing more fouls can lead to more victories.

3. Post Men Can Get More Three-Point Plays

Your post man is nearer the basket and is playing in a contact zone, therefore, he will be fouled more often while attempting to shoot. Since he is shooting a higher percentage shot, the post man will have more opportunities for three-point plays. Short bank shots and muscle lay ups are less affected by the contact of a foul, as compared to the effect of contact on a twenty foot jump shot.

4. Post Men Can Foul Out Opponents

In point number two, I suggested how you can draw more fouls with a post man. College and high school basketball allow only five fouls per player in a game before disqualification. If your post man can draw five fouls on his opposing center, then you have eliminated a vital part of your opponents' team. Without a post man, your opponents usually lose their rebounding and scoring punch. My teams have won many games because we eliminated a star from the game on fouls. It has often been said that my team would never have won a particular game if "Mr. Superstar" of the opponents had not fouled out. This may be true, but basketball is played at both ends of the court. If an opponent cannot play good post defense, then he has no business beating your team.

Sometimes you will not foul out the opposing center, but you will get him into enough foul trouble to alter his game plan. Three fouls on a center in the first half will usually result in one of two adjustments by the opposition. Either their center will slack off and play under extreme caution, or a substitute will take his place. In either case, your opponents have weakened their attack, and you have gained a big advantage.

My 1969 Jesuit High School team won the Sacramento Tournament of Champions from a more powerful Hiram Johnson High School team, due to fouls. The Johnson team featured 6-foot 11-inch Neil McCoy and 6-foot 6-inch Edison Hicks, who were two of the finest players to come out of Sacramento. My Jesuit team featured 6-foot 10-inch High School All-American Mark Wehrle.

Hicks and McCoy battled Wehrle for three quarters, and Johnson High School easily led most of the game. Late in the third quarter, Wehrle got his fourth foul. The two Johnson High stars were also in foul trouble, so it appeared to be a question of who fouled out first. I chose to rest Wehrle and go with my 6-foot 6-inch inexperienced sophomore, Ron Czarnecki. Ron turned to the basket the first time he got the ball, and Edison Hicks quickly picked up his fifth foul! With Hicks gone, it was anyone's game. Midway through the fourth quarter I put 6′10″ Wehrle back in, and he quickly fouled out a less experienced Neil McCoy. My Jesuit team went on to win 64-62, while Wehrle led all scorers with 32 points.

People often asked me afterwards what special instructions I had given my players. It was simple. "Give the ball to Wehrle." Mark Wehrle was a very intelligent ball player who knew his post moves well. Our game plan was always to force our opponents to defend and stop Wehrle. Usually Mark was unstoppable around the basket, but sometimes we beat better teams because he fouled out their stars.

It helps to have a great player like Mark Wehrle, but I have used lesser talents, shorter post men, and even guards at the low post to accomplish the same motives. If you use your post man, he will draw a lot of fouls.

5. Post Men Can Put Pressure on the Opponents' Team Defense

When your post man scores a lot of points under the basket, the pressure is on your opponents to stop him. They have to adjust their defense by sagging off of other players or by performing their normal defense perfectly. This will either leave your outside shooters open for easy set shots, or wear out the defensive man guarding your post man. Whichever the opponents choose, you have put them at a disadvantage.

If you develop your post man, he will have many moves to use on the opponent. This tends to put pressure on the opposition because their post man must concentrate on defense. Post defense is difficult to play because of its close relationship to the basket. While defensive post men can often help out a guard who has lost his man, there is usually no one to help the post when he makes a defensive mistake. Post defense is one on one at ten feet! It is the most difficult defense to play correctly, so you should force your opponent to show how well he can play it.

6. Post Men Can Provide the "Extra" Defensive Help

The post man is also very valuable on defense. A tall player can develop into a fine shot blocker and intimidator. Even if your center is only average sized, he can be very helpful in protecting the basket. When the guards happen to lose their men on driving situations, your post man has an opportunity to help stop easy lay ups. Most man-to-man defenses are based on turning the ball into the key area. This provides for weak-side help and good team defense. Turning a dribbler into weak-side help and a big center can be very effective. Even if the pivot man is not adept at shot blocking, he can discourage many small drivers.

If you are fortunate enough to have a very tall center, then intimidation is added to your defensive weapons. Offensive players sometimes change their shooting style when facing a tall opponent. The shots may be hurried, arched higher, or taken from a longer range. A big man can cause all of these shot discrepancies by his mere presence.

While few coaches are lucky enough to have a real tall center, they can still develop intimidation through post man help. Helping out on loose drivers, drawing offensive fouls, and containing the dribbler are all ways the average-sized post man can help his team's defense. The center often protects the key area for a basketball team just as a middle linebacker shuts off the middle in football. He is the key to sound team defense.

7. Post Men Can Provide the Edge in Rebounding

Having the tallest player on the court does not always mean your team will have the edge in rebounds. Collecting missed shots takes hard work and determination. Proper techniques in screening out and going for the ball can aid in rebound development. Whether your post man is 6-foot 2-inches or 6-foot 10-inches, he will only be a good rebounder if he is determined and has been taught the proper techniques.

Height is desirable in rebounding, but instead of waiting for a tall center to come into his program, the coach should develop his existing front line players. Good rebounding goes hand-in-hand with great defense. Limiting your opponents to one shot each time they have possession is a key to solid defense. Offensively, fast breaking is nearly impossible without domination on the defensive boards. Offensive rebounds provide your team with second and third attempts at the goal. Yes, strong rebounding from the post area is required because: *The team that controls the boards, controls the game.*

8. With a Post Attack, Close Games Are More Easily Won

This, I consider to be the key to my eight reasons for developing the post man. By developing your post man, you have a continuous threat throughout the game. Special defenses and plenty of hustle can thwart the efforts of a good post man, but special defenses and hustle have a way of breaking down at the end of games. Players get tired of putting forth the extra effort it requires to stop a good inside scorer. Suddenly, the post man breaks loose for five quick baskets at the end of a close game and leads his team to another victory.

I find it very comforting to know I have a post man to go to at the end of a close ball game. I know that my center will shoot a higher percentage shot, has a good chance of getting fouled in the act of shooting, and will often intimidate the opponents on defense. The only coaching that really needs to be done is convincing my team to pass to the post man. Any coach who is worth his salt can surely accomplish this.

Now that you have read the eight reasons why you should develop your post men, are you convinced? Well then, get busy! Look through your entire program and see if a future tall boy is waiting to become a superstar.

If after looking through the entire basketball program you still cannot find a big one, do not give up! Find the boys who are tough enough to play inside, even if they are only 6-foot 2-inches, and follow the principles discussed in the following chapters. Remember, the post is the key position in basketball, so develop your post man, no matter what size he is. I have had only one team with a player over 6-foot 7-inches in my ten years of coaching, yet all of my front line men have learned to be good scorers from the post position. Your biggest player may only be 5-foot 10-inches, but he can still be a good post player.

I guarantee that the principles and fundamentals in this book will not only develop your big man, but also make your short boys play "big" too. In a year or two *you* could be coaching an all-star post man, or better yet, a powerful championship team.

2

ESTABLISHING A LOW POST THEORY

The post man can be a very effective offensive weapon when he is used close to the basket. The constant threat of the pivot man standing and moving in the area near the backboard puts continuous pressure on the defense. This area around the basket is commonly referred to as the "low post." The "low post" can be defined as the area along the free throw lane, from the baseline up to and including the second free throw rebounding position. In extends approximately three feet outside the lane and ten feet in front of the basket. (Diagram 2.1.)

LOW POST PHILOSOPHY

Standing the center under the basket does not guarantee a good low post attack. There are eight important points that the coach must establish before the low post will develop into a scoring threat.

1. Your Post Men Must Spend Much of Their Offensive Time Under the Basket

An offense built around a high post will offer few inside scoring opportunities for the center. He should establish a low post position whenever possible.

2. Your Team Must Always Be Looking to Get the Ball Inside

This is the "Inside-Out Theory," where the offense is always looking to score inside first. When the defense jams the inside scoring areas, outside shots will be open and easier to make.

3. Post Men Must Look to Score Every Time They Get the Ball Inside

Post men who get the ball five feet from the basket, then pass it back out to a guard right away, are not effective low post men. I discourage my players from dribbling away or passing away from the basket once they have possession in the internal zone. The low post area is a "contact zone," so the ball should be taken to the hoop with the assumption that the shot will go in or a foul will be drawn.

4. Post Men Must Be Able to Read the Defense and Perform the Appropriate Move

Players must be aware of the defenders around the internal zone. Fakes may lead to easy lay ins and/or draw foul shots. Good shot attempts are also important. There is no excuse for "hope shots" or "fancy shots" in the internal zone. Every shot attempt is expected to go in the basket if the shooter is not fouled in the act of shooting. Through experience, players will learn to score around the basket even when fouled.

5. The Dribble Is Dangerous for Low Post Men and Should Be Used with Discretion

Dribbling wastes time: it slows the potential scoring move, allows the defense time to adjust, and provides smaller players a chance to steal the ball. The dribble should be used only when a post man goes directly to the basket. In most cases, no more than one dribble will be necessary.

6. Post Men Must Keep the Ball High When It Is in Their Possession

It is recommended that post men do not bring the ball below their chest. They should protect and keep it in a ready position for a quick shot.

7. Other Players Can Flash into a Low Post Position

This is a good way to take advantage of mismatches and weak defenders, however, one constant threat at the low post is the most consistent attack.

8. The Coach Must Devote Practice Time to the Development of Post Play

If a coach wants to strengthen his low post attack, then a segment of every practice must be devoted to this area.

This brings me to an area of discussion that you should consider right now. Do you want a stronger post attack? Obviously you do, or you would not be reading this book. Is it important enough to your team's future that

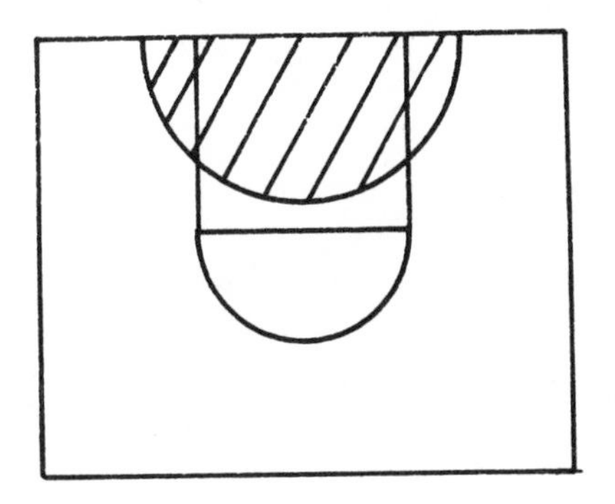

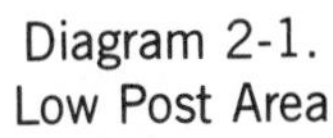

Diagram 2-1.
Low Post Area

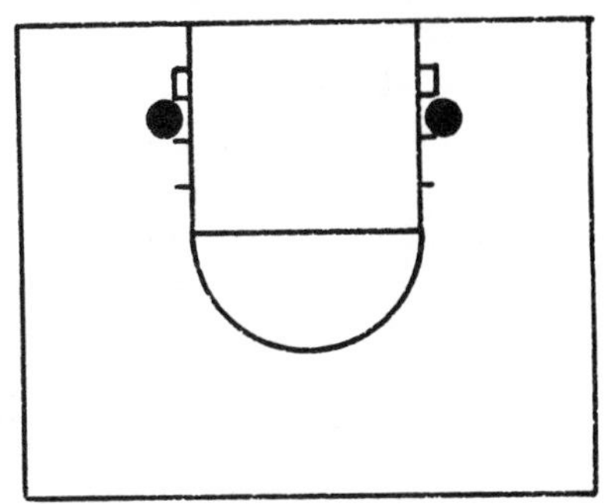

Diagram 2-2.
Relative Position of
Low Post

you will spend practice time on post play? If you are having trouble coming up with an answer, then consider this question. What position do you believe is the "key position" on a basketball team? Nine out of ten coaches I interviewed said "the post" was the key position. Do you agree? Do you treat post play as if it were the key to your team? Do you devote a fair amount of practice time to development of post play?

I spend fifteen to forty-five minutes during each practice on drills involving post play. The front line players spend more time on post moves than the guards, but every day all of my players practice scoring from the low post. Extra time is often spent at the beginning or end of practice with the post players. Quaterbacks spend extra time working out in football practice. Pitchers work longer and harder at baseball practice. They are the "key positions" in their particular sports, so the "key position in basketball" should also work longer and harder.

Many basketball coaches like to emphasize the amount of practice time they spend on defense, fast breaking, and conditioning. I contend that a fifteen to thirty minute session should be included in most practices to work on post play and post men. If you hope to teach your players a solid post attack, then you must work on it in practice.

RELATIVE POSITION OF LOW POST

Since the low post area is limited by the "three second rule," the best spot to establish low post position is the second free throw rebounding lane. The first and second free throw rebounding lanes are divided by a blocked-out rectangle. Post men should always try to establish a "relative position" above this rectangle. This affords the most advantages for low post moves, and it gives the player an easy visual spot to align himself. (Diagram 2-2.)

There are several reasons why post men should establish themselves just above the rectangle.

1. It offers an excellent angle for the short bankboard jump shot when a quick baseline front pivot is executed. This is a strong scoring move for a low post man and is a higher percentage shot than a baseline jump shot, which does not use the board.
2. The position offers a good angle for the drop-step, one dribble, muscle shot. This move is a straight power move used by many post men. The foot nearest the baseline is dropped to the basket, one dribble is used to position the player next to the hoop, and the post man lays the ball in the basket.
3. A drop-step toward the mid-key area, with the foot away from the baseline, sets up the post man for a simple hook shot over the front rim of the goal. From this angle, the short hook is as easily executed as a lay up.
4. The position suggested leaves the post man in an excellent offensive rebounding area. If a teammate shoots, the post man is already in position for a tap in. Too often, front line men get too far under the basket to be effective offensive rebounders. Above the "rectangle" is a good place to be positioned for retrieving missed field goal attempts.
5. In this relative position, the defense must choose whether to play the post man in front, behind, baseline side, or top side. This allows more passing angles than a lower post establishment can provide. The post man is near the basket, but he has room to move in any direction to receive a pass, to score, or to rebound.

Whether you wish to have a standing low post or a player moving to the low post, attention should be given to the relative position the post man establishes for himself. A post man operating from too low a post position will have difficulty finding room to maneuver. He will lose the bankboard angle for his jump shot, find himself floating away from the basket on hook shots, and have difficulty in getting passes from teammates. On the other hand, if the player establishes his relative position too high (third rebound lane), he will be operating from a longer shooting distance. The bankboard shot angle becomes smaller, the hook shot is no longer a lay up, and defensive help will jam the post man's moves in the mid-key area.

For simplicity, the relative position above the free throw lane rectangle will be referred to as the *low post* in further discussion.

CHOOSING A SIDE FOR THE LOW POST

Some coaches are successful with offenses which revolve around a double low post attack. Most coaches will find a single low post attack more beneficial, simply because they do not have two good post candidates. Assuming you want to establish a single low post attack, where will you station your post man? You will find that a right-handed player will operate better

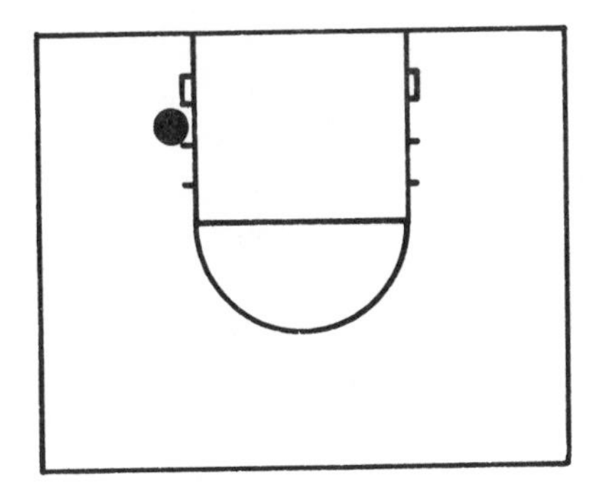

Diagram 2-3.
Left Low Post Position
for Right Hander

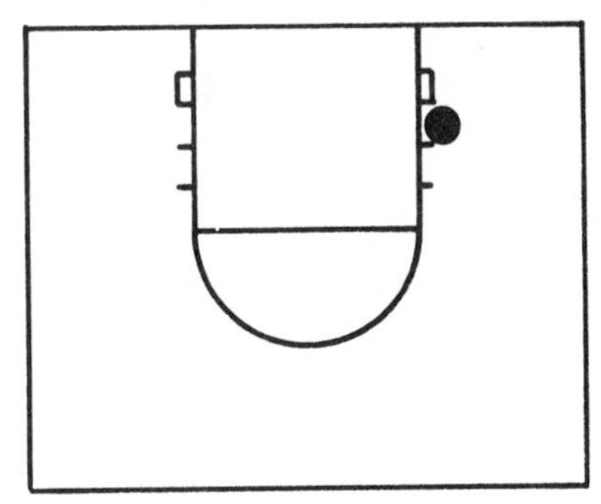

Diagram 2-4.
Right Low Post Position
for Left Hander

from the left low post position. This is the position on the left side of the key, when you are facing the backboard from the free throw line. (Diagram 2-3.)

The front pivot quick bankboard jump shot is easier for the right hander on this side. The shooting hand is next to the backboard, allowing a quick release and an excellent shooting angle. Right-handed players always shoot a better percentage on bank shots from the left side.

Establishing a low post on the left side also allows the post man to shoot a right-handed hook shot, when he turns into the lane. Naturally, right-handed players develop a better right-handed hook shot touch, so the left side low post allows players to shoot higher percentage hooks.

If you have a left-handed post man, place him on the right low post position. He will assume the same advantages on the right side that a right hander has on the left side. (Diagram 2-4.)

Strong consideration must be given to the development of both hands. Effective post men should be able to hook with either hand, tip with either hand, and score from either side of the lane. In order to give the defense "double trouble," a good post man is able to perform his scoring moves from either side of the basket. Make sure that post drills are run from both low post positions, and that players develop both hands.

MANEUVERING TO GET OPEN AT THE LOW POST

One objective of the post man is to receive the ball at the low post with his defensive man behind him. Then the pivot man can use his moves to play one-on-one with the defensive man. Often, good maneuvering will allow the pivot man to break free and receve a pass for an easy score underneath the basket. At other times, the player will be trying to establish himself at his relative low post position. There are essentially ten ways a player can get the desired post position.

1. Set up at the desired low post position and see if the defense challenges the passing lane. If the defense plays behind the low post man, he should have an easy time scoring.
2. Quickly get down to the low post spot before the defense arrives to challenge. This will often happen on a fast break attempt or late in a fast-paced game. Hustle is the key to this posting maneuver.
3. Attempt to gain the low post position. If this attempt is stopped, go away from the defensive challenger and then suddenly move back to the desired spot.
4. Move back and forth across the lane, attempting to gain advantage at one of the low post positions.
5. Set up away from the ball, then have it brought to the weak side. The defensive man must make a quick adjustment to cut off the new passing lane.
6. Roll or move quickly from the high post to the low post.
7. Flash into the low post from a wing position. This maneuver is very good for forwards who desire to post themselves, but it can also serve to deceive a defensive post man.
8. Exchange positions with another post player. This can be done between high or low post men.
9. Work a pick interchange with another post man. A good pick will force the defense to switch assignments and delay their efforts to cut off passing lanes.
10. Work a pick and roll with a guard or forward. This will often force a switch which provides the post man a mismatch situation. The shorter defender will have great difficulty defending against an established post man, and he will often give up an easy basket.

All of these moves are designed to open a passing lane to the low post. The post man will receive a quick pass for an easy lay up, or he will establish a low post position from which he can go one-on-one. Some or all of the ten moves should be incorporated in your offense if you want to establish a scoring threat with your center. I find the pick and roll play to be very valuable in my offense. The other maneuvers involve movement without the ball, which coaches always need to stress to their players.

It should be very apparent by now that the ten maneuvers mentioned can be valuable to all players, including the guards. To establish a total inside game, all players should be schooled in the art of getting open at the low post.

RECEIVING A PASS AT THE LOW POST

Once a player has maneuvered into an open low post position, he must instantly prepare to receive the ball and protect it. The following qualities should be developed in all players operating from the low post.

1. Face the Teammate Who Has the Ball

Post men should always attempt to keep visual contact with the ball. To offer an easy target, the player should keep his body square to the man with the ball.

2. Keep the Hands Up and Ready for Quick Passes to the Post

Showing a hand as a passing target makes it easier for teammates to see open passing lanes. This also indicates to the man with the ball that the post is ready to receive the pass. He has maneuvered to establish position and is now eager to score.

A low post man should offer the hand that is away from the defensive pressure. His palm is always facing the ball and exposing a very visible target. If the defender is positioned on the low post man's left side, he should show a raised right hand as a guide. The left arm, or off-arm, should be flaired out and held rigid. This serves to take up more room and keeps the defender away from the passing lane.

3. Move in the Direction of the Pass

This is one of the toughest habits to teach young post men. Once the player establishes a good low post position, he often feels compelled to hold that particular spot. Post men must realize that defensive men will do all they can to break up passes to the low post. If the defense is going to move to the ball, then the offensive player must also move and beat the defender to it.

4. Come to a Jump Stop, with Good Body Balance

As the player receives the ball, he must establish a solid post position. A jump stop should be performed as the pass is received. This jump stop serves to break the movement of the post man as he meets the pass. The feet should end up shoulder width apart with the weight on the balls of the feet. The jump stop is also important because it allows the player to choose a pivot foot. In the jump stop, both feet hit the floor simultaneously, so no pivot foot has been established. The post man can now move in either direction and pivot off of either foot. This becomes very important in reading defenses. (Photo Series 2-1.)

5. Catch the Ball Firmly, with Two Hands, and Bring It into the Chest Area

The player should receive the ball with his fingertips popping, rather than letting the ball slap into the palms. By catching it this way, he is able to shoot, dribble, or pass without difficulty. It is also important for the ball to be

Photo Series 2-1.
Receiving a Pass at the Low Post

brought into the chest area for protective measures. In this position the hands are still in place to shoot or pass, but the elbows are flaired out to protect the ball.

6. Stay Low by Keeping the Knees Bent

This provides a solid base, allows better maneuverability, and makes the post man quicker. He is in a ready position, and no movement will be wasted.

The same theory of positioning is used for a player receiving a pass inside the three-second zone, but he must be ready to move or shoot right away. In the key, the post man should turn and face the basket immediately, then shoot, drive, or pass off. There is no time to waste in the lane, so a post man must size up the situation quickly.

BASELINE THEORY

We have now maneuvered our player to a desired low post position, and he has received the ball. What next? It is time to score! Remember, the low post philosophy says that a player receiving the ball in the internal zone should always attempt to score. The guards did not work to pass inside just so they could get the ball back. It is the low post man's duty to score when he gets the ball inside, but we do not want a "fancy shot" or "hope shot." We want a high percentage attempt that will result in a field goal or two free throws.

The post man must know what to do once he gets the ball inside. He cannot panic, but he must be relaxed and read the defense. Some great post men can score inside because they have superior skills or size. The average basketball team does not have a "superstar" post man, so intelligent moves must be used. My post men have been very successful using the "baseline theory." This system is based on reading the defense and then making the appropriate move to score. It limits the post man to three basic moves, each based upon reacting to the defensive man's position. I like the system because it gives every player a plan of attack that he can use inside. It is a simple system, but it requires constant practice to keep the reaction time sharp.

What is the baseline theory? Let us backtrack to our post man who has the ball in his possession at the low post. The player has his weight on the balls of his feet, no pivot foot has been established, and the ball is tucked into his chest and protected. Now we want him to score. Right? What is the shot you prefer this post man to score with first? The high percentage lay up shot, of course! To do this, the player will usually have to make a quick and direct move to the basket, around or past the defense. From the low post position, the quickest and shortest route is a one dribble move to the baseline side. Hence, the "baseline theory."

As soon as a player receives a pass at the low post position, he should turn his head and look at the baseline. If the defense is not in position to stop the baseline lay up, then the player should take one dribble directly to the basket and muscle the ball in. Whenever the defense plays the passing lane from the top side, the baseline will usually be open. (Photo Series 2-2.)

The low post man should always look baseline as soon as he gets the ball. He must not move his feet or any other part of his body, except his head. A quick look to the baseline will tell the player which of three basic post moves he can use to get an easy basket.

Besides the baseline driving muscle shot, the post man has two other excellent scoring moves. If the defense is playing off of him to prevent a drive, then the post man should pivot on his foot nearest the baseline and shoot a bankboard jump shot. As mentioned earlier, the low post position provides an excellent angle for the bankboard shot. Through constant practice, the post man can shoot this shot with remarkable accuracy.

If the defense is playing tight and on the baseline side, the player will see this when he turns his head to look. The situation now calls for a drop-step pivot and hook shot. This is an almost forgotten shot in basketball today, but one that is very effective. Shorter post men find the hook invaluable against taller opponents. With a minimum amount of practice, players can add this weapon to their repertoire.

That is the "baseline theory." It is very simple, but very effective. It makes short post men play big, and it makes tall post men almost unstoppable. By turning the head to look at the baseline, a player can immediately decide which high percentage shot to shoot. The system takes practice, daily practice, but it can give your team an "awesome" inside attack. The "baseline theory" can be incorporated into any offense and used by guards and forwards, as well as centers.

It is a proven theory, as many of my former out-sized and out-classed post men can attest. Bill Walton used a similar theory during his fine career at U.C.L.A. The "baseline theory" is the key to developing a successful low post attack.

ELIMINATING UNNECESSARY MOVEMENT

The foot movement used in performing the three basic post moves requires only two types of pivots. These are:

1. The drop step and pivot, which is used on the baseline muscle shot and the hook shot.
2. The front pivot, which is used on the bankboard jump shot and in advanced moves.

The importance of the jump stop should be mentioned again at this time. Pivoting and performing appropriate moves are much easier when the player has a choice of pivot feet. A lot of practice and drill may be required of post

Photo Series 2-2.
Player Looks Baseline for Opening—Defense on Top

men who have poor foot movement. Without proper footwork, low post scoring will be difficult.

The "baseline theory" not only gives a post man some moves to score with, but also serves to eliminate unnecessary movements. Three shots have been recommended to be used by players at the low post. The "baseline theory" suggests a logical order to the shots that a coach desires.

1. The muscle lay up shot.
2. The bankboard jump shot.
3. The hook shot over the front rim.
4. An advanced one-on-one move.

The baseline is the best direction in which to attack the basket because there is little defensive help. Most defenses try to turn the driving opponent into the key where help is available. Often, a post man will be jammed up and forced to shoot an off-balanced shot in the key. The baseline is relatively free of traffic once the offensive player gets by the initial defender. The quick muscle shot move from the low post is the most desirable shot. It is a high percentage shot and is very seldom challenged by helping defenders.

The second most desired move is also a baseline move—the bankboard jump shot. The post man turns to the baseline and notices his defender is playing off to prevent the drive. Since the pivot is to the baseline and no drive is involved, the offensive player can be almost certain his shot will be unchallenged.

The third shot in the sequence is the hook over the front rim. When the baseline is sealed off, the offensive player responds with a quick pivot to the middle of the lane, and then a shot attempt. Although the post man is entering the often congested key area, the quickness of his move should provide an unmolested shot attempt.

The advanced low post moves are covered in chapter 3. They should be introduced only after a player has mastered the "basic three."

The "basic three moves" from the low post give the player control over his situation in the internal zone. He knows exactly what to do with the ball, and the coach knows what he will do. This gives the coach some control over his post men and allows player and coach to work together in defeating opponents. You have rules for players to follow on defense, in offensive patterns, and against pressure defenses. It only stands to reason that you should have rules by which your post men can operate.

Post men often join a basketball team and have no inside moves, or worse, they develop moves which do not offer good scoring opportunities. By presenting the "baseline theory" and the "basic three" post moves, you can give players a strong offensive attack and eliminate poor shot attempts. Unnecessary moves and "fancy shots" usually lead to lower shooting percentages and less effective low post play. Some of the most common of these low percentage moves are:

1. The Cross Under the Basket Lay Up

This is wasted movement that allows more time for the defense to adjust and contest the shot attempt. I insist my players always muscle the ball into the basket from the side they originally started. This challenges the defense immediately and often pressures them into fouling during the shot attempt.

2. The Turn-Around Baseline Jumper

This shot usually comes about because the post man receives the ball too low. He is below the bankboard angle and must shoot directly toward the rim. While many post men seem to develop quite a touch with this shot, I do not like it because it is a lesser percentage shot than a bankboard shot. It should also be considered that defensive contact does not bother the board shooter as much as the rim shooter. Also, the baseline shot leaves the post man in poor rebounding position, if he should miss the shot.

3. The Baseline Hook Shot

This shot was often used twenty years ago and has recently been popularized by Kareem Abdul Jabbar. It provides the same disadvantages as the baseline jump shot.

4. The Fall-Away Jump Shot

This is a favorite of short post men. The fall-away shot is very pretty when it goes in the basket, but it is against my philosophy of "putting pressure on the hoop." Moving away from the basket increases the difficulty of the shot, and again lowers the percentage of its going in. Defensive men are not likely to foul a player shooting this shot because the player is moving away from the target.

5. The Underhanded Flip Shot, or Finger Roll Shot

A coach's nightmare is the best way to define this move. The player attempts to be quick and deceptive with the move, but all he really does is expose the ball to the defense. This shot is often "rejected" by alert defenders, or it spins out of the basket due to its own disastrous english.

I once coached a player at Montana Tech, who loved to shoot this shot. He amazed everyone when one of his "finger rolls" went in the hoop. He was a 6-foot 5-inch 180 pound post man who was not an effective scorer until he stuck to the "basic three." As a "finger-rolling junior," he was not much of an offensive threat. However, during his senior year, he mastered the "baseline theory" and suddenly became a high scorer. He was rewarded by his teammates when he was voted the most valuable player during his final season.

These are the five dreaded low post moves. I want it made clear that I do not condemn players who are successful with any of the previously mentioned moves. I just do not believe in them, and I do not teach them. I certainly would not tell Kareem Abdul Jabbar to forget his "sky hook," or Elvin Hayes to forget his "fall-away jump shot." These players have mastered their shots and are superstars because of the particular move. The "basic three" are for young post men or players who have no effective post moves. This encompasses about 99% of the players from elementary through college basketball.

Teaching the "baseline theory" requires time and patience on your part. I have found that it takes about half of the basketball season before my new players catch on. After one year of exposure to the "baseline theory," most players usually can perform quite well from the low post. High school coaches should instruct their freshman and sophomore level players in post theory. With this basic foundation, the varsity coach will have strong and experienced post players arriving each season. At the college level, we spent a lot of time developing post moves throughout the freshman year. Generally, our centers and forwards were ready for advanced moves during their sophomore or junior year.

Like everything else in basketball, you cannot start teaching post theory too soon. The earlier in the program that you develop good post players, the stronger your varsity will become.

3

COACHING THE LOW POST

Having accepted the low post philosophy and baseline theory, you are now ready to teach the post men how to score. Theories and philosophies in basketball are worthless unless they lead to points on the scoreboard. Since I limit my players on the moves they can use, it is only natural that I teach them solid techniques of scoring. The following pages present detailed descriptions of the proper way to score with the "basic three" and some selected advanced moves.

THE MUSCLE SHOT

The muscle shot is the most important offensive weapon that front line players can develop. It is a power move and is difficult to defend when executed properly. This represents the post man's version of a lay up shot. Since contact is so prevalent around the basket, the muscle shot is the only sure way a post man can protect his right to score in the internal zone.

The muscle shot should always be the first choice of a player receiving the ball at the low post. As the baseline theory states, a player must take the baseline route if it is left unprotected by the defense. Muscle shots are high percentage attacks offering few possibilities for defenders to block the attempt. They often draw fouls and can lead to many three-point plays. The muscle shot is also a great weapon for offensive rebounders. It is the only feasible shot attempt which challenges opponents in the congested rebounding area.

The muscle shot is the first move I teach my post men when introducing the inside attack. It should be used by all players when they find themselves under the basket with the ball. Elementary and junior high coaches can instruct their players in the art of muscle shooting, as it is never too soon to learn. The earlier a player develops the shot, the more of an offensive threat he will be around the hoop.

From the low post, the player should take his normal look to the

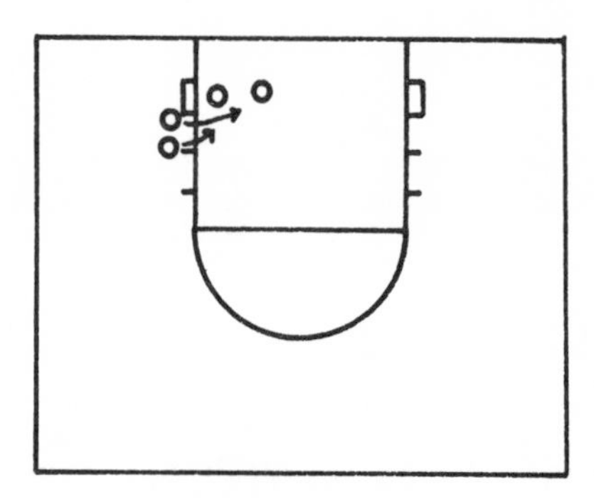

Diagram 3-1.
Foot Positioning of
Muscle Shot

baseline. If a lane is open to the baseline side, the player drop steps to the basket with the foot nearest the baseline. On the left low post side, this would be the right foot. It should be a fairly long step and aimed directly at the basket. This opens the body to the baseline itself but allows the player to protect the ball from the defense with his entire body.

The ball is still in the chest area with the elbows flared out, but the arms are preparing to take one dribble. This one dribble is actually a simultaneous move with the lead step. It is all that is needed to position the offensive player underneath the goal. The dribble should be taken with the hand away from the baseline. This prevents a player from bouncing the ball off of his lead foot and out of bounds. On all post moves, dribbling is discouraged and held to a minimum. However, the muscle shot from the low post is one move that does require a dribble.

The pivot, or back foot, is moved up closer to the lead foot after the dribble is executed. The player should now be parallel and in line with the backboard. (See Diagram 3-1.) His body will come to a jump stop, and he will bring the ball to the chest area again. The knees are flexed and ready to spring, the head is up with the eyes fixed on the basket, and the arms and elbows flaired to protect the ball.

The defender will either be left behind or pinned behind the man with the ball. The offensive player now only needs to concern himself with making a strong move up and to the basket. It is no time to get lazy because contact is imminent.

The offensive player should jump straight up and toward the basket. Both arms must go up with the ball as protection, and the shot is released with a flick of the wrist at the top of the jump. (Photo Series 3-1.)

Muscle shooters should never twist during the jump, but rather stay parallel to the baseline throughout the entire shot. At the conclusion of a muscle shot, check to see that the player has finished parallel to the backboard or baseline.

Photo Series 3-1.
Muscle Shot

During muscle shot attempts, defenders will often try to block the shot from behind. If the offensive player is parallel to the backboard, has his arms flared out, and keeps the ball out and in front of his head during the release, then few muscle shots will be blocked without a foul occurring. More often than not, a three-point play will result if the muscle shot is performed properly.

Players must often be reminded that the muscle shot is a power move and that they should explode toward the basket. They must leap high and hard, as if they were jumping through a barrier. Often there will be a barrier of descending bodies who will try to deflect the shot. The good muscle shooter is never intimidated and will accept contact willingly. He will pride himself in his ability to take punishment and still score. He will realize the advantages of drawing fouls while shooting a muscle shot.

High school coaches will find that football players learn the muscle shot rapidly, and usually become quite adept at scoring with it. If you coach a group that seems to dislike the punishment that goes with muscle shooting, then drill on it daily. One-on-one drills under the basket accustom players to internal contact, and also increase offensive rebounding skills. Basketball is a contact sport, so you might as well condition your players to take it.

THE PUMP FAKE

Before moving on to the two other basic post moves, I feel it necessary to introduce the "Pump Fake." This fake is very useful under the basket following offensive rebounds. It can also be a valuable aid to shorter post men when they try to get off a muscle shot. "The Pump," as we often call it on my ball clubs, throws the defense off balance and renders useless the high-leaping shot blockers.

To be successful, "The Pump" must in all ways appear to be a muscle shot attempt. The offensive player obtains his parallel position in front of the backboard. While keeping his knees bent and butt extended, the shooter fakes a muscle shot by showing the ball to the defense. The feet must remain stationary and the arms should be extended fully overhead. This gives the defender a good look at the ball, and in all likelihood will force him to leave his feet. It is very important to stress to players that the ball must go above the head on the fake. A head or shoulder fake is not needed to draw defenders off their feet. Showing the ball is the key! The body should remain still and ready to power up with the muscle shot once the defender has committed himself. (See Photo Series 3-2.) A good fake will sometimes provide an uncontested shot because the defender will fly completely past the shooter. At other times, the defender will jump on top of the offensive player because he has been thrown off in his timing. No matter what the situation, the offensive player must be ready to shoot once the defender leaves his feet. Three-point plays are only possible when a shot has been taken during a foul.

Photo Series 3-2.
The Pump Fake

Encourage your players to muscle a shot attempt even when the defender is about to land on their backs.

Since the muscle shot usually takes place inside of the three-second lane, an offensive player generally has time for only one "Pump Fake." Encourage your players to challenge the defense with a shot attempt, even if the fake did not draw the defender into the air. Remember, it is better to attempt a shot inside than to back away from the basket. Put "pressure on the hoop" and pressure on the defense. A second fake is not advised because the three-second violation will usually be called. It is better to attempt a well-defended muscle shot, than to lose possession of the ball through a violation.

"Pump Fakes" will also be incorporated in future moves such as the bankboard jump shot and some advanced moves. Faking is an important weapon of all post players, and it goes hand-in-hand with reading and reacting to the defense.

THE BANK SHOT

When the defense becomes wise to the baseline muscle shot, they will often back off and prevent the drive. The short bankboard shot is immediately taken by the post man who reads "loose defense." As long as the offensive player receives the ball above the rectangle, he will be in position to shoot a bank shot.

The post player who flashes across the lane to receive a pass will often be far enough ahead of the defense to shoot an easy board shot. This becomes especially true when the offensive man has a height advantage. A very tall post man will find the bank shot an easy point-getter, even when he possesses a "quickness problem." The quickness of the pivot and release of the bank shot is important, but it becomes less of a factor for a very tall center who towers over the opposition.

The bank shot is easy to learn and should especially be taught to awkward and fast-growing young centers. The visual target is a spot on the board, which is easier to hit than the horizontal plane of a rim. I teach all of my players the board shot because it is easy to learn, requires no great shooting form for consistency, and it takes the pressure off of short shots. I have seen some terrible shooters become excellent marksmen when they use the bankboard. Again, I feel the key is the ease with which a shooter can hit a spot on a vertical plane, rather than lofting a ball out, over, and through a horizontal plane.

If you have never thought the bank shot important, then consider how you teach lay up shots. Most basketball coaches insist their players use the bankboard on lay ups. If you ask yourself why, you will probably come up with the same theory I just explained for the bank jump shot. It is easier to hit a spot!

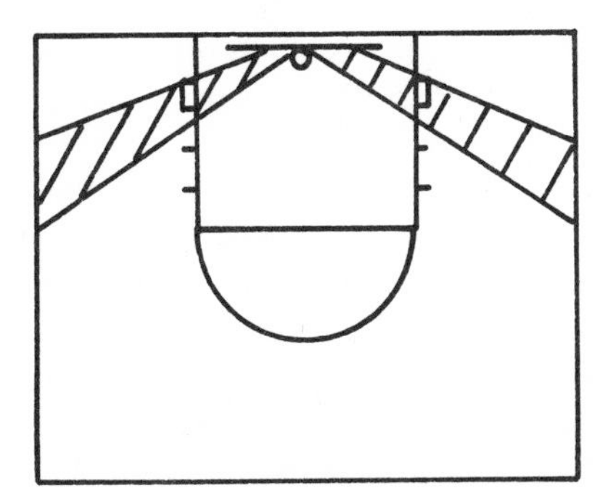

Diagram 3-2.
Bankboard Shooting Angles

Bank shooting can increase the field goal percentage of all players, not just low post men. All it requires is the correct angle. Diagram 3-2 shows the desired areas of accurate board shooting. Notice that the area under the basket includes the release point of good bankboard lay up shots.

Coaches of elementary teams should teach the bank shot to all of their young players. Most youngsters are too small and weak to develop the accuracy and arch needed for set shooting on a ten foot rim. Developing a bank shot will be easier for them and provide enough accuracy to keep them interested in basketball. The habit of aiming at a particular spot on the board will develop the hand-eye coordination necessary for shot development in advanced stages. The youngster who learns a bank shot early will have a valuable weapon throughout his playing career.

Scoring from the low post against loose defense can be as easy as shooting lay ups, when the bank shot is mastered. Following a quick glance to the baseline, the post man realizes the defense is playing off or is late arriving. The player makes a quick front pivot on his foot nearest the baseline. Only a quarter of a turn is necessary as the post man assumes a position parallel to the baseline and bankboard.

For a player on the left low post position, the pivot is on the right foot. The left foot is brought up parallel to the baseline. The opposite is true for the right low post position. The pivot is on the left foot, and the right foot is brought up parallel to the baseline.

The pivot is always made on the ball of the foot; the knees remain flexed and ready to spring; and the ball is protected in the chest area by flared elbows. The arms take the ball up and in front of the head in a position to shoot. This occurs simultaneously with a straight jump up into the air. During the baseline pivot, the eyes should be focused on the proper spot on the bankboard.

Proper shooting style dictates that the shot should never be taken behind the head. Make sure your players keep the ball in front of the head as it is released. The low post bank shot is much the same movement as a muscle shot. The difference lies in the distance from the hoop and the idea of substituting quickness for power.

The continuation of the board shot should bring about a wrist shot. The shooting arm extends straight out with a locked elbow, and the wrist appears broken upon complete release of the shot. This follow-through will provide the soft touch necessary for high shooting percentages. (Photo Series 3-3.)

The shooter should come down in approximately the same general area that he took off. Sometimes, a player flashing across the key will fall away slightly on his turn-around board shot. Because momentum carries the moving player, this is acceptable. However, the player who has established a low post should avoid the fall-away shot. Floating and falling away lead to lower shooting percentages, which all coaches can do without.

The "Pump Fake" can sometimes aid the post man in shooting a board shot. This should be held to a minimum, however, because the "baseline theory" provides easier ways to score against tight defense.

The low post bank shot is an important weapon that should be mastered by all players. It requires a minimum of footwork, provides an easy target, and demands no great shooting touch. If possible, the side-angle board shot should also be used on all inside shot attempts, rather than an over-the-rim technique. Demand this of your players and watch the inside shooting percentages rise.

THE HOOK SHOT

Modern defensive philosophies often call for tight baseline pressure on opponents receiving the ball at the low post. If a defender is continually successful stopping offensive moves to the baseline, then the "muscle shot" and "bank shot" will be difficult to perform. This leaves the obvious attacking zone, the mid-key area. A simple reverse pivot to the middle allows the alert offensive post man to score on a simple hook shot. If the defense is read quickly and the pivot executed immediately, the hook shot often becomes a lay up over the front rim.

The hook was once a very popular shot in earlier days of basketball, but lately has become almost a forgotten art. The hook is a very important member of the "basic three" because it is the counter move for the other two. A good hook shooter is nearly impossible to stop, especially if he is equally effective with his baseline attack.

After a quick look to the baseline, the low post man realizes the defense is overplaying too much. He takes a large back-step into the key, with his foot farthest from the baseline. (See Diagram 3-3.) The step should be straight back into the key, parallel to the baseline, and never away from the hoop.

The back-step should be on the ball of the foot, to allow a smooth and

Photo Series 3-3.
Bank Shot from Low Post

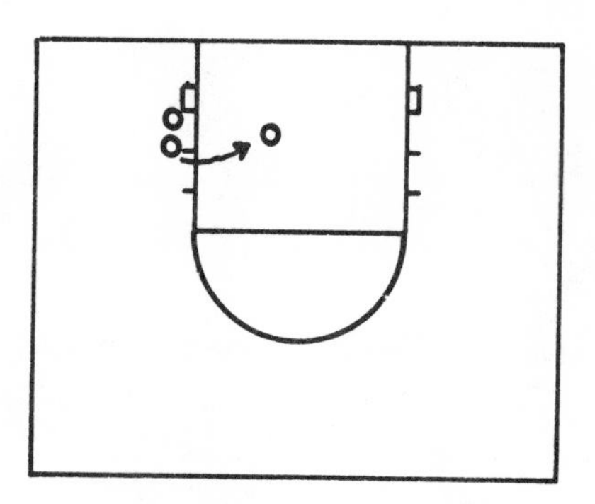

Diagram 3-3.
Drop Step for Hook from
the Left Side

simple pivot. The body swings into the key, using the left leg as an axis. (Left side, right-handed hook shot.) The player must avoid dropping down onto the heel of the left foot, as this could lead to awkwardness or a traveling violation.

The quick drop-step and pivot will place the baseline defender on the post man's back side. The ball should be held about 12 inches from the right side of the head. Both arms bring the ball up so it is protected until released. The body continues to pivot on the left foot, and the ball is released with the body approximately perpendicular to the baseline. (See Photo Series 3-4.)

The right-handed hook shot is a flip of the wrist at the top of the right arm's reach. The left arm is released as the right arm straightens, then it stays out and in front of the head to serve as protection from would-be shot blockers.

The head and eyes are very important to good hook shooting. Players can often get away with last second glances at the target when shooting muscle shots or bank shots, but early visual contact is desired for the hook. The hook shooter must get his head up, and his eyes on the rim as soon as possible during the pivot. Many hook shooters have poor percentages because they fail to look at the target, or they sneak a needless look at the defender. By getting my players to concentrate on the basket immediately, I have improved their percentages.

The hook shot is a soft shot and should be released quickly, yet smoothly, with a flip of the wrist. Since the hook is taken over the front of the rim, a soft touch will allow more shots to bounce into the basket. High arch on the shot is the key to a soft hook shot. With the head and eyes up, right arm extended, and a wrist snap, the hook will usually be soft. Do not allow players to sacrifice quickness for softness in shooting touch. When the guidelines are followed, a quick and soft hook shot is obtainable.

The hook shooter must not be afraid to challenge opponents. Pivoting away from the basket or the defense will not only lead to more missed shots, but also more blocked shots. The offense must go to the basket and try to stay

Photo Series 3-4.
The Right-Handed Hook Shot

close to the defender. The more daylight between hook shooter and defender, the more room the defense has to locate and react to the ball. By keeping the defender on his back side, a hook shooter protects the ball and the shot attempt.

Hooks will seldom be blocked when the defense is on the hip of the shooter. Shot blockers will either foul or react too late. If the defender is allowed enough daylight to take a step to the shooter and leap, then the shot is in danger of deflection. Challenge the defender and go to the hoop! The defense will be at a severe disadvantage.

The hook is a great counter move to the baseline attack. The post man must either look baseline or feel defensive pressure on the baseline, before attempting to attack the middle with a hook shot.

Post men will find the hook shot valuable as a height-equalizer. An offensive man can give up quite a few inches in size and still shoot hook shots over opponents. Coaches with short teams would be wise to develop this weapon for a stronger inside attack.

The side-key hook going toward the baseline is not a good percentage shot. The bankboard is of no visual help at this angle, and offensive rebounding is decreased. By limiting hook shots to the mid-key area, players will always be challenging the defense. This leads to more field goals, higher shooting percentages, extra free throws, and more VICTORIES!

ADVANCED LOW POST MOVES

The "advanced low post moves" should only be introduced after the "basic three" have been mastered. Learning the "basic three" is enough offense for most inside players, and only the more skilled post men should attempt new moves. At the high school and college levels, varsity players should be the only ones introduced to advanced options. Freshmen and junior varsity coaches need to stress fundamentals, which should always include the "basic three." If the fundamentals are learned at the lower levels, varsity coaches will then have sound players to work with. It is up to the head coach to decide what advanced moves will be added, if any.

The coaching personnel should understand that the goals in coaching are to teach players to develop their skills, cooperate and play as a team, and to enjoy the game of basketball. The staff must work together with goals in mind for each level of competition. Again, the basic fundamentals are the key at the lower levels. Fundamentally sound varsities are the result of teaching the fundamentals at earlier levels and reviewing after they have reached the varsity.

THE STEP-THROUGH MOVE

A great counter move to the bank shot is the step-through move. It is very effective against quick, leaping defenders who love to block shots.

Sometimes a low post man may be covered by a quick defender who plays straight up defense. This defender likes to stay between his opponent and the basket, but he uses his speed to step in the path of offensive moves. The step-through is a faking move which momentarily confuses the defender and opens the path to the basket.

The step-through should be set up by scoring off of the basic bank shot first. If the offensive man notices he is being played straight up, the step-through should be considered next.

The post man pivots on his baseline foot and turns as if to shoot the bank shot. Both feet are now parallel to the baseline. Instead of shooting, the offense shows a "pump fake" which should draw the defense to the ball. As described earlier, the knees must remain flexed, the butt low, and the ball should be presented above the head. The fake must, in every way, appear to be a bank shot, but the offensive man must be ready to step by the committed defender.

As the defender leaves his feet or leans toward the ball, the post man steps through and to the basket with his non-pivot or outside foot. When working from the left low post, the left foot is the step-through foot. (Photo Series 3-5.)

The pivot foot is always the one closest to the baseline, just as it is for the bank shot. The offensive man must be sure he does not move this pivot foot during the fake, or a violation will result.

The move requires no dribble, it is quick and quite deceptive. The shot attempt is a short-hook lay up over the front of the rim. Again, the player must be reminded to go to the basket, shoot softly, and never cross under the basket. Sometimes, in practice drills, I allow my taller players to dunk the ball on this move. They like to stuff the ball, of course, and this teaches them to go aggressively to the hoop. It challenges them to jump higher and also to focus visual contact on the rim early.

The step-through is one of my favorite moves to teach because it involves no dribble and attacks the baseline. This minimizes any weak side defensive help and cuts down on turnovers. Remember that the move should only be taught to the more advanced post men because it does require agility.

THE CROSS-OVER MOVE

Facing the same quick, straight-up defender requires a counter to the hook shot, also. The cross-over move was designed to relieve pressure put on hook shooters. After two or three consecutive hooks have been taken, some defenders will anticipate the next one. They will stand on the baseline side of a player at the low post, but mentally they will be geared to swatting away the impending hook. When the offense uses the cross-over move, the defender will be left helplessly flying away from the post man shooting an easy lay up.

Photo Series 3-5.
The Step-Through

While the "basic three" are moves dictated by the position of the defense, advanced moves require thought and planning before initiation. The cross-over seems to work best after two or three successful previous hooks, or after a block or near block of a hook.

To use the cross-over, the post man fakes a hook shot by pivoting on his top foot without stepping back into the key. Since the defender is anticipating a hook, he will be watching the ball and will react to it. Usually the defensive man will leap up and out toward the ball in an attempt to block the shot. This leaves the man with the ball free to cross-over with his lead foot and go to the basket.

The faked hook must be good enough to draw the defender out of position. The leg nearest the baseline should swing around with the arm action as the ball is faked. From the left low post position, the left foot is the pivot and the right leg swings up with the right shooting arm. As the defender sails by, the right leg crosses over the left and toward the basket. This move requires one dribble to position the post man under the hoop for a muscle shot. From the left side, the ball should be placed down with the left hand to avoid the crossing right foot. (Photo Series 3-6.)

A muscle shot is best used at the end of the move because it insures proper balance, take-off, and protects the shooter from defensive help.

You have probably noticed that the counter to the baseline shot is a hook, and the counter to the hook is a baseline muscle shot. The post moves must be kept simple, and I try to keep that in mind. A lot of fancy moves and shots are not necessary to score inside. You have been presented five scoring options using only three very simple shots: the bank shot, hook, and muscle lay up. When the defense is read and analyzed, scoring at the low post can be quite simple. Do not let your offensive post men be their own downfall by attempting moves and shots that are of a low percentage. Limit their inside moves and have them master the techniques. This eliminates confusion and improves your inside attack.

THE JUMP HOOK

Another low post shot that I often teach is the "jump hook." I have found this shot to be quite valuable to the short, heavy post man that we often find at the high school level. It is also an excellent move for the forwards and low posts who flash into the key and receive passes from a high post.

The jump hook uses the entire width of the body to protect the ball from shot blockers. The arm also extends the ball farther away from the defense, as the ball, arm, and body form a straight line to the basket. The non-shooting arm is used the same way as in a regular hook shot—to lift the ball and provide additional protection against defenders.

The offensive man should limit the jump hook to a confined area in front of the hoop. A pass should be received with a jump stop and no pivot foot

Photo Series 3-6.
The Cross-Over

established. The jump hook gets its name because the shooter jumps off of both feet in his attempt at the goal.

Receiving the ball in front of the hoop forces the offensive man to react right away. He has three seconds to shoot, or pass and get out of the key area. Since it is senseless to pass out, once getting the ball underneath the basket, the jump hook becomes very valuable.

Having possession of the ball in front of the basket, the offensive man immediately looks to go to the hoop. If the defense is between the ball and the basket, then a quick shot is needed. By immediately jumping off of both feet, the shot is often on its way before the defense can react. Since the body and hook motion protect the ball, the defense has nothing to block.

The shooting arm should remain straight until a flick of the wrist upon release. The eyes must look up and find the target right away, as in shooting a regular hook shot. If the defense is tight or contacting the offensive man, then the shooter leans slightly into the defender. *Never, never should the shooter fade away or jump backwards.* Challenge the defender by going to the hoop. As long as the forward movement is ever-so-slight, the defender will get the foul call because he is going to the ball. (Photo Series 3-7.)

As mentioned earlier, the jump hook is great for players who flash into the key and receive a pass. Offensive rebounders find this move valuable too, especially when out-sized. The muscular but shorter post men are very successful with the jump hook. They are often too slow to score effectively with a regular hook against taller opponents, but they can protect the ball with their physical size using a jump hook.

Like any other advanced move, the jump hook should only be taught after the "basic three" have been mastered. It is a valuable weapon when properly used by inside players.

PICKING BY THE LOW POST

Although it is best to get the ball to inside players as much as possible, the low post can also be used as a pick setter. The following are suggested ways to use the low post in pick situations, thus opening new avenues of scoring.

1. The low post can pick cutters coming to the ball from the weak side.
2. The low post can form a double pick to free cutters or jump shooters.
3. The low post can pick for the man with the ball to free him for a drive or jump shot.
4. A pick and roll by the post can free him for a pass and easy score.
5. A pick will often force a "switch" by defensive players, thus presenting a mismatch. This allows the low post man to work on a smaller defender.
6. The low post can pick for a high post man or another low post man, thus opening a big man near the hoop.

Photo Series 3-7.
The Jump Hook

The picking post man must be willing to use his body when establishing the "pick and roll." Contact is imminent, so sacrifice is called for. If the picker uses the width of his body, the defender will be lost trying to get around, and a switch will occur. This generally presents the desired mismatch, so the post can go to the hoop and use his height advantage.

The pick by a post man should be perpendicular to the path of a dribbler. This helps the man with the ball to maneuver his defender into the pick and force the switch.

After seeing a switch take place, the picker should pivot on the foot closest to the basket and roll in that direction. The pivot must be a reverse, so the roll man can maintain visual contact with the ball. The lead hand should be raised during the roll to the basket. This gives an easy target for the dribbler to see and pass toward, plus it prepares the roll man to receive a quick pass.

Post men must practice their timing and positioning on pick plays. This will eliminate needless fouls on the offensive end of the court. The pick must remain stationary until the defense has been stopped or performs a switch. The picker should be firmly planted on two feet and motionless a full step before the defense on the dribbler or cutter arrives. Moving picks and illegal picks cause needless turnovers that teams can do without, but a well-executed pick and roll will produce many easy baskets.

FEEDING THE LOW POST

The first rule a coach needs to establish in a post attack is: "Always look inside when first receiving a pass on the offensive end of your court." This will make your team pass and post area conscious. It makes no sense to have a man under the basket if his teammates are ignoring him.

A second rule should be: "Avoid bounce passes to post men." I do not like my teams to use bounce passes at any time, but the feed to the low post is the last place I want to see a bounce pass attempted. A bounce pass is slow, harder to control for passer and receiver, and is too low to the floor for big men to handle. All feeds to the low post should be crisp passes aimed somewhere between the chest and the top of the head. This is the best area for a big man to maintain visual contact with the ball and then grab it.

The third important rule when feeding a low post is: "Hit the target hand; pass away from the defensive man." Young players see the man they want to hit at the low post, but they often fail to notice the position of the defense. A pass carelessly thrown can be knocked away or even intercepted, if the defense is not noticed. When the low post men are taught to put up a target hand away from the defense, a passer can key on this visual aid.

No pass should be forced into a low past man. Post men have means by which to open new passing lanes, so guards and forwards do not have to risk turnovers on poor pass attempts.

Rule four: "Avoid lob passes if possible." They are slow moving and allow the defense too much time to adjust and bat them away. If feeds to the low post are crisp and direct, the defense will be at the mercy of the offense.

The best type of pass to throw to a low post man is a two-handed overhead pass. The feeder does not have to worry about passing around bodies and feet. Only the hands of the defenders will be interfering in the overhead passing zone. The receiver sees the ball as it leaves the passer's hands, and he can maintain visual contact until it is caught.

Fancy passes, trick passes, and surprise passes are poor risks to post men. The congestion and contact under the basket gives the post enough trouble, so keep the feeds simple. Faking, of course, will often be required to open a passing lane. If the feeder puts the ball head-high as he looks inside, he can fake or pass easiliy from this position. (Photo Series 3-8.)

If the defense fronts the low post, the lob pass becomes a possibility. This pass should also be thrown from the overhead position.

A proper passing angle should be considered when feeding the low post. A player on the wing attempting to feed inside should line up with the low post man and the rim. An imaginary line can be drawn from the passer, through the low post, and to the basket. This gives the post man the best chance to create passing lanes and puts the defense at a disadvantage. The best feeding angle is the same court areas used for bank shots. (See Diagram 3-2.) It is not desirable to throw passes of more than fifteen feet, passes from the corner, or from the top of the key. Generally, feed the low post from the wing and turnovers will be decreased, defenders will be disadvantaged, and the low post will score more.

DRILLS FOR IMPROVING THE LOW POST PLAYER

Timing, ball handling, and coordination are three areas that all basketball players need to condition and develop. I try to start each practice session with twenty minutes of individual work. Each player is given a list of drills or fundamentals to work on. These usually include rope jumping, tipping, and review of the "basic three." The players generally work in pairs or groups of three, according to their position.

Some of the drills that I use for low post men are outlined below.

1. Rope Jumping

Jump 200 to 500 times repeatedly, emphasizing quickness one time and raising the knees another time.

2. Tipping

Have your players do ten consecutive tips with one hand, trying to tip the last one into the basket. The ball should be tipped with the fingertips and

Photo Series 3-8.
Feeding the Low Post

never slapped by the palm. Control is important in tipping, and control comes from the fingers. The ball should be tipped six to twelve inches above the plane of the rim. Emphasize development of both the right and left hands. We usually do three sets of ten with each hand, or 60 tips.

3. Medicine Ball Pass

The medicine ball is a fine aid in development of grip. The fingers and wrists are strengthened, if the players catch and pass with the fingertips. When the medicine ball slaps into a receiver's hands, he is catching it wrong. We throw 25 to 50 passes, using both the chest pass and the two-handed overhead pass.

4. Mikan Drill

This drill has been used for many years to develop coordination and timing in big men. The player starts under the basket and alternates shooting a right-handed hook and then a left-handed hook. The proper footwork should be emphasized, and the ball should never touch the floor. This is a great drill for junior high and other beginning players.

5. Explosive Shot Drill

This drill is a good conditioner for the muscle shot and offensive rebounding. The player stands in front of the basket while a teammate tosses the ball off of the rim. The rebounder then takes the ball immediately back up for five consecutive muscle shots. The shooter must always use the bankboard on the shot attempt. He should jump as high and strong as he can each time.

Variations to the drill are also used to improve offensive rebounding. A "pump fake" can be used before the third and fourth muscle shot attempts. I also like to use a small football blocking pad to bump the players as they go up. This gives a game-like effect to the drill and the players always seem to enjoy the contact.

6. Post Moves by Yourself

I teach this drill so that players can work on the "basic three" by themselves. The player starts in front of the rim and lobs the ball toward one of the low post spots. He runs toward the ball, comes to a jump stop as he grabs the ball back, and then performs one of the low post moves. He should immediately follow his shot, and tip or muscle it into the basket if the original attempt missed. After scoring, the player takes the ball out of the net and lobs the ball to the other low post spot. He then runs to the ball and repeats his previous move, this time from the opposite side.

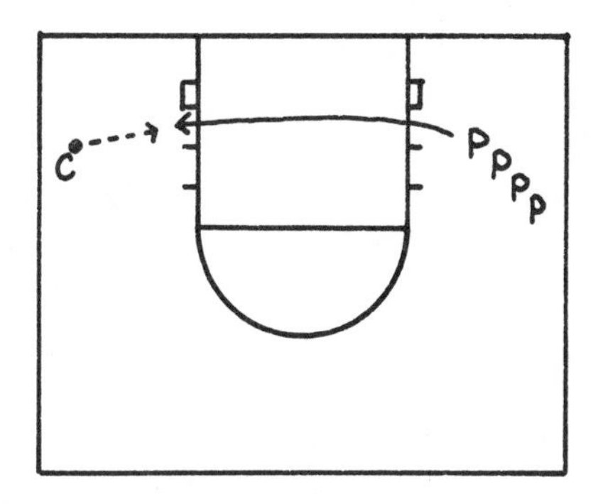

Diagram 3-4.
Group Post Moves

7. Group Post Moves

This is the drill I use to teach post moves and to check up on my players during the season. The group forms a single line at the wing position. The coach has the ball at the opposite wing. (See Diagram 3-4.) The first player cuts across the key with his hands up as a target. He tries to cut to a low post spot above the square. The coach passes and checks for the jump stop, ball protection, baseline look, and proper move. After each post move, I have the shooter follow his attempt with a strong muscle shot. This makes him offensive-rebound conscious and gives him an extra attempt on each turn.

After the coach is satisfied with the progress on one side of the court, the line switches sides and works from the other low post.

8. One-on-One Post Moves

This drill is the same as group post moves, except a defensive man is added. After playing offense, the player becomes a defender on the next man in line. The offensive man now must work to get the ball at low post, and he must read the defense after receiving the ball. The coach can stand behind the backboard and let a manager be the feeder. This will give a better view of the action and make it easier to instruct.

9. Intimidation Drill

I first used this drill at Jesuit High School early in my career. My team was facing a very strong Del Campo High School team which featured a 7-foot center. In order to teach my players to attack the big man and still get quick visual contact on the basket, I played defender and used a tennis racket to block shots. Players often get intimidated by the size of defenders and forget to concentrate on the goal. I use this drill to condition them to seeing the hoop.

I incorporated the tennis racket into some of our group post move drills while at Montana Tech. It helped the players to improve the arch on their hook shots, so it has become a regular part of my drills. If the shooter looks at the racket or hooks a flat shot, I just swat the ball away to the delight of the team. The shooter is allowed another chance to perform correctly, and he generally does.

10. Pressure on the Hoop Drill

This drill is used to teach players to go to the hoop rather then fade away on shot attempts. It is one-on-one at five feet from the basket. The coach has the ball at the top of the key. An offensive man breaks from a low post position to the mid key and receives a pass. He must then turn to the basket and score immediately. (See Diagram 3-5.)

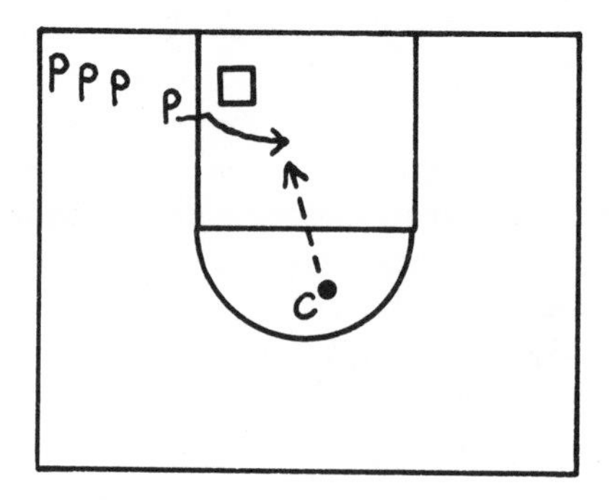

Diagram 3-5.
Pressure on the Hoop Drill

The three-second rule must be firmly implanted in the players heads. There is time for one fake or one dribble, but not both.

A defensive man should be added as soon as the players are attacking the basket correctly. The defender must play behind or to the side of the flash post man. The offense should always go to the basket, and any fade-away attempt is received with displeasure.

These are a few of the drills that can be used for teaching low post moves. You can develop more of your own by creating drills from parts of your offense. Breakdown drills taken from a coach's own offense can be the best practice post men can get. Make post drills that will fit your needs.

4

DEVELOPING BASKETBALL'S HIGH POST

As stated in chapter 3, a low post man is used as a scoring threat at all times. Coaches, however, have flexibility in their use of a high post player. The high post can be used as a pick setter, feeder, and outside shooter, but the basic traits of a low post player are also desirable.

Height is welcomed in a high post man, but is not necessary. Often a mid-sized player makes a much better high post then forward, especially if he is a poor outside shooter. His quickness can be utilized to drive and to position for offensive rebounds. A slow but well-built player also makes a good high post. He can use his bulk to set solid picks for teammates and also to bounce opponents around on the boards.

The single post attack works best with a tall, yet agile high post man. This player is free to move to the low post and use his height, or to work one-on-one from the free throw line. The offensive attack should center around this type of player, as his abilities must be utilized. Pro stars Dave Cowens and Bob McAdoo are superior examples of the agile high post man.

POSITIONING THE HIGH POST PLAYER

A stationary high post could be set up in any one of three spots along the free throw line. (See Diagram 4-1.) The most common choice is the middle of the free throw line because the player can utilize more court space when attacking. This balances the offense and puts the most pressure on the defense.

Stationary high posts are used mostly in multiple-post attacks, such as the double post alignments. These include the 1-3-1, or high-low offense; the 1-4, or double high post offense; and triple post offenses. A more detailed explanation of these set-ups is available in chapter 8.

A player can also flash to the high post from the low post or from a wing position. This movement will create passing lanes and prevent defenses from

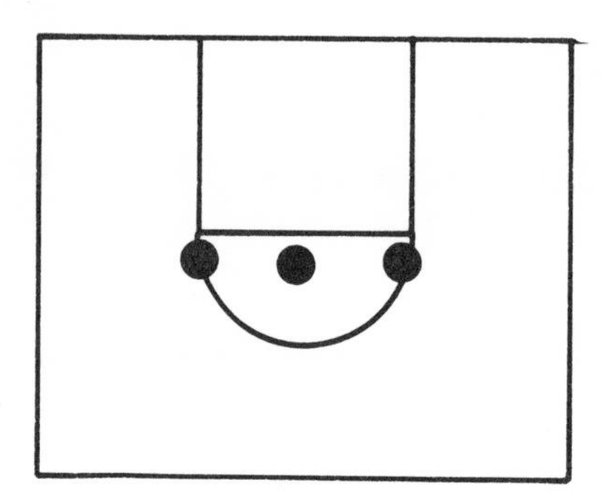

Diagram 4-1.
Relative Positions for
High Post Men

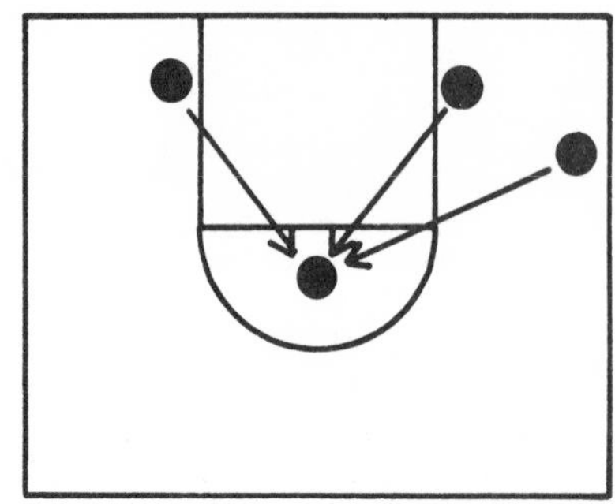

Diagram 4-2.
Flashing the High Post

jamming the high post area. By keeping the free throw line open, the helping defenders cannot sag off and bother your post man. The smart offensive player will then break to the high post with a minimum of opposition. (Diagram 4-2.)

When a player is stationed at the high post, he can use a quick cut to get open at the low post. However, if the defense offers little resistance at the free throw line, then the high post should receive the ball. He can then shoot, drive, or pass to cutting teammates. Every pass made by a team causes the defense to shift and adjust. The high post is the middle of the court and can serve as an effective relay position.

Whether the high post player is moving or stationary, he must meet all passes using a jump stop. Both feet should hit the floor simultaneously to provide a firm base and a choice of a pivot foot. This allows the offensive man to turn in either direction, according to the design of a particular play or the position of the defense.

Whether the high post has the ball or not, he should try to take up as much space as possible. This makes him an easier passing target and also presents a possible pick for cutting teammates.

The high post should put up a hand when he is ready to receive a pass. The defense dictates which hand will be used as a target. If the offensive player feels defensive pressure on his left side, he will offer his right hand as a guide to the passer. Often, the high post will receive no pressure, so the offensive man should offer both hands overhead. This lets his teammates know that he is wide open and anxious to initiate a scoring play.

Some opponents may elect to front your high post and shut off the passing lane. By faking quickly to the ball and then cutting towards the hoop, the post man will free himself for a lob pass and easy lay up. (See Diagram 4-3.) The guards must recognize this situation immediately and be ready to throw the lob. One or two quick lay ups will soon convince your opponents to leave the high post man alone.

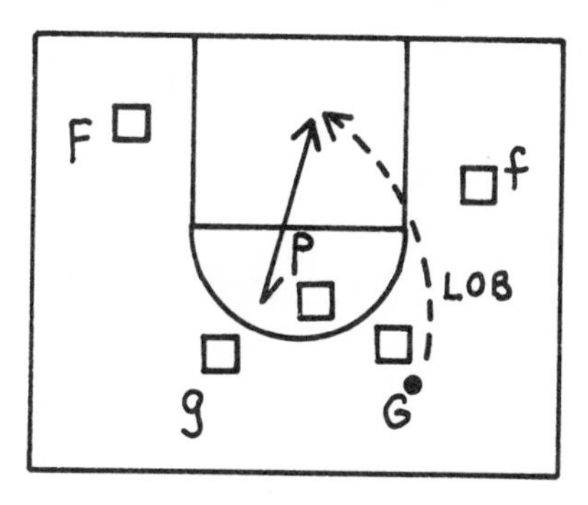

Diagram 4-3.
The Fronted High Post
"Automatic"

The two-handed overhead pass is the best feed to use with high post players. Like the tall low post man, high post men can see the ball better when it is passed at eye level. The more agile post man can handle bounce passes and chest passes.

Passing is another fundamental area that coaches often ignore. Instruct your guards as to the type of feeds you expect them to make to the high post, then work on them in pracitce. Remember, a good passing team will commit fewer turnovers, and thus win more games. Make sure your team knows what type of passes you want used in your attack. It will help you and the team to work better as a unit.

THE HIGH POST AS A FEEDER

One of the important functions of a good high post man is feeding teammates. Unlike the low post, who is under the basket and must always look to score, the high post is 15 to 18 feet away from the basket. He should look for teammates under the hoop or cutting to the goal. If the defense jams the key, the high post can feed another player who may be open for an outside shot.

The high post should have good peripheral vision. This will allow him to quickly see and analyze situations. He must know the intended offensive patterns so he can anticipate the next moves of his teammates.

Pivoting is a key fundamental move of a high post player. Since he will generally be receiving the ball with his back to the basket, the high post man must pivot to become a real threat. When facing the hoop, a player can shoot, drive, or see open cutters. The high post man must "put pressure on the hoop" by facing it!

A pass at the high post is received the same as at the low post. The ball is kept head high with the elbows flaired out. This protects the ball from blind

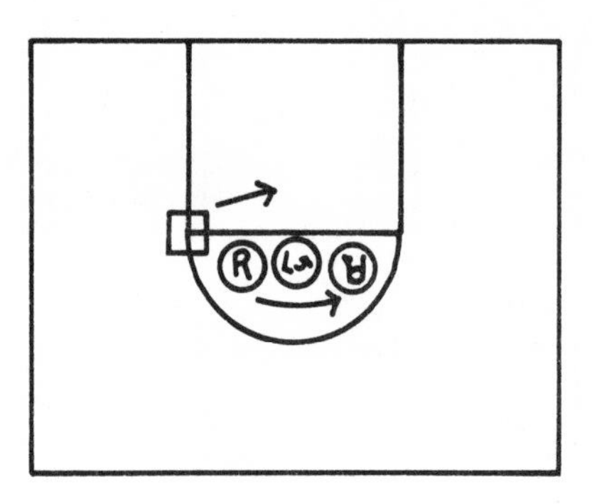

Diagram 4-4.
The Front Pivot for
the High Post

side defenders who will try to poke it away. This position also allows the player to pass or shoot quickly after he pivots to face the basket.

The pivot will usually be a "front pivot" away from any defensive pressure. If the post defender is pressuring the high post man's right side, the offensive man would pivot on his left foot. This is accomplished by crossing the right leg in front of the left and pivoting until facing the basket. (See Diagram 4-4.) The opposite movement would take place if the defense pressured from the left side. If no pressure is felt, the post man has a choice of the type of pivot used. It is important that he face the basket right away, so a front or reverse pivot is acceptable.

The front pivot moves the offensive post man quickly away from defensive pressure. The lateral movement forces the defender to shift quickly, or an easy drive is attainable. The more adjusting required by the defense, the easier it is for the high post to do his job.

The only time I do not have my high post men pivot immediately is on the "backdoor play." I have the post look at the cutter before he pivots. If the cutter is open, he will receive a quick feed for the lay-up shot. When the "backdoor" is covered, the high post pivots rather than passes. This opens many new options and puts pressure on the defense.

After facing the basket, the high post should shoot the jump shot when the defender backs off. If a lane is open to the bucket, then the offensive man has the option to drive. In all instances, the high post man must be alert to possible passing lanes. As the defense adjusts to defend the shot or drive, new scoring options open up. The "assist" is as good as a basket and should be valued as such by the whole team.

The two-handed overhead pass is the best one for high post men to use. The ball is protected, easy to handle, and is exposed only momentarily to the defense. The bounce pass should be learned for "backdoor plays." The chest pass and lob are also important weapons of a good high post feeder.

The post man must be a versatile passer, much like the guards. He can make or break an offense with his passing skills. Drill on this important fundamental area.

SHOOTING FROM THE HIGH POST

The high post player must be skilled in low post moves. He will often move inside and is expected to score when he receives the ball. Besides the hook, bank shot, and muscle shot, the high post man should develop a good jump shot from eighteen feet. This will give him the range needed to force defenders outside, thus opening the potential passing lanes to the low post areas.

High post men who cannot shoot well from the free throw line area are destructive to team offenses. Their defenders will sag off and concede the outside shot, thereby jamming the inside attacking areas. There is hardly anything worse than watching your offense bog down, while the center holds the ball at the high post. It would be foolish to guard the non-shooter; so a poor shooting high post is a detriment to any offense.

In my initial season at Montana Tech College, I ran a single, high post offense. At the center position I substituted two players, 6′6″ Gary Weber and 6′7″ Paul Pryor. I considered both to be inexperienced post men. We had a pressing and fastbreaking attack, so alternating the centers seemed to be the best way to keep a fresh big man on the court.

Pryor was fairly quick and shot well outside. Weber was slower and a poor outside shooter. He was a good rebounder and defender, but "he couldn't hit the ocean if he stood on the beach." It did not take long for our opponents to realize that they could sag off of Weber and stop our offense. As the season progressed, both players developed to the point where I decided to start them together. Pryor made an excellent high post man and Weber was tough at the low post. Our "High-Low Post Attack" (see chapter 8) was a key to a strong finish in the conference that season.

If you use a high post attack, make sure your high post man can hit the outside shot. If he cannot, get him to the low post as soon as possible. Teach post men to shoot in the off season and while they are in the lower programs. Instruction and observation are always needed at every level, but be sure to teach the fundamentals of good shooting early. Aim to have a whole varsity team of good shooters.

The jump shot is fairly simple to learn around the free throw line area. The distance and visual background is very similar to the free throw shot, so a high percentage can be expected. After pivoting to face the basket, the player should be standing comfortably on both feet with his weight evenly distributed. The feet are shoulder width apart, the knees flexed, elbows flaired, and the ball is in front of the head. If the player wants to shoot, he should jump straight up and take his jump shot. No dribble is needed and should be discouraged unless driving inside. A shot is quick and deceptive enough to baffle defenders. Emphasize a straight jump with no float forward, sideways, or backwards. The shooter should come down in approximately the same spot he took off. If your players float on jump shots, work to correct the flaw. The shooting percentages will go up and confidence will soar.

Jump shooting fundamentals require the ball to be taken up with both hands and released with the shooting hand. The off hand serves as a guide to steady the ball and position it for release. The elbow of the shooting arm is kept in near the body and pointed toward the target. The ball rests on the upper half of the fingers and should avoid touching the palm. This gives the feel and control needed to be a good shooter. The shooting arm extends out and toward the target. The ball is released off of the fingertips as the wrist snaps down and the elbow locks straight. (Photo Series 4-1.)

I consider the wrist snap and straight elbow to be keys in teaching shooting. I have my players hold their position after shooting and check for a "broken wrist" and "locked elbow." This allows them to analyze their own shots and forces a good follow-through. The "broken wrist" and "locked elbow" are positions the shooting arm should resemble at the completion of any shot.

The same checkpoints are used when I teach free throw shooting. The follow-through is the key to foul shooting under pressure. By giving my players a personal checklist and requiring them to repeat it over and over, they form good habits that are automatically followed in games. In my four years at Montana Tech, we never shot under 70% as a team at the free throw line. Our high point was a second place finish in the N.A.I.A. free throw statistics during the 1972-73 season. Our team shot 76.8% and featured N.A.I.A. Individual Free Throw Champion, Ted Ackerman.

Shooting can and should be taught at all levels. Have a series of checkpoints and review them often with your team. They can follow your instructions when working on their own or during practice. Remember: "A good coach builds on a series of fundamentals, thus forming good habits." *Do not ignore shooting,* because you cannot win without points on the scoreboard.

DRIVING FROM THE HIGH POST

Besides passing off or shooting, the high post man has the opportunity to drive to the basket. The purpose is to position the ball in an area more favorable for high percentage shot attempts.

A quick start is important to high post men that drive. This allows the offensive man to elude his defender and score before help arrives. The driver should be low on the drive for balance and maneuverability. The ball is handled by the fingertips for good control. The high post man must develop both dribbling hands so he can attack on either side of the defense.

When a high post man is tightly guarded on one particular side, he should drive the open side. (See Diagram 4-5A.) If the pressure is straight up (defender directly in front of offensive man), then the driver should attack

Photo Series 4-1.
The Turn-Around Jump Shot

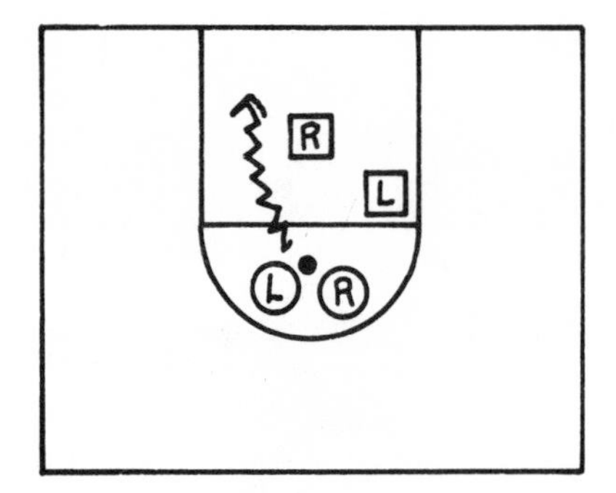

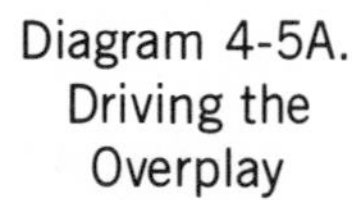
Diagram 4-5A. Driving the Overplay

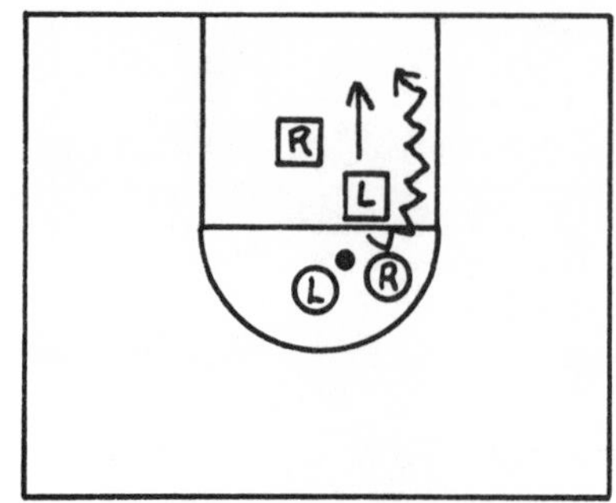

Diagram 4-5B. Driving the Straight-Up Defender

the defender's weak side. The weak side is determined by defensive foot positioning. If the defender has his left foot forward, then the high post drives to the right. (See Diagram 4-5B.) This forces the defensive man to open up (pivot) and retreat. Any time a defender must open, he is at a distinct disadvantage. He moves slower and is often beaten to the basket.

Faking is very important to the high post who wishes to drive. A fake of a pass, shot, or drive can confuse the defender so areas of penetration will open. The defense reacts to the ball, so good fakes will keep the defenders guessing.

I teach my entire squad the "rocker-step moves," which are the keys to good one-on-one basketball. They include the "rock and shoot," "rock-cross-and-drive," and the "rock-lean-and-go" moves.

The "rock and shoot" is merely a large step to the side of the defender, a return to the original position, and a jump shot. (See Photo Series 4-2.) The rocking forward motion caused by the step forces the defense to retreat or lean. By quickly stepping back to the original position, the shot is open. A good offensive man can "rock and shoot" in either direction.

The "rock-cross-and-drive" is often called "the rocker-step." The player steps outside the defender with one foot, then crosses the lead leg around the defense and drives the opposite side. (See Photo Series 4-3.) The offensive man actually fakes a drive in one direction, then crosses over and dribbles around the opposite side. The defense is often left with tangled feet, as the driver scores an unmolested two-pointer.

The "rock-lean-and-go" is a counter move to the "rock and shoot." It works very nicely after a couple of successful "rock and shoot" moves. The offensive man steps to the side of the defender, then leans his upper body back while keeping the lead foot forward. The defender will be enticed into thinking a jump shot is coming, so he will lean forward. The offensive man merely drives past the off-balanced opponent. (See Photo Series 4-4.) This move is a real point-getter when performed properly. Be sure your players

Photo Series 4-2.
The Rock and Shoot

Photo Series 4-3.
The Rock-Cross-and-Drive

Photo Series 4-4.
The Rock-Lean-and-Go

keep their lead foot out. The body will be stretched out and low. The lean back is a movement from the waist up. The feet and legs hold position until the player is ready to dribble.

Work your post men at the one-on-one game. "Rocker-step moves" will make your players tough drivers. Quickness is important on the drive, but good moves can get anyone open.

The high post is a position where you can use players of modest stature. Especially in multiple-post offenses, short men can do the job. A quick and scrappy forward often makes a good high post because the free throw line is a great place to go one-on-one.

In my third season at Montana Tech College, I coached a 6′5″ forward by the name of Ken Pressley. Ken was quick and liked to drive, but he was not a forward type. His outside shot was poor, and he was known as a "one-dribble-driver." (That is the kind of player who seems to always lose the ball on the second dribble.)

After a rather poor non-league season at the forward spot, I tried Pressley at the high post. He loved to get the ball, turn, and drive right by the slower defenders. During league he often started games with a drive, and it resulted in a three-point play. Pressley served us quite well as a high post man, but would have seen a lot of time on the bench as a wing man. He was a hard worker and a good scrapper. Do not be afraid to use such a player inside, as not everyone is a good outside shooter.

THE PICK-AND-ROLL

The high post is stationed in the center of offensive attacks, so his relative position provides opportunities to pick for all teammates. Diagrams 4-6A through 4-6F illustrate ways you can use your high post man as a picker.

As can be seen in the diagrams, many styles of offensive play can be developed using the high post as a pick. An inexperienced big man can be used primarily as a picker for his teammates. The entire offensive pattern would revolve around the high post man freeing other players. Versatile pivot men can be used as scorers or pickers. This creates a balanced offensive attack.

The same coaching points mentioned in chapter 3 on picking by the low post should be followed by the high post. Because of the congestion in the pivot area, a picker must turn and locate the man he wishes to pick before moving. This helps the player avoid unnecessary fouls and also aids in consistency. By finding the man first, a pick-setter will be able to run directly to the defender and set a good pick. More offensive men will get open and good shots will result.

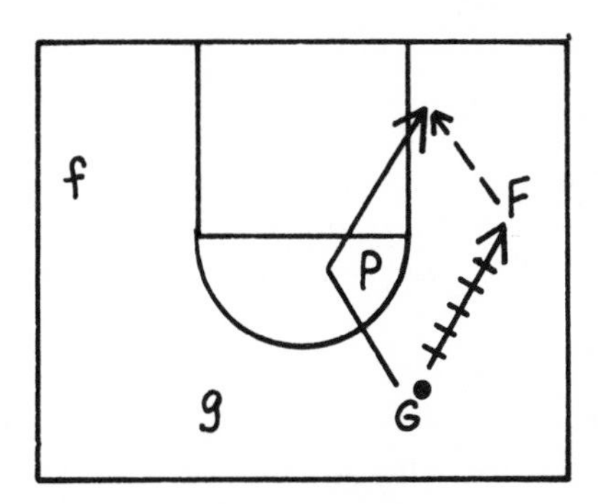

Diagram 4-6A.
The Strong Side
Rub Out

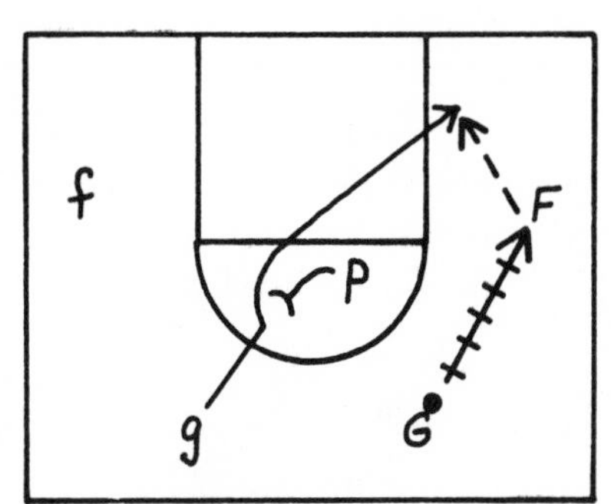

Diagram 4-6B.
The Shuffle Cut or
Weak Side Cut

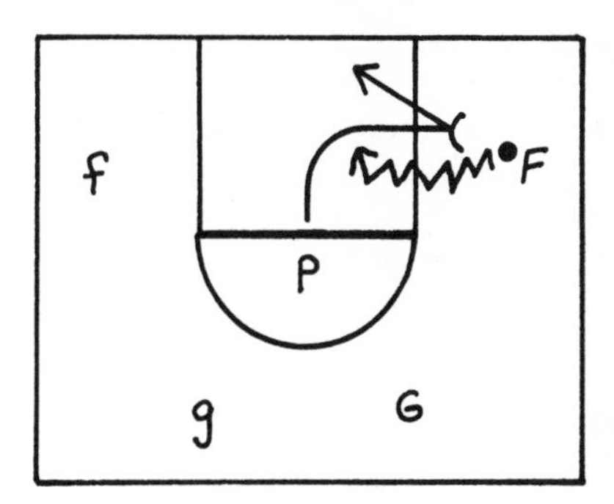

Diagram 4-6C.
Pick-and-Roll
from a Wing

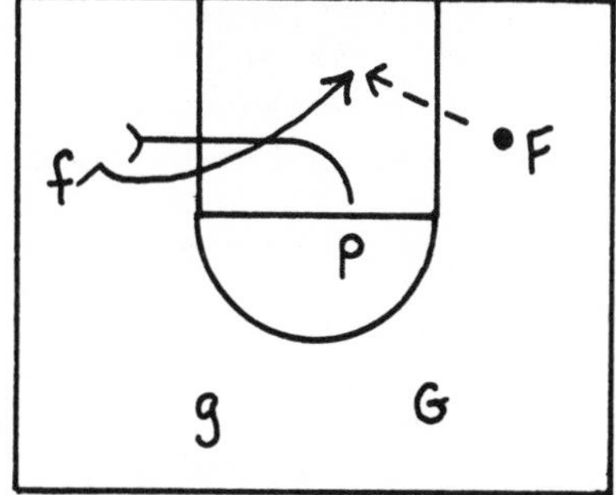

Diagram 4-6D.
Reverse Action or
Pick Away

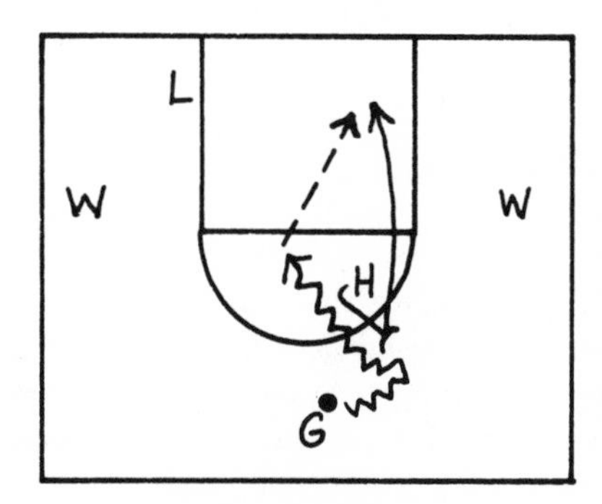

Diagram 4-6E.
Pick-and-Roll
for Guard

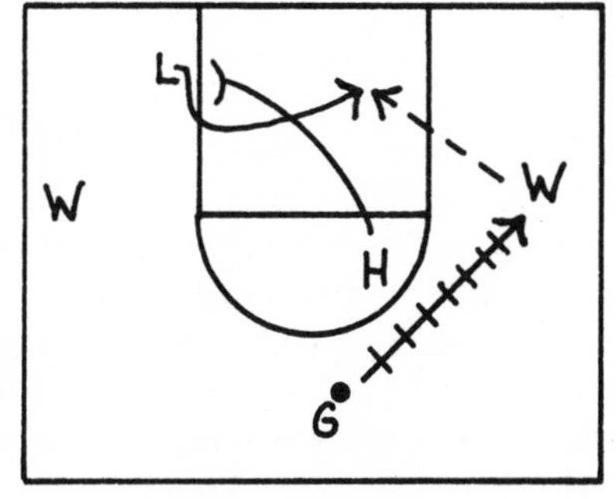

Diagram 4-6F.
High-Low Post Pick

DRILLS FOR IMPROVING THE HIGH POST PLAYER

Since the high post man must also be able to function at the low post, he should work on the drills listed at the end of chapter 3. Other drills that I use for high post players are outlined below. Since forwards and guards sometimes flash into the pivot area, I include all players in these drills from time to time.

1. Passing Drills

Ever since the first basketball was filled with air, players have been bouncing the ball too much. Passing is a key fundamental that is weak throughout basketball. Since the high post is often used as a "relay position," any form of passing drill will aid your team.

Group passing drills are generally helpful to the coaching staff because all players can be involved. I like to break my team into groups of three and let each group work with a ball. Then I instruct them as to what pass to throw, while I cruise around the groups and watch techniques.

Another passing drill that I like is illustrated in Diagram 4-7.

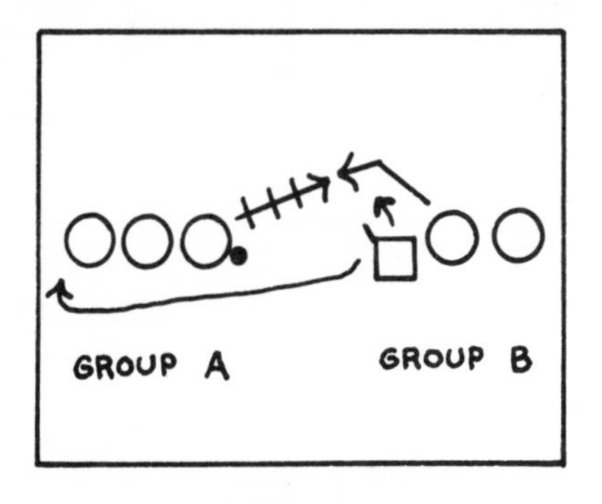

Diagram 4-7.
Passing Drill—Hit
the Open Side

Two groups form a straight line facing each other. If group A has the ball, the front man of group B defends against the second man in group B. The defender plays on one side or the other and attempts to deflect a pass from group A. The player wishing to receive a pass offers a target hand away from the defense. The pass should be thrown crisply to the open side. The receiver must make a V-cut and catch the ball. The passer in group A now becomes a defender to the second man in group A. The drill is repeated. After playing defense, a player rotates to the end of the opposite group.

The coach should check to make sure all two-handed passes are thrown correctly. The arms must be extended to the target with an outward rotation of the hands and wrists. The thumbs will point to the floor and the palms outward at the completion of a good pass. This extension and wrist snap provides the power needed for strong passes.

Reception of the ball should also be watched. A pass must be caught with the fingertips of both hands. The ball is then tucked to the chest area with elbows flaired for protection.

Passing drills need to be reviewed quite often to assure your players of developing proper passing habits. A team of good passers is tough to beat. They can fastbreak well, attack zones easily, and seldom rattle against pressure defenses.

2. Rocker-Step Moves

The rocker-step moves mentioned earlier in this chapter can be worked on in groups or by individuals. The moves should be taught and reviewed one at a time from a single line group. The coach can observe, instruct, and correct all players with this method.

After the rocker-step moves have been learned, the coach can allow some one-on-one competition. Limit the players to using only the rocker-step moves and nothing else. Players should learn the moves while facing the basket before attempting the next drill.

3. High Post Pivot Drill

This is a drill designed to teach high post men to face the basket immediately after receiving a pass. An offensive player breaks up from the low post area and gets a pass. He must quickly pivot to face the hoop and perform the instructed move. The coach may call for a shot, drive, or rock-step move.

A defensive man can be added once the coach is satisfied with the progress of his players. The drill then becomes one-on-one with your back to the basket. The stress is always on pivoting and facing the hoop before making any offensive move.

I like to use this drill as a shooting drill quite often. The players just pivot, shoot, and follow any missed attempts with a muscle shot. The free throw area jump shot should be practiced often, as it can be a high percentage attempt.

4. Two-on-Two—Pick and Roll

This drill can be either "two-on-two" or "three-on-three." Any offensive player can pick for the man with the ball. The driver must use the pick and attempt to get open or force a defensive switch. The picker rolls to the hoop after the dribbler passes the screen. The roll man must be alert for feeds and opportunities to post against small defenders.

5

INCREASING REBOUNDS FROM THE POST POSITION

> You can pass too much; you can dribble too much; you can shoot too much; but you can never rebound too much.

The above quote is a good philosophy for coaches of front-line players. The post player has the opportunity to assert himself as a rebounder, because he cruises the territory around the basket. Consequently, he has a "front row seat" to all action. The coach's job is to make sure the big man gets out of "his seat" and joins in the action. To be totally effective, the post player should play the lead role in the rebounding game.

The team that controls the backboards, controls the game of basketball! It would be great to coach a giant, muscle-bound, aggressive leaper who can sweep the boards for your team at both ends of the court. Unfortunately, few coaches are that lucky. Teaching fundamentals and a hard-nosed attitude are the answers for the average coach who has average players.

There are two areas where a non-scorer can excel and bring glory to himself in basketball: (1) defense, and (2) rebounding. A post man who can dominate or even just grab a good share of the rebounds is a valuable member of the team. He is just as important as the top scorer for the success of the ball club. No team can score without the ball, and rebounding missed shots provides the most chances for possession.

Rebounding can be broken into three separate areas for discussion. These are: (1) defensive rebounding, (2) offensive rebounding, and (3) rebounding free throw attempts. This chapter deals with each area as a part leading to the total rebounding game.

DEFENSIVE REBOUNDING

Controlling the defensive boards improves both the defense and offense of a team. Good defense ends by securing possession of the ball without allowing a score. This goal is more likely to occur when the opponents are limited to one shot at the hoop. A good defensive rebounding team allows the oppenents very few tips, follow-ups, or extra possessions.

Offense starts once a team gains possession of the ball. On the defensive end of the court, the fastbreak attack begins when a missed shot is gathered in. A good defensive rebounding team is much easier to program into a fastbreaking style of play. To improve both the offensive and defensive aspects of the game, a coach should instruct his players on the fundamentals of defensive rebounding.

I like to break DEFENSIVE REBOUNDING into four basic parts. They are:

1. Mental Preparation
2. Position
3. The Grab
4. The Outlet

To be a good rebounder, a player must realize the close relationship that exists between each part. A letdown in any one area will weaken the rebounding ability of the player.

Mental Preparation

George Raveling has written an excellent rebounding manual called *War on the Boards*. In it, Coach Raveling discusses the "aggressive nature of rebounding." Since rebounding is such a physical part of basketball, WAR is a good way to describe the contact.

In order to physically take the pounding, colliding, and hurting involved in rebounding, the post man must be mentally tough. He should fear no opponent or collection of opponents who challenge for the "right of possession." The post man must not be discouraged when faced with a size disadvantage, physical aches and pains, or even exhaustion from the game's tempo. A mentally tough rebounder will value the loose ball and rebound no matter what the conditions. He will constantly attack all possible rebound situations and seek the possession for his team.

Along with the desire to compete physically for the ball, a good rebounding post man must assume all shots are missed. Since the post player is generally stationed near the hoop, he is in good rebounding position. If the big man is to take advantage of this natural good positioning, then he must anxiously await a stray shot.

In order to get my players in the habit of assuming all shots are missed, an assistant coach or myself watches the frontliners on all shot attempts during scrimmages. Any player who cruises or hangs outside and away from the rebounding area is immediately reprimanded.

Mental preparation, in essence, means the post man is ready to go after the ball, take a physical pounding, and win the BATTLE OF THE BOARDS!

Position

When a shot is taken by an opponent, the defensive player must first concentrate on the movement of his assigned man. Whether the offensive man goes right, left, stands still, or retreats determines the counter move of the defensive rebounder. In order to block-out the opponent's move and get into position, the defender must use a pivot. The two most common methods of blocking-out are: (1) the front pivot, and (2) the reverse pivot.

THE FRONT PIVOT is most often used against opponents on the strong side, especially low post men. It is quick, and it allows the defender to step in immediately to draw contact.

Photo Series 5-1 illustrates the proper movement by a post man using a front pivot. The defender remains low in his defensive position and starts the pivot with a cross-over step. In the example, the right leg and arm of the defender quickly move in front and across the offensive man. Next, the defender swings his left arm and leg back. The man blocking-out has moved 180°, halfway around, and should now be facing the hoop. The defender must draw contact so he can feel the position and movement of the opponent.

Deciding which arm and leg to lead into the cross-over should rest with instinct. Whichever lead gets the defender into a front pivot the quickest is the answer. Generally, when the shot goes up on the defender's left side, he will execute the front pivot as previously described. This helps him to maintain visual contact with the ball. If the shot goes up on the defender's right side, he will execute the front pivot by crossing the left leg and arm across the offensive man. Again, the all important visual contact can be maintained.

The front pivot requires the defender to go at his opponent, providing immediate contact and an aggressive block-out. This type of block-out works well on the shooter, slow reactors, and stationary opponents.

THE REVERSE PIVOT is generally used against opponents on the weak side of the court—away from the ball. It is also valuable to use on quick opponents who like to run around block-outs. The post defender will find occasion to use the reverse pivot, especially against active big men.

Executing the reverse pivot requires the defender to maintain a low defensive position as the shot goes up. He waits for the offensive player to take a step to the basket. This movement keys the execution of the reverse pivot. The defender slides his foot nearest to the direction of the opponent's movement. This foot then becomes a pivot off of which the defender reverses. The opposite leg and arm swing behind the body until the player has reversed himself. The defender is now facing the hoop and searching for the flight of the ball. Contact must be made and held on the opponent until the rebounder knows where the ball will go. (See Photo Series 5-2.)

Teaching the front pivot and reverse pivot is not as difficult as it may first seem. Both techniques require the defender to move toward the potential

Photo Series 5-1.
The Front Pivot

Photo Series 5-2.
The Reverse Pivot

offensive rebounder. If your players can get the habit of moving to opponents and drawing contact, the front and reverse pivots become natural moves.

Stopping the movement of an opponent is the objective in positioning. The defensive rebounder must learn to step to the stationary opponent, then pivot and block-out. He must also learn to step in the direction of a moving opponent and reverse pivot. Defenders who turn and run to the basket without blocking-out, too often watch their opponents sail by them and tap in an easy two points. When your players become conscious of stopping the crashing offensive rebounders by direct contact, the "battle of the boards" advantage shifts to your team.

The defensive post man must be careful not to get pushed too far under the basket. Proper position is approximately six feet from the hoop. This gives the rebounder a legitimate chance at all caroms, including long or short bounces.

Coaches should pay particular attention to the positioning of extra tall players. These big men often get in the bad habit of rushing under the hoop and then using superior reaching ability to gather rebounds. This works fine until your team faces an opponent with physical frontliners who like to push and shove. Suddenly your big man will end up under the net, exhausted, and ineffective. Positioning is the key for all rebounders, big and small. "Good blocking-out is the equalizer when you lack height, and the dominator when you have height."

The defensive post man defends against a very powerful and potentially dangerous rebounder. The offensive pivot man has only one thing on his mind as a teammate shoots: "Get inside and pick up an easy two points." If the defender does not block-out and contain this anxious opponent, the easy two points soon become a reality.

Blocking-out the shooter is another area of consideration. The shooting post man generally works from the internal zone. Whether the offensive man shoots from three feet or twenty-three feet, the defensive post man has a responsibility to block him out.

Defending the shooting post player requires close connection between defensive fundamentals and rebounding techniques. The defensive man maintains the proper defensive position—between the ball and the basket. As the shot is being taken, the post defender puts a hand up and hollers "Hey." The combination of hand and voice distracts the shooter's vision and concentration. Some coaches like to use the term "Shot" when a man shoots. This term serves to alert defensive teammates that a rebound is imminent. I prefer "Hey," because it is directed to the shooter rather than the rebounders. Of course, any teammate hearing "Hey" knows that a rebound is coming.

After the shot is released, the post defender should step to the shooter and perform a front pivot. The block-out should be quick and the defender must stay low and alert. Slight contact into the opponent is the goal of the front pivot. The contact serves two purposes: (1) to disturb the shooter and to give him something to think about the next time he shoots; and (2) to prevent quick movement to an offensive rebound position by the shooter. A good block-out position should be held until the defensive post can tell where the rebound is headed.

While guards and forwards usually shoot and fall back to the defensive court, offensive post men generally hit the boards after shooting. By preventing the offensive pivot man from crashing the boards, many second shots will be eliminated. The shooting post man is a very dangerous rebounder because he is close to the basket, knows where the shot is likely to bounce, and has a good view of the ball's flight. He also has added incentive from the frustration of missing the initial attempt; and therefore, he is anxious to correct the mistake.

Once contact is established and the shooting or non-shooting opponent is blocked-out, the defensive post man must hold position and prepare to get the ball. The rebounding stance is as follows:

1. Feet spread about shoulder width apart to provide a firm base.
2. Weight on the balls of the feet, ready to move quickly.
3. Knees flexed and ready to spring or move.
4. Back fairly straight and never hunched over.
5. Elbows out to take up space and protect the position.
6. Hands and fingers pointed up in a "ready position."
7. Eyes search and focus on the ball.

The defensive rebounder must be prepared to hold the block-out position up to four seconds. The rebounding stance should not be sacrificed in the struggle for position. Quick, choppy steps laterally will keep the rebounder between the offensive opponent and the basket. The butt of the blocker should contact the upper legs of the opponent, while the elbows serve as messengers telling the defender which way to move. A defensive rebounder cannot afford to take his eyes off the ball or his hands out of "ready position."

As soon as the rebounder sees where the ball is going, he moves in its direction. When the ball comes to his area, he must go for it. If the ball bounces to another area, the rebounder should move a step or two toward it while analyzing the situation. A loose ball may occur, so an alert player can gain possession.

The Grab

A rebounder must never wait for the ball to come to him, but rather, he must go after the ball. From the rebounding stance, the post man should leap quickly and aggressively after any ball in his area. The leap should be timed so the rebounder can grab the ball at the top of his jump. The arms must be extended to their fullest length in the direction of the ball. A well-timed leap and a maximum reach can make the difference between a successful rebound and a hopeless attempt.

The rebound should always be grabbed firmly with both hands. This assures possession and protects the ball from being knocked loose. The one-handed snatch rebound is quite impressive to see, but it can only be performed consistently by a few great players with big hands. Even those few have their troubles rebounding when the "going gets rough." Going for the ball with two hands provides the protection of both elbows, both arms, and both hands. (See Photo 5-3A)

A defensive rebound should never be tipped or slapped, unless the player is out of position and has no chance of grabbing the ball. Even tipping the loose ball to a teammate is risky business. An opponent may step in and steal the intended tip, or the ball may stray out of bounds.

Once the post player has grabbed the ball, he should jerk it out of the air quickly. The ball is then brought down in front of the head with the elbows out for protection. The player must land in a spread eagle position, with the ball never going below the chest area.

The Outlet

A proper defensive rebound is never completed until the ball is passed out to a guard or forward. It does no good to successfully grab a missed shot only to fumble the ball away, lose it on a violation, or pass it to the opponents. The post man has an obligation to get the ball quickly to the guards so the offensive thrust may begin.

As soon as he grabs the ball, the rebounder should turn and look for an outlet man. This search must take place as the player is descending to the floor, so he may pass the second he comes down. (See Photo 5-3B)

During descent to the court, the rebounder should make a half turn in the air toward the nearest sideline. This will position the player so he is facing the outlet man, thus aiding in a quick and effective outlet pass. Vision and passing position are both improved through this simple half turn maneuver.

As the rebounder hits the floor, he must be sure to maintain good body balance. Body weight should be evenly distributed on both feet, knees flexed, and upper body slightly arched. The ball remains head high, but is next to the ear because the head has turned to look down court. (See Photo 5-3C)

When the player has spotted an open teammate, he should execute a sharp and direct pass to him. The two-handed overhead pass is the safest and easiest to control. The one-handed baseball pass is also used for long outlets, especially by fastbreaking teams. Both passes can be safely executed without bringing the ball down below the shoulders. This negates the chances of the ball being slapped away or tied up. (See Photo 5-3D)

The post man must not use his dribble immediately following a rebound. It should be saved as a last resort to relieve the pressure of two-timing defenders. Most post players are poor dribblers on an open court, so dribbling in a congested rebound area is even more dangerous.

Photo 5-3A.

Photo 5-3B.

Photo 5-3C.

Photo 5-3D.

The Defensive Rebound

If the rebounder cannot find an open outlet man, he can resort to the dribble to break clear of pressure. He must move quickly and aggressively away from the defenders, while searching for an open teammate. A poor dribbler should take no more than two dribbles upcourt. This is usually enough to open the court and free teammates who eagerly await the ball. One dribble can easily get the post man to the top of the defensive key, which is certainly enough to open many new passing angles. Any more than two dribbles by a big man will make him "open season" for the smaller and quicker guards. Since big men usually dribble with their heads down, using one dribble, stopping, and then looking is the best way to avoid trouble. The dribble should always be directed to mid-court, and never to a corner or the sidelines. Mid-court offers many passing angles; the sidelines offer many troubles.

When the outlets are covered, the only open area is at mid-court. If the rebounder can "bust out" of his congestion, then the deep defenders will converge to mid-court looking for a steal. This now frees the outlet men who have remained on the sidelines. An easy fastbreak situation arises and the defenders are outnumbered. (Diagram 5-1)

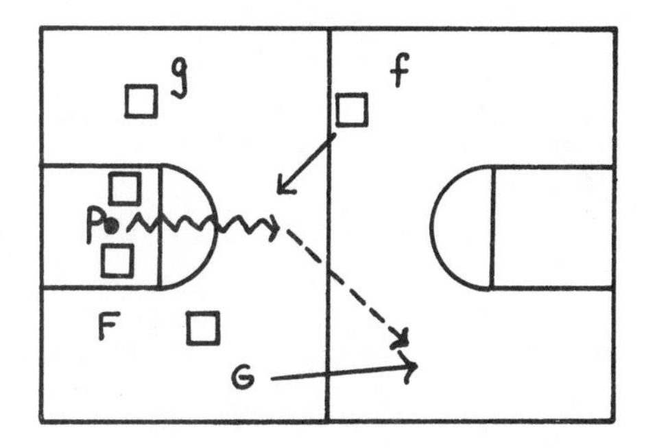

Diagram 5-1.
"Busting Out of Pressure"

In order to clear a two-time effectively, I run a "Bust-Out Drill" regularly in practice. The players learn to protect the ball, look for outlets, and then "bust out" of the tight situation. The key is to dribble low and keep the body low. High dribbles expose the ball to defenders, resulting in turnovers. The low dribble provides better control and maneuverability.

Along with controlling the dribble, rebounders must be able to control their passes. A smart post man never forces outlet passes into congested lanes. A quick and senseless turnover is the last thing needed following a hard-fought rebound. It is better to be forced into a jump ball or a "ten-second violation" than to shift momentum with a bad pass.

The individual techniques discussed in this section work better in man defenses than in zone defenses. In man-to-man defense, each player has an assigned opponent to block-out. Zone defenses require the defenders to choose an opponent in the immediate area to block-out. Overloading zone offenses sometimes cause a swamping of rebound areas, and the defensive rebounder is outmanned. The rebounding game then becomes a scramble to see who can get to the loose ball first. Personally, I like the control man-to-man defense gives my team on the boards. If one particular opponent is constantly sneaking around my defender and getting offensive rebounds, I know who to correct or replace.

Post men generally have the responsibility of screening the opponent's big man in both man-to-man and zone defenses. They have to keep the opposing post player off of the offensive boards and still gain a vast share of the rebounds. A combination of good mental preparation, positioning, grabbing, and outletting is the only way the big man can do the job.

OFFENSIVE REBOUNDING

A good basketball team must also have a strong offensive rebounding attack. While holding the opponents to one shot per possession, your team should get two or three attempts if needed.

"Offensive Efficiency" is a term I use to measure my team's effectiveness on each possession. Instead of concerning myself with field goal percentages and total points scored, I check how successful my team is at scoring on each possession. This is found by dividing the total number of points scored by the number of team possessions. When the team shoots and misses but gets the offensive rebound and scores, the efficiency is no different than if the original attempt was made. When a team averages more than 1.0 points per possession, the "offensive efficiency" is considered good.

To increase "offensive efficiency," a team needs strong offensive rebounders. Again, because of his relative position around the hoop, the post man can and should be a tough competitor on the offensive boards. Frontliners, especially double and triple post men, can form a powerful attack under the basket. If two or three men fill the key rebound spots, then the chances of repossession increase tremendously. The key again is the big man, who often has the height and reach to challenge anyone.

The post man becomes a strong offensive rebounder when he develops the following four basic traits.

1. **Desire.** The player must want to get the ball and be willing to put forth the extra effort needed.
2. **Aggressiveness.** Fighting a block-out requires rough play. An offensive rebounder must be willing to get knocked around and still come back for more.
3. **Quickness.** This trait applies to both foot movement and thought analysis. A good offensive rebounder sees the opening and gets through it immediately.

4. **Experience.** A player gains knowledge of the game each time he plays. Offensive rebounders learn to sense where the ball will come down, through the experience of seeing many shots bounce off the rim. Technique also improves with playing time, as practice makes perfect.

An active post man is the best type of offensive rebounder; however, desire to get the ball can make any big man effective. The offensive rebounder should not stand still and wait for the ball to come to him. He becomes too easy to block-out when he is not moving. Because the big man is often standing under the basket on offense, it is easy for him to become complacent. Unlike the defensive rebounder, the offensive rebounder always has the freedom to go where he thinks the ball will come down. A good post man takes advantage of this opportunity to help his team.

Through charting of scrimmages and my team's games, some interesting statistics were found. On the average, sixty-five percent (65%) of all missed shots originally taken from one side, bounce over the basket to the other side of the court. This is the natural result of momentum left over from the shot. Missed shots taken from in front of the basket tend to bounce back toward the shooter, also at about a two-out-of-three rate. Thus, the knowledgeable post man can position himself favorably when on offense. His movement will be an added distraction to the opponent attempting to block-out. This distraction may be enough to give the offensive rebounder equal or better position to tip in a stray shot.

Avoiding a block-out by the defensive post man can be aided through the addition of the following three "offensive rebounding techniques."

1. **The Fake and Go Away.** By appearing to go in one direction, the offensive rebounder may entice the defender to block too soon. The commitment by the defensive rebounder allows the offensive post man to change directions and head to a desirable rebound area. A head, shoulder, and leg fake works the best to invite an incorrect pivot out of the defender.
2. **The Roll-Off and Hook.** When the offensive man finds himself already blocked-out, this method is effective for getting free. The player pivots off the foot which is closest to the direction he wants to move. The pivot is a reverse, allowing the offensive man to roll across the back of the defender. As the far foot swings around, the offensive man plants it outside the defender's stance and continues a full pivot around. This should place the offensive player beside the defender and give him good position to contest for the rebound. (See Photo Series, 5-4A, B.)

   The "hook" part of this maneuver involves swinging the opposite elbow around and over the opponent's arm during the pivot. As an example, if the offensive man pivoted around the defender's right

Photo 5-4A

Photo 5-4B

Photo 5-4C

The Roll-Off and Hook

side, his left elbow would swing around and over the defensive man's right arm. This puts the offensive man in a better position to grab or tip a rebound. (See Photo Series 5-4B,C)

3. **The Dummy Move.** This is also a very effective move to gain position, as it involves outsmarting the defensive post man. As the shot goes up, the offensive post man stands still and gives a lazy appearance. The idea is to convince the defender that no attempt will be made to position for the ball. As the defender turns to locate the ball, the offensive man makes a quick and aggressive move to the desired area of rebounding. The element of surprise and lack of block-out by the defender gives the offensive rebounder a great opportunity to gain position.

At Montana Tech College I coached a player named Gary Becker who was a master of the "dummy move." Becker would often surprise his opponent by standing on the perimeter looking bored, and then fly over or around defenders for a neat tap-in. He was a rare young man that never stopped battling, and his biggest plays seemed to come during the crucial parts of games. Gary Becker was a perfect example of what determination can do for a rebounder.

While it is not a good idea to run over or climb the back of defensive rebounders, offensive post men should not be afraid to move aggressively to the hoop. Seldom are offensive fouls called on players charging to the basket, because of the normal movement and collisions that take place. The one or two fouls the post man may get will certainly serve to let the opponents know who is in charge. By picking his spots, the experienced post man will avoid any needless fouls.

An offensive rebounder does not need inside position to be effective on the boards. Moving to a parallel position, or next to the defensive rebounder, gives the offensive player a good chance to tip the ball back in the basket. If a controlled tip is impossible because of position, the offensive rebounder should attempt to keep the ball alive. The ball can be tipped toward the hoop, toward a teammate, or up into the air for another chance at control.

Many of the key steps to defensive rebounding are the same for offensive rebounding. The player's head should be up with his eyes focused on the ball. The arms must be extended with elbows out and hands open. The tap is best executed at the top of the jump, so timing is very important.

There should never be any slapping or palming while attempting a tip. The tip is with the fingers, and the thumb is used as a balancing agent. A cupped formation of the hand will prevent improper hand action. The fingers remain rigid and a slight wrist action controls the direction and distance of the tip.

I prefer my players to always tip with one hand. I also expect them to be able to tip effectively with either hand, as needed. A player can reach five inches or more while raising one arm, as compared to raising both arms. This extra bit of reach can allow the tipper to get many more rebounds each season. Practice will allow the player to control the ball as well with one hand as he can with two.

Remembering that a good rebounder should assume every shot is missed, the offensive tipper must be ready to execute a second, third, and fourth effort. A great offensive rebounder pursues the ball until he sees it safely dropping through the net.

Rebounds that bounce more than six feet from the basket are quite difficult to tip effectively. These caroms should be caught, brought to the floor, then immediately taken back up to the hoop. The "pump fake" and "muscle shot" mentioned in chapter 3 become powerful weapons in this situation. A post man who gathers in an offensive rebound should always take the ball back to the hoop. His size and strength give him the advantage over most defenders. Quite often, a three point play results because the frustrated defenders foul. When a post man gets the ball inside, whether it is by a pass or a rebound, he must power up a shot. The only possible exception would be late in the game when delay tactics are required.

Offensive rebounding sparks a team; it gives them momentum; and it increases "offensive efficiency." The post man is a constant offensive threat because he is a potentially dangerous rebounder. Even the big man who cannot shoot well can learn to score off tips and follow-up shots. What better way is there for a post man to fire a team up, than to turn a missed shot into a quick two points?

REBOUNDING MISSED FREE THROWS

I am the type of coach who feels that tending to the "little things" can make a "big difference." Although recent rules have eliminated one-shot free throws in basketball, there are still plenty of opportunities to rebound missed free throw attempts. While sitting on the sidelines watching my team play a crucial league game one winter, my confidence in tending to "little things" was shaken.

The opposing Western Montana College team continued to miss their free throw attempts. More amazing to me was that the Western players kept coming up with the offensive rebound. In fact, the whole situation became downright disgusting after we lost a close contest. Needless to say, the next day's practice plan contained plenty of discussion and drill on rebounding free throws.

Since that fateful game in 1973, I have paid particular attention to offensive and defensive free throw rebounding. Giving the opponent a free shot at the basket is bad enough, without the added burden of giving them another possession when they miss. And of course, if the opponents fail to block-out when your team shoots free throws, it pays to have your players ready to take advantage.

The key to successful free throw rebounding, like regular rebounding, is to "assume every shot is missed!" This is often a hard concept for players to develop, because the free throw seems an easy shot. However, statistics show that good free-throw shooting teams miss about three out of every ten attempts (30%), and average teams miss four or five out of ten tries (40-50%).

Because of the softness of most free throw attempts, approximately half of the missed shots fall to the inside rebounders. Since the post man generally occupies an inside rebounding position, a coach can easily see the need to teach him sound free throw rebounding techniques.

The post man should line up close to the block separating the first and second rebound positions. This places him close to the opposing rebounder in the next lane, and it provides a better chance of successfully blocking-out the opponent. The knees are flexed, hands are up, elbows are out, and the eyes focused on the ball and shooter. The rebounder's feet should be about six inches apart. One quick step by the top foot places the player in excellent position immediately.

In college and high school basketball, a rebounder must stay in his lane until the ball hits the rim. As soon as the ball does make contact, the post man should thrust his top foot and arm quickly into the lane. He should make immediate contact with the offensive rebounder and block him out. Visual attention must never leave the ball during the free throw block-out. From here on, the defensive rebounder follows the same steps mentioned earlier in the chapter. They are: time the leap, grab the ball with two hands, half turn in the air, and outlet the ball.

Post men must be cautioned against stepping to the basket, rather than stepping out and back into the lane. (See Diagram 5-2.) Moving to the hoop puts the big man out of the best rebounding area and allows the offensive rebounder to move into a good spot.

From the offensive standpoint, inside positioning by the opponents does not guarantee they will get the missed free throw. Many teams fail to cover free throw rebounding in practice, because they assume position should provide enough advantage. Consequently, alert offensive rebounders can often gain possession and tip in stray shots.

The offensive rebounding post man has two choices when lining up along the free throw lane. (See Diagram 5-3.) He can move close to the block next to the inside rebounder, or he can move close to the hash mark at the top of his lane. An offensive rebounder should never stand in the middle of the lane, but move to either side, depending upon his strategy for getting the rebound.

When standing next to the inside defensive rebounder, the post man must step quickly and aggressively into the lane. His goal is to get there first and not be screened out. A parallel position next to the defensive inside rebounder is advantageous. As in defensive rebounding, the top foot and arm should lead the offensive rebounder into the key. Since most missed free throws bounce softly back in front of the rim, an offensive rebounder

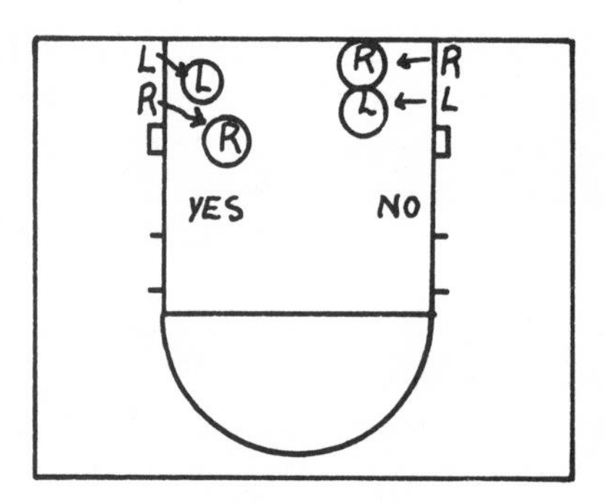

Diagram 5-2.
Defensive Rebounding of
Free Throws

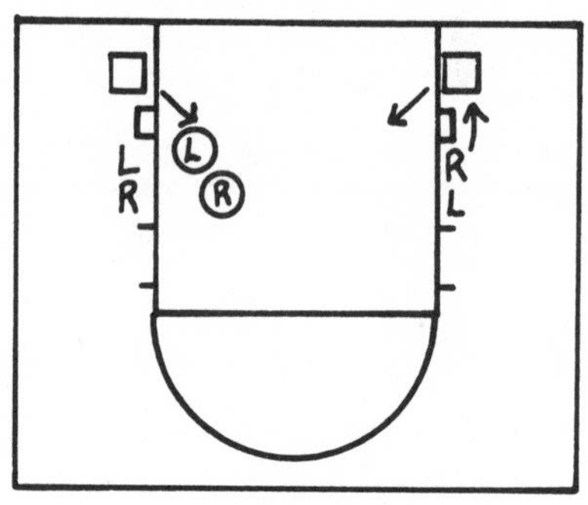

Diagram 5-3.
Offensive Rebounding of
Free Throws

with the slightest room to reach the ball will have an excellent chance to put it back in the basket.

Standing at the top of the offensive rebounding lane offers two other strategies. One, the post man can avoid the immediate block-out of the inside rebounder. If the opposition is slow moving or fails to block-out properly, then the offensive man is able to gain good position by moving freely into the lane. Secondly, the post man can fake in and then step behind the defensive rebounder. This move will often catch the opposition unprepared, thus allowing an extra attempt at a score.

Any free throw rebounded by the offensive post man should immediately be tipped or gathered in, and muscled back up to the basket. And, as in field goal rebounding, the big man must be ready to execute a second, third, or fourth effort.

The coach's strategy should call for a big, physical post man to line up opposite the opponent's post when on offense; and next to the opponent's big man when on defense. The reasoning behind this is simple. Avoid the opponent's biggest man when trying to score, and be in position to block-out their big man when on defense.

Whether a shooter is attempting a field goal or free throw, the post man must be prepared to rebound the shot. A big man who crashes the boards consistently throughout the entire game becomes a serious threat to the opposition. To have a powerful rebounding attack, the post man must be the leader.

DRILLS TO IMPROVE REBOUNDING SKILLS

It is quite common for coaches to have daily drills for offense and defense. Too often, however, rebounding fundamentals are ignored. I try to incorporate some specific rebounding drills into every practic session. Following are the ones I use to increase rebounding techniques in post men and in other members of my teams.

1. Tipping

Tipping drills were mentioned in chapter 3 as integral to the development of low post players. Hand and finger control are very important to the offensive rebounder. Strength, ball control, and coordination are improved when tipping is part of the everyday work-out routine. Players at all levels, from junior high leagues to professional leagues, should learn to control-tip with each hand.

Post men can develop their tipping abilities through the simple warm-up drill outlined in chapter 3. The suggested ten count tipping sequence can be altered to fit beginners, by cutting the number to three. Whatever the number, the player must remember to work with each hand.

2. Two-Man Rebounding Drill

Two players position themselves on each side of the basket. One player overshoots the ball off of the backboard, attempting to hit some part of the rim on the other side. The second player times his jump, leaps to the ball, and attempts to complete a fundamentally sound rebound. After hitting the floor, the rebounder shoots the ball back over the basket in the same manner as the first player. The first player also completes a strong rebound. The two players repeat the drill until each has grabbed ten rebounds. After a brief rest, the sequence is repeated twice more. The coach serves as an observer, correcting any technical faults of the participants. (See Diagram 5-4.)

Most gyms have six baskets around the main court. A twelve man squad can divide up and utilize all of the baskets. This allows the coach to float around or stand at mid-court and observe the whole team working at one time. Three sets can be performed by the entire group in about five minutes.

3. Four-Man Outlet Drill

This drill is an extension of the Two-Man Rebounding Drill. Outlet men are added at the appropriate positions, as required by the coach's philosophy. The position may be around mid-court or near the short outlet area in the corners.

As the post man pulls down a rebound, the half-turn in the air should place him in position to see the outlet man. A two-handed overhead pass or a baseball pass can be used to clear the ball out. The outlet man then returns the ball to the rebounder so he can shoot it back over the basket. (Diagram 5-4.)

4. Block-Out Around a Circle

To teach players the proper blocking-out methods, I use this group drill. Three to five defensive players are lined up on a jump circle, facing a ball which has been placed in the middle. (See Diagram 5-5.) An equal number of offensive players are assigned to the defenders. The offensive players start

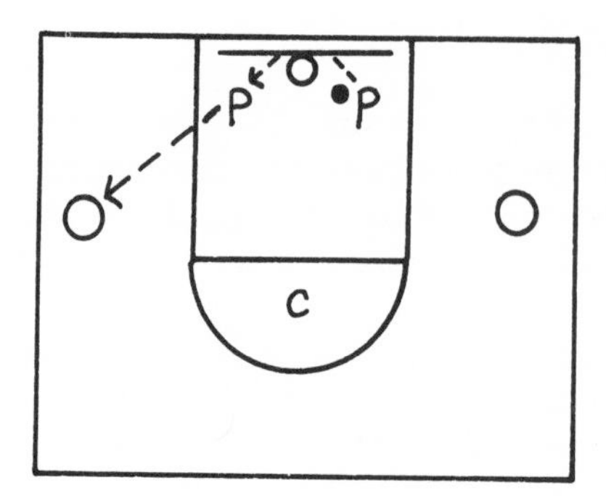

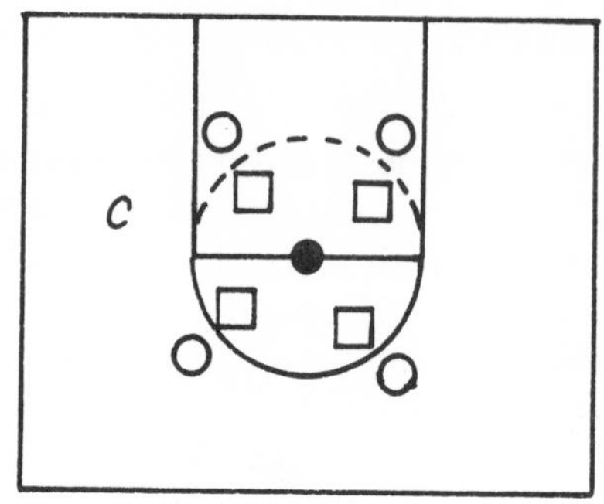

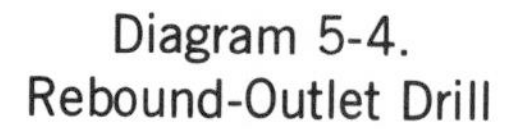
Diagram 5-4.
Rebound-Outlet Drill

Diagram 5-5.
Rebound Around a Circle

outside the circle. The defenders make contact with an opponent, holding a proper block-out position. When the coach blows the whistle, the offensive players try to get to the ball. The defenders must keep the opponents from touching it for four seconds. The coach counts "1-2-3-4" out loud to encourage the participants. The defenders have to keep their knees flexed, elbows out, and hands up at all times. Contact on the opponents should be made with the butt and held by quick movement of the feet. When one group successfully defends the ball for four seconds, the offense moves into the circle and becomes the new defenders.

I also use this drill to teach the reverse pivot and front pivot methods of blocking-out. This is an advanced part of the drill and should be attempted only after blocking-out is learned. The defenders face the offensive men, just like in a scrimmage situation. When the whistle blows, the defenders check their oppenents with one of the pivot moves. They must then block-out as in the previous drill. A count of five is used in this drill. The coach should check all of the defender's techniques, watching for players who constantly let their opponent slip past.

This drill is also good for practicing the offensive rebounding maneuvers mentioned in this chapter. They include: faking, roll-off-and-hook, and the dummy move.

5. Three-on-Three Block-Out

Three offensive players line up at various positions on the court. Their defenders stay with them, defending according to the position of the coach who has the ball. (See Diagram 5-6.) When the coach shoots, the defenders block-out the opponents and then go for the rebound. An outlet pass to the coach must follow any successful defensive rebound. If the offense comes up with the ball, they must immediately take it back up to the hoop. (The exception would be if the shot were rebounded more than six feet from the basket).

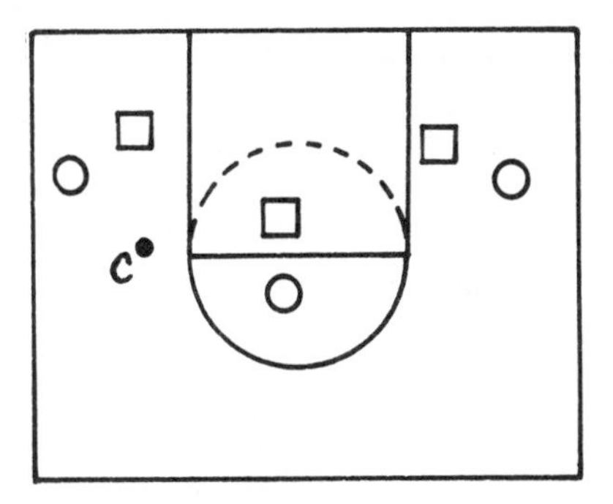

Diagram 5-6.
Three-on-Three Block-Out Drill

I like to make this drill competitive by giving each team five chances on defense. The team with the least defensive rebounds pays a penalty such as twenty finger-tip push-ups or some wind sprints.

The drill can be repeated as time allows. I usually play three times and have the defenders switch assignments each game. Such competitiveness in drills helps to make practice fun, and there certainly is no law saying practice cannot be enjoyable.

6. War

The players often cringe when they hear me say, "The next drill is WAR!" While it is a rough, physical drill, I believe it is beneficial to the development of good inside players. A post man must be able to take the rough play under the boards, so this drill serves that purpose.

Players are broken into groups of three, according to their size. The coach throws the ball onto the basket to start a game. The players must rebound and score to get a point. After each point, the contest starts over until one player gets three baskets. The losers then pay a penalty: push-ups or wind sprints.

The contestants are allowed to foul, push, hack, and just about anything else within reason. The coach should guide the action to make sure it does not get out of hand. At the end of this drill, the coach will have three mighty tired players. This is tremendous conditioning, both physically and mentally. You can tell who the "real players" are and who the "quitters" are through this drill.

While this drill may sound dangerous, I have not seen anything other than simple bruises result from the action. If you want a physical ball club, WAR will help condition your team.

7. Two-Man Full Court Drills

I often use these rebounding drills as part of the warm-up to open practice. The drills are: (1) Rebound-Outlet and Fill a Lane, and (2) The Bust-Out Drill.

Two lines are formed by the team, as shown in Diagram 5-7. The player under the basket throws the ball off of the bankboard, pulls it down with proper rebounding techniques, and looks to the outlet position.

If the coach instructs the rebounders to throw the outlet pass, the outlet man must dribble to the middle of the court. The rebounder goes behind his pass and quickly fills the outside lane. The drill continues as diagrammed in 5-8. Not only does it involve rebounding techniques, but passing, dribbling, and fastbreak fundamentals.

When the players are instructed to "bust out," it is assumed the outlet passing area is covered. The rebounder looks to the outlet man, then reverse pivots and takes two dribbles. This will get the player above the top of the key and out of congestion. The outlet man should move down court after the rebounder starts to dribble. The drill continues as diagrammed in 5-9.

For teaching purposes, the Two-Man Drills can be terminated at mid-court. This allows the coach to run the team through more rebounding fundamentals in a shorter time span.

8. Five-on-Five Team Rebounding

In order to work on the entire team as a rebounding unit, Five-on-Five Team Rebounding is often used in my practice session. Five defensive men are assigned to five offensive players. I usually start out by mismatching each player to add to the challenge. The post man sometimes is paired with a quick and pesky little guard. This forces the big man to move fast to hold inside position. Later, I assign the post man to a quick but taller forward. Finally, near the end of the drill, the post gets to defend the opponent's big man.

As in Three-on-Three Rebounding, the coach shoots the ball and then watches the players' techniques. Defenders outlet when they rebound, and offensive men attempt to score right away when they get the loose ball. This drill provides an excellent opportunity for the coach to suggest likely rebound spots. Recall that 65% of all side shots bounce over the basket when missed.

9. Blocking the Shooter and Following the Shot

During shooting drills, I like to work on blocking-out the shooter. Two or more players are grouped at a basket. The defender has the ball and starts the drill by passing to a shooter. The defender must contest the shot, then execute a front pivot and block-out. The offensive man can work on his offensive rebounding by attempting to shake loose from the block-out.

Post men can work on offensive rebounding by having the defense alternate at passive and active play. The defender can allow the offensive big man

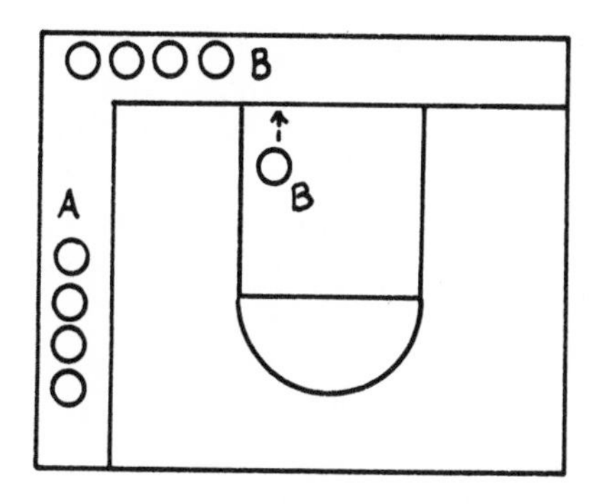

Diagram 5-7.
Two-Man Outlet Drill—
Positioning

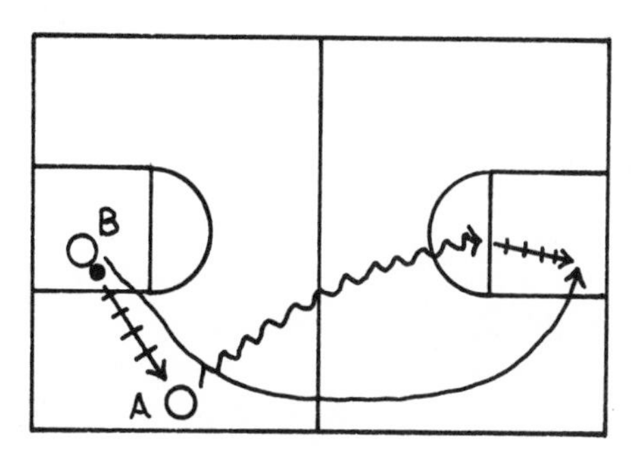

Diagram 5-8.
Outlet and Fill a Lane

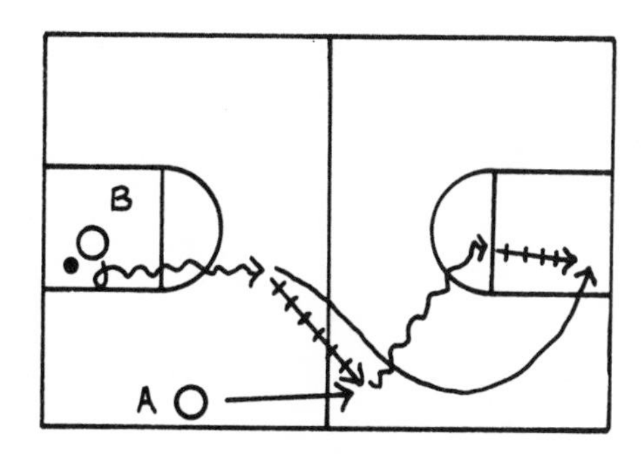

Diagram 5-9.
Bust-Out Drill

to regain his rebound with minimal resistance. A muscle shot is the goal of the offensive rebounder, so the defender can challenge tough after possession is gained. The next shot attempt should result in a strong block-out and aggressive rebound by the defender.

10. Free Throw Game called "Twenty-One"

I often use this drill as a "fun break" or to sharpen skills around the free throw line the day before a game. The players always seem to enjoy this drill, and the values gained are worth the time required to play it.

Four to six players are needed to play effectively. One player starts the game by shooting a free throw. The other players line up around the lane, looking to rebound a missed attempt. If the free throw is made, the shooter can continue shooting until he misses a shot or makes five in a row. Each free shot counts one point.

When a free throw is missed, everyone attempts to tip the ball in the basket. A successful tip gives the player two points, and the opportunity to make five consecutive free throws. If the rebound is caught or hits the floor, then play is dead and the next man in line becomes the free throw shooter.

The rotation of shooters is clock-wise. Thus, the player who misses a free throw goes to the left side. The top man on the right side moves to the free throw line. Of course, a successful tipper bypasses all competitors and moves to the free throw line.

A total score of "21" points wins the game. If two contests are going on at the same time, then a championship game involving the top finishers can be arranged.

Earlier in this chapter, I mentioned a particular game where poor free throw rebounding beat my team. This drill was used periodically from that time on, and our rebounding improved. Because my team was composed of excellent free throw shooters that year, the players began to assume all shots would be made in practice. However, when we got into the pressures of a game, many more free throws were missed. Because of a coaching oversight, my players were not assuming shots would be missed—the key to successful rebounding. The "Twenty-One" game keeps everyone alert and ready for missed attempts. Good habits are formed because of the personal competition.

6

UTILIZING THE POST IN YOUR CURRENT OFFENSE

There are many offensive attacks used in the modern game of basketball. All forms involve some kind of single or double post responsibilities. As mentioned earlier, the coach who uses his post men effectively will have a powerful game-winning weapon.

The patterned man-to-man offense, the speed game of fastbreak attack, out-of-bounds plays, and the opening tip-off can be turned into scoring opportunities for the big man. It is up to the coach to utilize the post man in the entire offensive attack. This chapter points out some important areas of offensive play where post men can take advantage.

THE FASTBREAK

Modern basketball is a fastbreaking game. Opponents are constantly looking to get the ball upcourt quickly, so they can gain an advantage over the defense. The advantage may come in three basic forms. These are:

1. **Beating all defenders down the court:** leaving an unmolested shot attempt for a streaking offensive player.
2. **Outnumbering the defenders:** thus, leaving one or more offensive players free to shoot.
3. **Forcing the defense to retreat quickly:** therefore, wearing them out and leaving them less effective as the game progresses.

A fastbreaking team is a threat in scoring many points in a relatively short time. Unlike the control-type teams, the fastbreakers can turn games around in a matter of minutes. Large deficits can be wiped out quickly, or close games can suddenly turn into "routs."

In chapter 5, the importance of the defensive rebound was discussed as a key to successful fastbreaking. The post man must be a good rebounder to help start the break, but he can also be an offensive threat. Hustle and proper movement with teammates are the essentials needed.

Since the post man is usually around the defensive basket and contending for rebounds, he will serve as a trailer on most fastbreaking thrusts. The big man should not consider his job finished after outletting a rebound. His assignment now switches to that of an offensive player, so he must be prepared to help his team attack. Following a rebound and outlet, the post man should perform the following sequence of duties.

1. Head for the sideline and go behind the man to whom he threw the outlet pass. (Diagram 6-1)
2. Serve as a trailer (second man down) in his lane. (Diagram 6-2)
3. Prepare to fill the outside lane if it is vacant. (Diagram 6-3)
4. Serve as a safety while trailing. The big man stays behind the ball and prevents an easy layup if a turnover occurs. (Diagram 6-4)
5. Attack the basket as a second cutter, after the first wing crosses under the hoop. (Diagram 6-5)
6. Set up at the low post if the initial break is stopped. (Diagram 6-6)

To be an effective fastbreak player, the post man must develop his full-court skills. These include running, cutting sharply, passing, receiving passes, and shooting. Lay-up shots should be learned from both sides of the court, with either hand, and at full speed. This is an area that tall, uncoordinated big men often show weaknesses. Full-court drills and involvement with smaller team members will help develop the post man for the running game.

Being able to stop quickly and shoot a ten to fifteen foot shot is also a requirement of an active post player. A feed to the big man on a wing should result in two points. A lagging defense will often concede the outside shot on the break, especially to the post man. I drill my players daily on the medium-range bank shot off of the break. Since the post player is required to learn a bank shot as part of the "basic three," he can rapidly develop it for fastbreak purposes. The keys are landing on both feet in a jump stop and stopping in the bank shot angle areas.

Some teams employ fastbreaks off of made shots—both free throw and field goal attempts. This adds to the quick attack, as fastbreak opportunities are possible in every change of possession.

Many coaches assign the post man to take the ball out-of-bounds after a made shot. This has some obvious advantages. The big man can see down the court and over most defensive pressure. He is able to pass over a defender who may challenge his inbounds pass, and he is already back to defend in case a turnover occurs.

I prefer to use my post man in a slightly different fashion on the "Made-Shot Break." I picked this method up from Coach Ralph Miller while I worked under him at Oregon State University. The next tallest player, usually a tall forward, takes the ball out of bounds. The best shooting guard

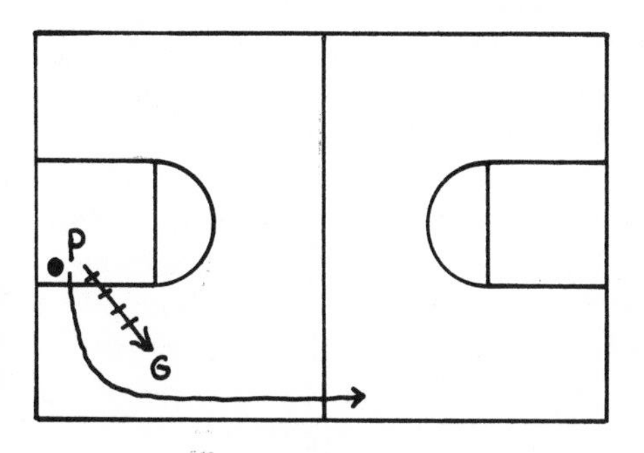

Diagram 6-1.
Go Behind Outlet Pass

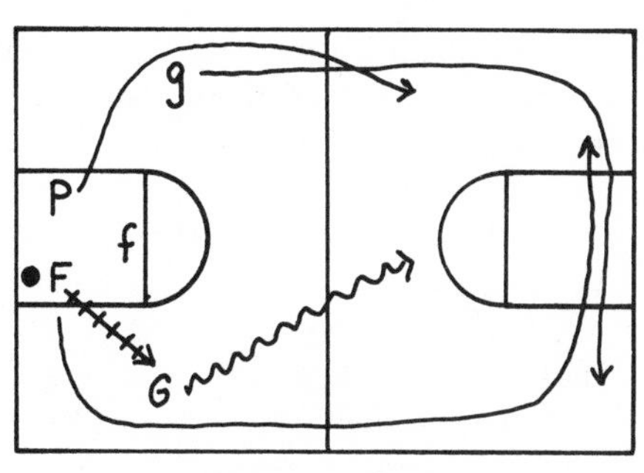

Diagram 6-2.
Post as a Trailer

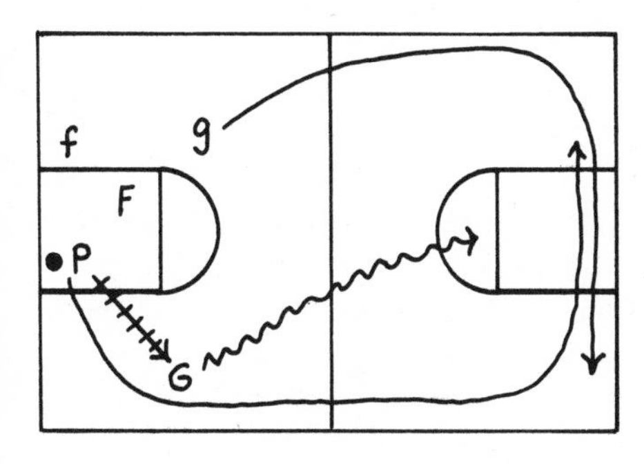

Diagram 6-3.
Post Fills Lane

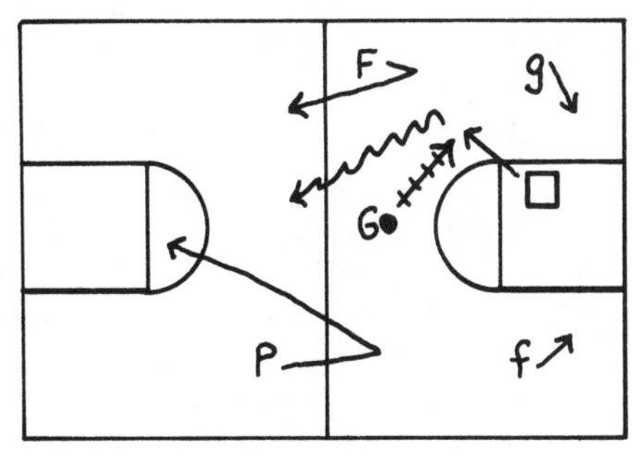

Diagram 6-4.
Post as a Trailing
Safety

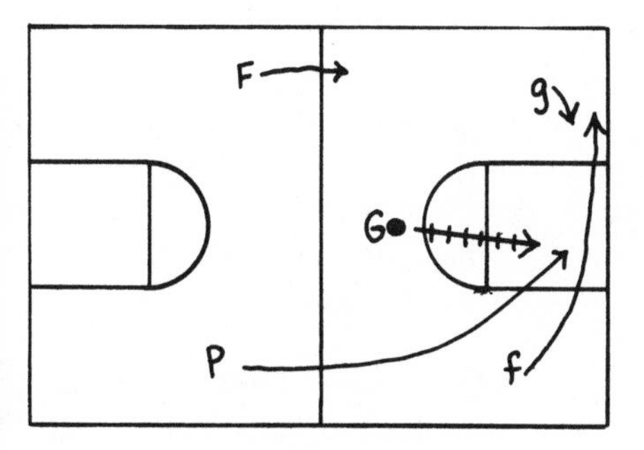

Diagram 6-5.
Post Cutter after Cross

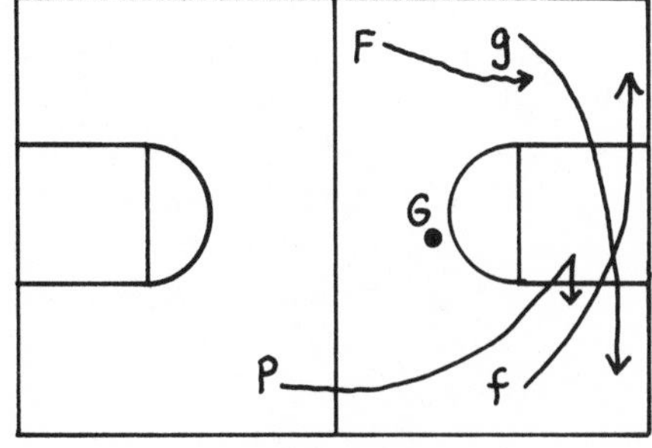

Diagram 6-6.
Set Up at Low Post

streaks down the court and heads for the right corner. The short forward goes to the mid-court, right side area. The other guard serves as an inlet on the right side. The whole left side is left open for the post man to streak down. (Diagram 6-7)

All players on the right side should be alert to the possibility of passing to the streaking post man. Should his defender decide to loaf back on defense, an easy two points may result. If the ball goes all the way down to the flash guard (g), he has the option to drive or shoot. When the guard puts the ball over his head, this keys the post man to cut across the key and establish low post position. A quick feed may catch the defenders off balance and an easy muscle shot will result.

Any team that alternates its post men a lot will wear the opponent's big man out with this attack. Even a good, hustling post man who plays the entire game can get some easy shots once in a while. Whatever the case, it surely beats walking the ball up the court!

SINGLE POST OFFENSES

Single Post Offense has been the most widely used attack by basketball teams in the past forty years. Because of its adaptability, the single post setup can easily be revised to fit the talents of most teams. It is a balanced attack, having two forwards and a post man in good position to score or rebound, and two guards in position to retreat quickly on defense.

Many of the plays used by single post teams were illustrated in Chapter 4, dealing with the high post player. Others are mentioned in Chapter 10, which covers my man-to-man offense. The key to utilizing the post man in any of these attacks is to get him under the basket as much as possible. The big man can start at the high post, but he should end up under the hoop at the end of the play. This positions him for a feed and an easy score, or puts him in excellent offensive rebounding position.

Starting the post man at the low post makes an interesting situation for the defense. (See Diagram 6-8) They must worry about a quick feed inside, a lob pass to the basket, or a quick cut to another position by the big man.

Any play that requires the big man to move out of the low post should end with him moving back to the low post area. Diagram 6-9 demonstrates a side post split with a guard shooting. The post man hands off and then goes to the internal zone looking for a return pass or rebound.

The single post player has the territorial right to move in the internal zone. By setting up or moving to the low post, he becomes a powerful offensive threat.

THE SHUFFLE OFFENSE

The Shuffle Offense has been a popular attack in many areas of the country since the 1940's. Bruce Drake, former coach at the University of

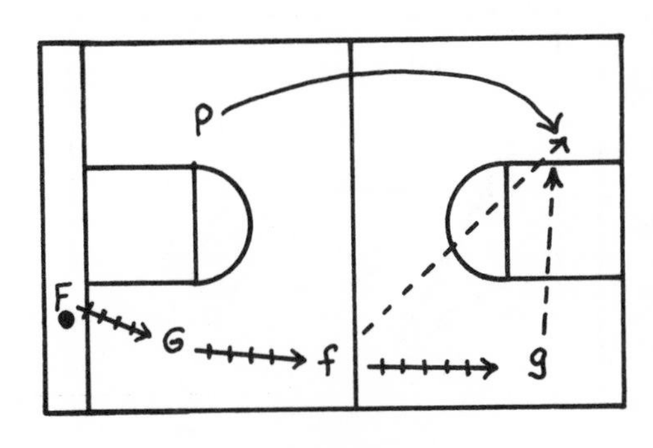

Diagram 6-7.
The Made-Shot Break

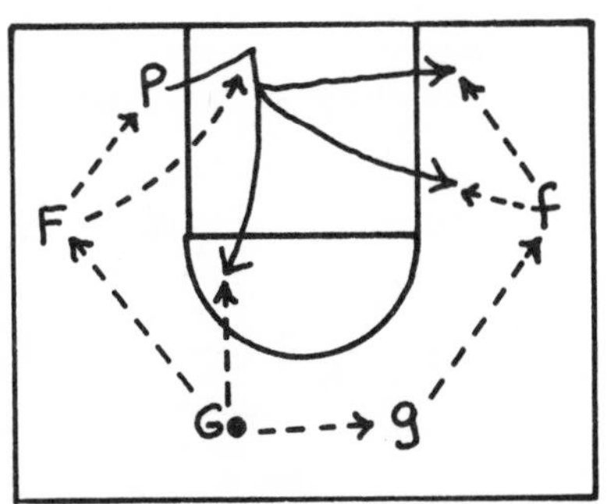

Diagram 6-8.
The Single Post Set-up

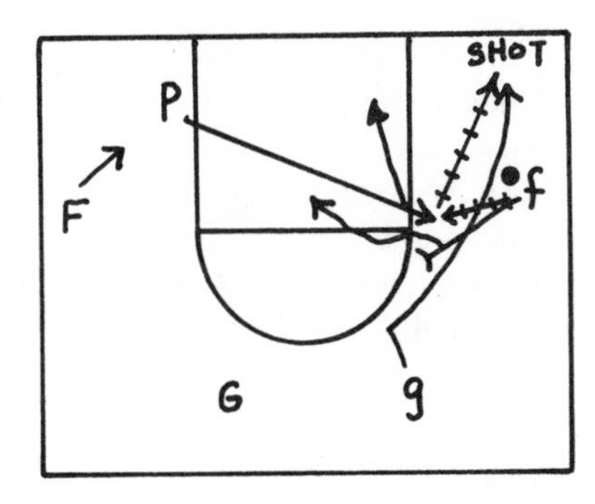

Diagram 6-9.
Side Post Split

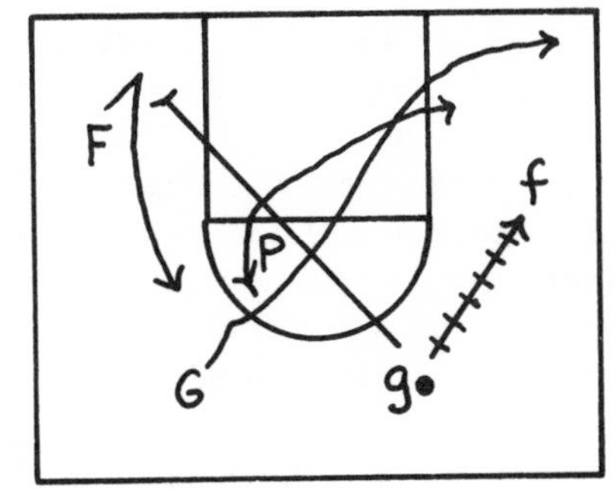

Diagram 6-10A.
Four Man Shuffle

Oklahoma, is credited as the innovator of the Shuffle. Joel Eaves, former coach at Auburn University, wrote a complete book of the offense in 1960. The title of his work was *Basketball's Shuffle Offense* published by Prentice-Hall, Inc.

While the Shuffle Offense basically found its success through the patterned movement of five middle-sized players, it can be adapted to fit the tall post man. Rather than rotating the big man in all positions as the Shuffle requires, the coach can elect to run a "Four Man Shuffle." This keeps the post man where he belongs: around the basket! Diagrams 6-10 A and B illustrate the "Four Man Shuffle" with an active post man.

After setting the screen on the cutter, the post man follows him to the basket. If the defensive post switches to the cutting guard, a mismatch will result for the offensive big man. A feed from -f- will result in an easy shot attempt for the low post man.

In Diagram 6-10B, the "change of sides" occurs. As -f- cuts off of -P-, the post again follows to the strong side low post position. The cutter always

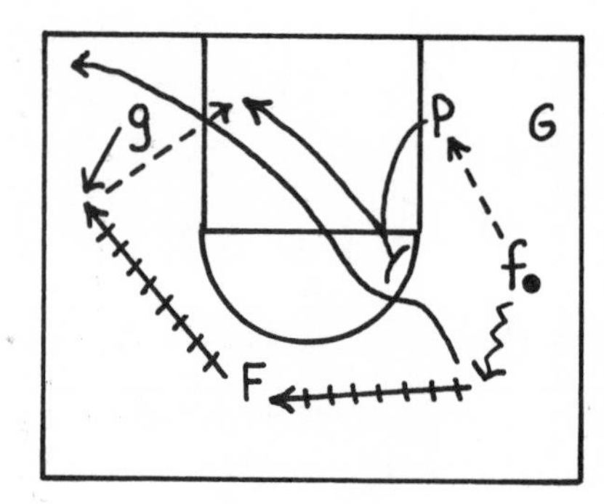

Diagram 6-10B.
Change of Sides

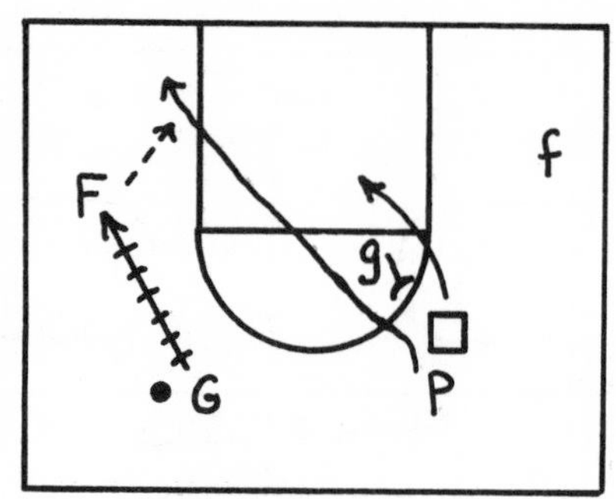

Diagram 6-11.
Rubbing Out the
Post Man

takes his defender to the corner, thus freeing the internal area for the post. Player -F- should pick for -G- after passing to -g-, thus completing the "change of sides."

Coaches of agile big men may wish to use the regular "Five Man Shuffle" from time to time. I have found it very effective to bring a defensive big man out to the guard position, then rub him off on a screen. (See Diagram 6-11). Involving the post man in patterned play now and then will often confuse the opponents and spark your offense.

THE PASSING GAME

The offense of the 1970's has been the *PASSING GAME*, especially on the West Coast. It has spread rapidly through the college ranks and recently found its way into many high school programs.

Passing Game simply means "if you pass, screen opposite." It offers continuous movement, many picks, and free-lance opportunities. The offense can be run from one or two guard fronts, and there is also a four man version for coaches who like to leave the post man under the basket. Coaches often adopt their own rules and options for the Passing Game. It can be designed to set up one key player, or provide a balanced five man attack. The Passing Game offers freedom to the coach and players, while keeping the attack balanced and moving. The constant motion of weak-side and strong-side players presents a very difficult assignment to the defenders.

Diagram 6-12A illustrates one version of the *Four Man Passing Game* attack. The post man sets up away from the ball and waits until a pass goes to the forward position. He then breaks across the key and establishes a new low post position. A feed inside should result in a one-on-one move from the "basic three." The weak-side defenders are involved in fighting through picks; therefore, they cannot provide much help on the post player.

Diagram 6-12B shows the ball reversing sides, allowing the post man to

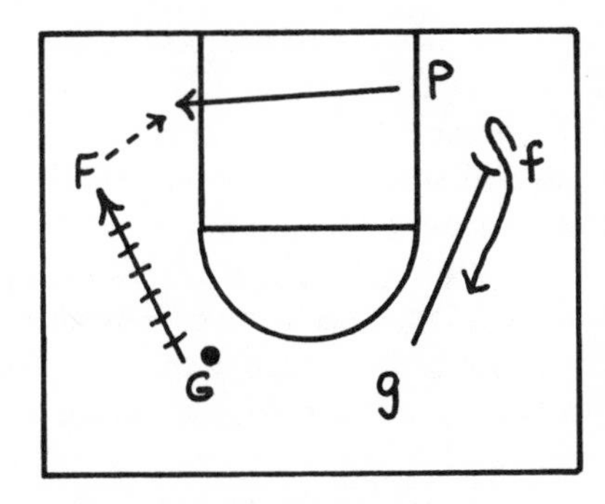

Diagram 6-12A.
Four Man Passing Game

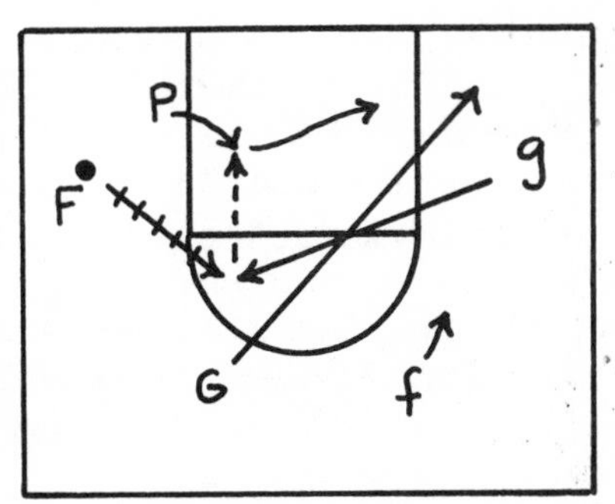

Diagram 6-12B.
Four Man Continued

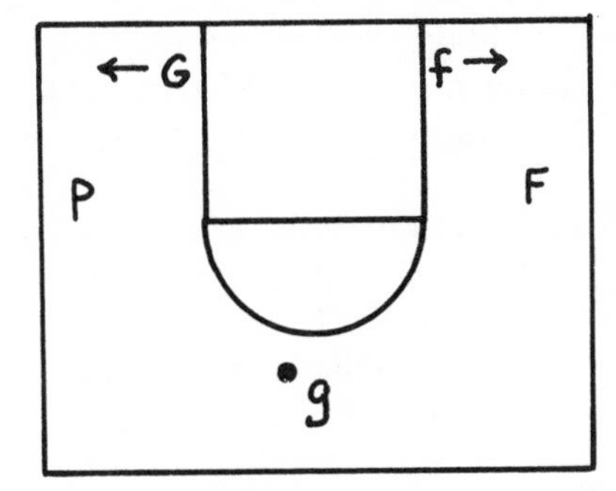

Diagram 6-13A.
Five Man Passing Game
Setup

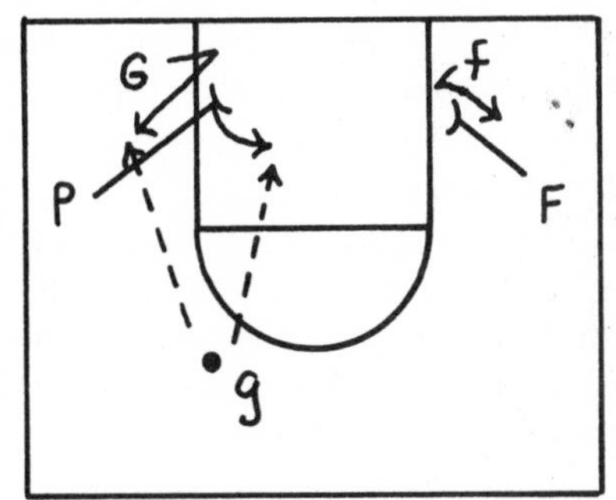

Diagram 6-13B.
Initial Pick-and-Roll

again flash across the key. The perimeter players must remember to continually "screen opposite" after passing the ball. The picks will also open shooters for fifteen foot shots around the free throw line. The big man is always in good rebound position.

The *Five Man Passing Game* is usually run from a one guard front. A 1-2-2 alignment is the most popular setup. (See Diagram 6-13A.) The baseline man can start at the low posts or the corners.

By putting the big men on the wings, the initial picks of the offense often free the low post players. Two quick passes may result in a shot at the low post. Sometimes, the point man can feed directly to the rolling post. (Diagram 6-13B).

OUT-OF-BOUNDS PLAYS

When a team gets possession of the ball underneath its own basket, the opportunity arises for a quick score. Again, utilization of the post man can play a big part in the effectiveness of "out-of-bounds plays."

Since the ball is taken out under the basket, the shortest pass is to a player under the hoop. The big man has the size and reach necessary to receive a pass inside. He should be set up by having him cut to the ball from the perimeter, or by picking his defender. I have used my post as a picker on "out-of-bounds plays," then rolled him to the hoop. This involves movement of other offensive players, thus confusing the defense enough to free the post man. Diagrams 6-14 A and B illustrate two of my favorite plays involving the big man.

In both plays, the post man picks and rolls under the basket. The first cutter receives the ball if he is open. Usually the defenders will switch, thus freeing the rolling big man.

Because of the success many teams have had with "out-of-bounds plays," defensive teams have gone to the zone as a method of stopping picks and rolls. I have used one particular "zone out-of-bounds play" for years, and it has paid off handsomely. While appearing quite simple to execute, it nevertheless produces easy shots inside. Diagram 6-15 shows the "zone out-of-bounds play."

The post man lines up on the side of the ball near the free throw line. Player "F" represents a strong inside threat, "g" is the best corner shooter, and "G" is the safety release. At the slap of the ball, "F" breaks under the basket and "asks" for a pass. If open, he should immediately receive the ball for a muscle shot. Player "G" lopes up to the top of the key, while "g" moves quickly to the corner and sets up to shoot. When the zone defense shifts to cover this movement, "P" can cut to the hoop for a lob pass. It is amazing the number of times "P" is open for the shot. When the defense adjusts, "g" is usually wide open in the corner. Since he is the best corner shooter, the open attempt is a high percentage shot.

Because the rules were changed and one-shot free throws eliminated, "sideline out-of-bounds plays" have become important offensive weapons. Again, I favor a picking and cutting post man who moves to the hoop. Diagrams 6-16A and B show my favorite sideline play.

The pattern is similar to a "Shuffle Cut" from out-of-bounds. The post man follows the cutter and receives a pass if the defenders have switched. The post also serves as a safety inlet man, in case the guard is covered.

Against zones, sideline plays are unnecessary. I usually choose to just inbound the ball and set up in a regular zone offensive attack.

TIP PLAYS

The tallest player on the court can be an effective weapon during tip situations. With a little thought and planning, the post man can turn jump ball plays into quick scores. Diagram 6-17 shows a favorite tip play of mine to start a game. The center tips to the open forward, then sprints to the offen-

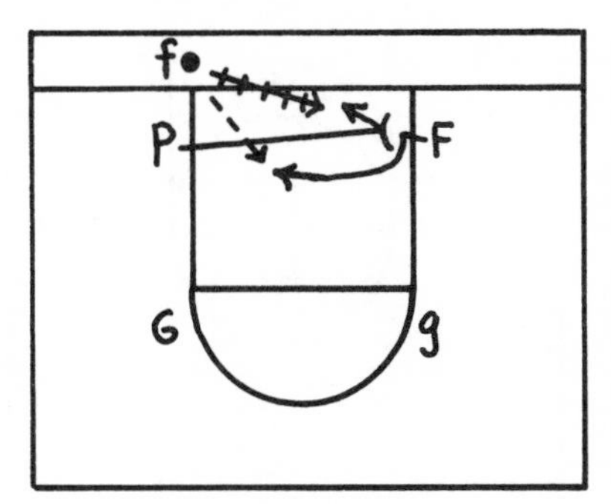

Diagram 6-14A.
Lateral Pick
Out-of-Bounds

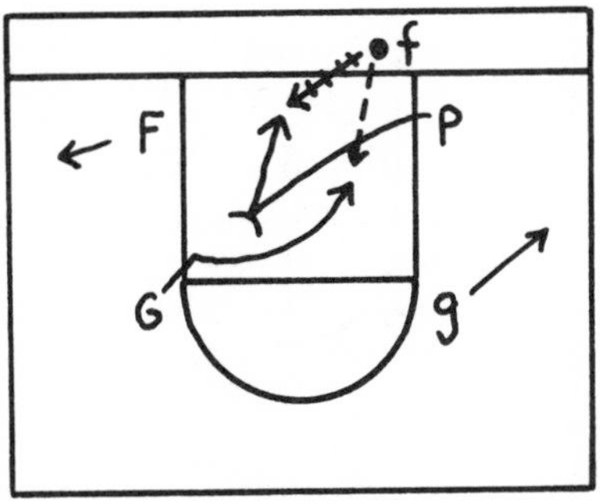

Diagram 6-14B.
Diagonal Pick
Out-of-Bounds

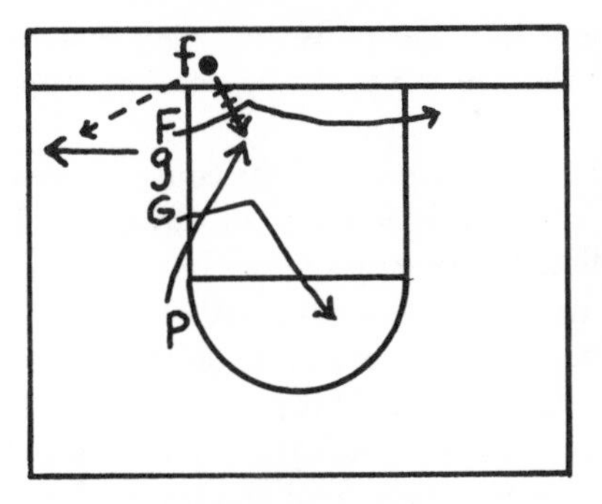

Diagram 6-15.
Zone Out-of-Bounds Play

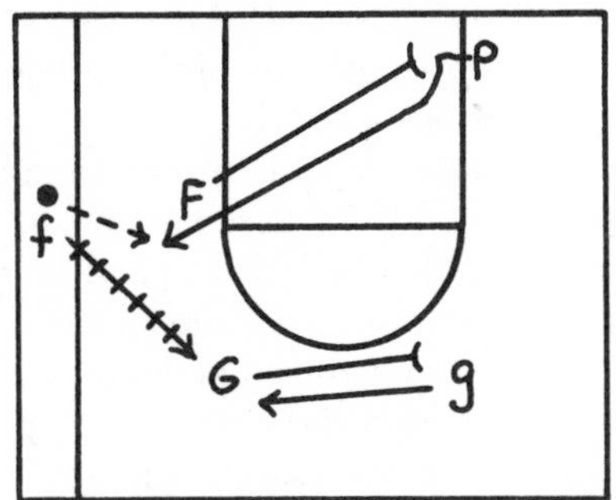

Diagram 6-16A.
Sideline Play

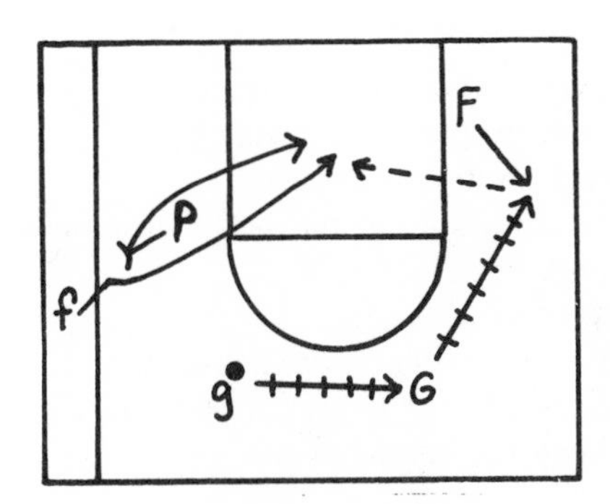

Diagram 6-16B.
Sideline Continued

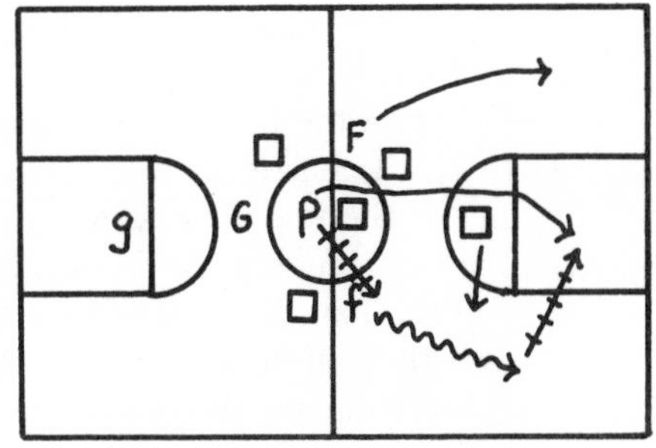

Diagram 6-17.
Tip Play for Post

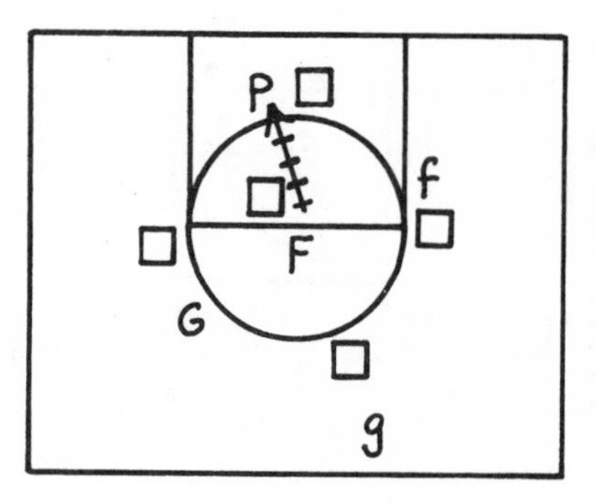

Diagram 6-18A.

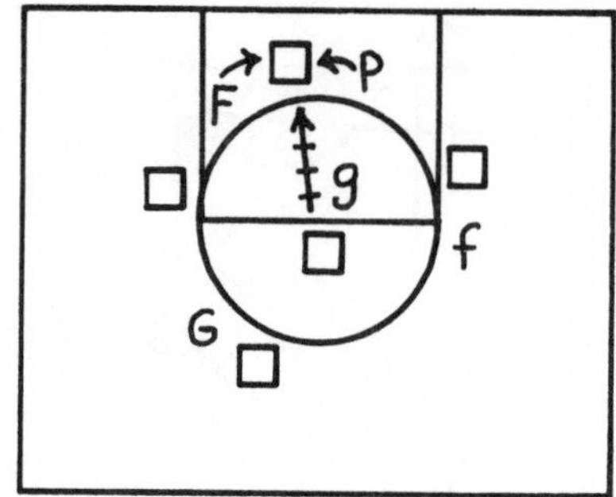

Diagram 6-18B.

sive basket. The forward dribbles to the side and pulls the safety man out. This frees the post man for a quick feed inside, provided he beats his opposing center down court.

The same play can be used from the defensive end of the court whenever the post is involved in the jump ball. The guards and forwards would switch areas, thus allowing the best ball handlers to drive up the sideline. The taller forwards are then available for defending the opponent's basket.

When not involved in the tip itself, the post man should position himself under the basket and next to the opponent's center. This provides him with a chance at a quick scoring attempt under his own basket. When under the opponent's basket, the big man is in position to defend the internal zone. (See Diagrams 6-18A and B).

Gaining possession in a jump ball situation requires the post man to prepare himself physically and mentally. Some suggestions for good tip control include:

1. Check the placement of all players for possible open gaps.
2. Get low by bending the knees and preparing to spring up.
3. Focus on the ball and concentrate on its movement.
4. Keep the hands off of the knees. Freedom to move the arms will enable the jumper to extend himself higher.
5. Tip with the fingers; do not slap or grab the toss.
6. Tap the ball firmly and directly to the intended teammate. Never slam the ball hard, as it may be fumbled or go out of bounds.
7. Practice tip situations often to keep the timing sharp.

7

DEFEATING ANY DEFENSE WITH EFFECTIVE POST PLAY

There are a variety of reasons why basketball teams use defenses other than basic man-to-man coverage. Lack of quickness, height, or experience lead coaches to install special defensive philosophies. A team must be prepared to meet these challenges so the inside game will not be disrupted. Effective post play is the key to defeating any defense, including straight zone coverage, match-up zones, and full-court pressure. This chapter will deal with some of the many "specialty defenses" in use today.

ATTACKING ZONES

Zone defenses are very popular at the high school level and are gaining respect in the colleges. Lower-level coaches often employ zones because they require less time to implement than man-to-man defense. With the conflicts today for practice space and time at all levels, the zone can be a life saver to the coach. More time can be used in learning how to put the ball in the basket, along with other offensive fundamentals.

Zone may also be installed to slow quicker opponents, to save star players from foul trouble, or to force the opposition to shoot from the outside. If the adversary is successful at accomplishing any of these objectives, then the offensive post men are *not effective!*

Zones must be attacked internally. This can be accomplished through quick ball movement, cutting action of the offensive players, and a conscious effort to look and pass to inside players. It is the coach's responsibility to see that his team has these necessary tools to handle zones.

A zone offense should be similar in its initial lineup to a team's man-to-man offense. This allows for smooth transition against the two defenses and eliminates confusion on the part of the offensive team. The same basic alignment should be used against all half-court defenses. Only a slight adjustment to the weak areas is necessary to get good shots against the 2-1-2, 1-2-2, or 1-3-1 zone half-court defenses.

The fastbreak is a great weapon to beat the zone, but the offense must accept only high percentage inside shots. If the defense is able to convert quickly enough to stop the lay up or short shot, then the offense must set up and work the half-court attack. Impatient teams that shoot quickly and from long range will often have trouble against zones.

Penetration with a dribble can be useful in drawing defenders away from the post men. While I like dribbling to be held to a minimum, the guards can disrupt the zone with quick penetration. This draws the defenders to the ball and opens passing lanes to the big boys inside.

Quick passes, especially from one side of the court to the other, often free the post men inside. The defenders must shift and adjust each time the ball is moved to a new area of the court. A combination of good passing and movement by the post men internally will result in open passing lanes.

All perimeter players must be conscious of teammates who are working to get open inside. Each player should look to pass inside before moving the ball to a new perimeter man.

As mentioned in chapter 4, the high post is a great area to attack a zone defense. The potential passing angles are considerable and the shot or drive threat is always there. I try to keep a player stationed at the high post, or constantly move players in and out of this attacking area. A pass to the high post, who in turn feeds a floating low post man, is a very effective play.

I like to face zones because they are generally weak on the boards and on baseline defense. The defenders in a zone defense are assigned areas to rebound, so very little blocking-out takes place. This allows my offensive men the freedom to "crash and cash" as we like to say. (i.e. "crash the boards and cash in on the scoreboard!" The baseline defense is weak, due to lack of coaching time spent on this important area. Zone defenders usually "dance on their toes" with both arms extended overhead when guarding the ball at the low post. A quick fake and drive often result in a muscle shot or two free throws.

There are many fine zone offenses used by coaches across the country. Some teams employ two or three offenses against zones, using a different attack for each defensive alignment. I have used only one zone offense the past five years, and it has worked well against all zones. It is called "The Stack" and can easily be adjusted to fit the personnel of various teams from year to year. The initial setup is shown in Diagram 7-1.

The two tallest players are lined up in a stack on the left, low post area. Since this is the best spot for a low post man to operate, this offensive setup takes full advantage of the territory.

The best outside shooting forward plays the wing spot -f-. Basically he is a feeder, a board crasher, and perimeter shooter. He keeps the opponent honest by hitting the outside shot if the defense jams the middle or sags. Sometimes a guard can be used at this position, especially an immobile one.

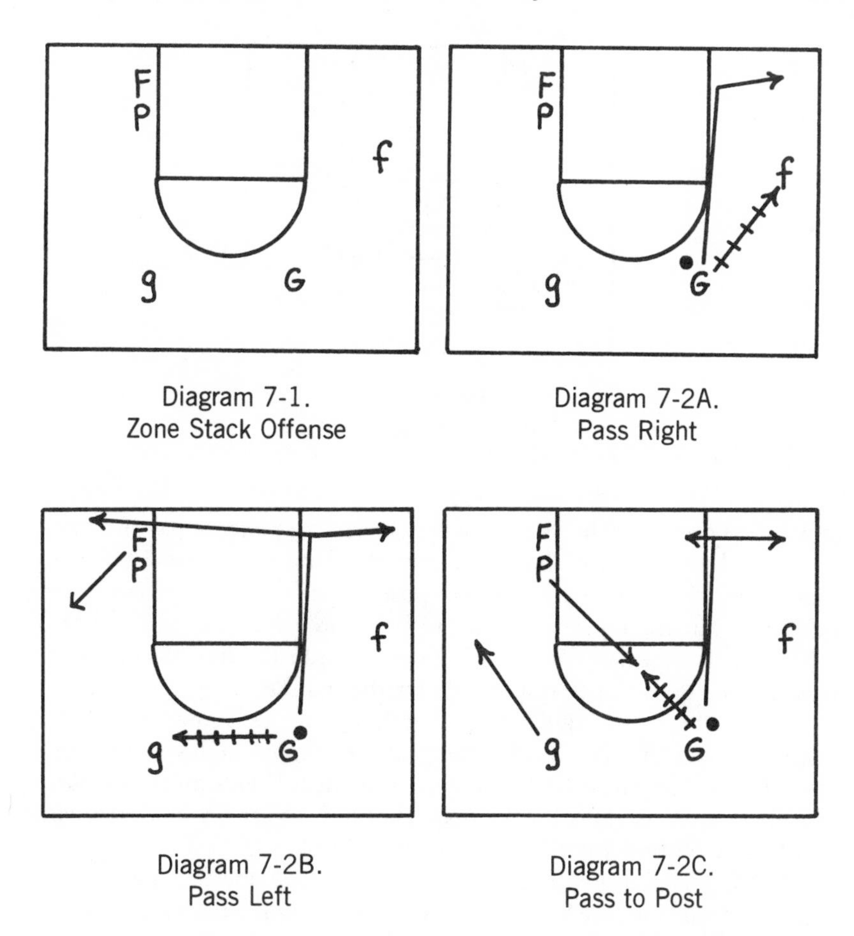

Diagram 7-1.
Zone Stack Offense

Diagram 7-2A.
Pass Right

Diagram 7-2B.
Pass Left

Diagram 7-2C.
Pass to Post

This spot requires very little movement, but a talented player can be devastating here. Free-lance movement is possible and can be utilized easily in this offense.

The guards always start out as a two-man front, but quickly shift to a single guard point. The reason for a two-man front is simple. Two players can handle the initial pressure of an attacking zone much easier than one point man. Once the ball is passed to someone on or below the free throw line, one guard cuts to the baseline and serves as a floater. (See Diagrams 7-2A, B, and C). This sets up overloads and possible open shots from the vulnerable corner areas.

The guard who is designated as the cutter and baseline floater falls into one of three categories. These are: (1) the best low posting guard, (2) the best corner shooter, or (3) the man with the hot hand. The third category often develops as a game progresses. By sending your hot shooter to float the baseline, you take advantage of his total value to the team. His presence in the corner draws the zone out and opens the inside game. If the defense

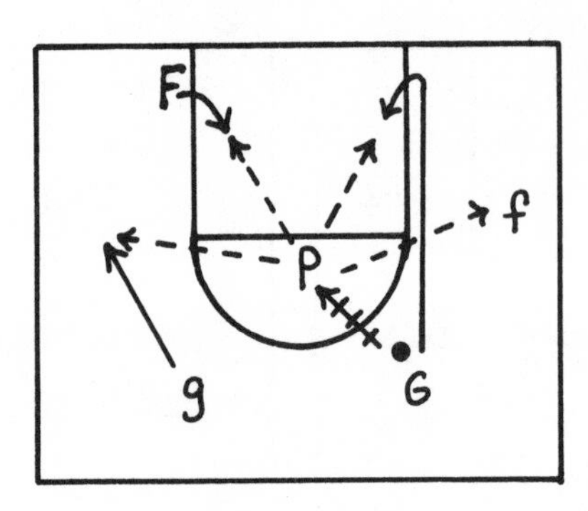

Diagram 7-2D.
Hitting the High Post

refuses to come out, the shooter will make the opponents pay the price.

The "Stack Offense" has three key attacking areas that set the inside game in motion. These are the high post, the left side wing, and the right side wing. The high post is a powerful attack area as mentioned earlier. The 1-2-2 zone is especially vulnerable to passes into the free throw line area, since no one defender is responsible for the middle.

Any player receiving a pass at the high post must immediately pivot to face the basket. In "The Stack," the post man breaks high when the area is open. Upon receiving the ball, he must immediately look for the big forward -F-. He should also look for the open shot himself; and as outlined earlier, look for the cutting guard. (See Diagram 7-2D.)

A tall, physical guard can surprise many zones by posting low on the high post feed. The big forward -F- is also tough when flashing from behind the defenders. Since I often use a double post attack, -F- is usually a very effective low post scorer.

The point guard -g- moves to the left wing for a possible shot, while the forward -f- also looks for an open shooting spot. The high post has four possible passing options. If the ball goes to the wing, the floater -G- moves to the ball-side corner and initiates the overload. (See Diagram 7-3A and B.) The offense then requires the strong-side low post to be filled by one of the two post men, -F- or -P-. The overload now has a shooter in the corner, on the wing, and wide on the weak side. The high and low post positions are filled by the two big men.

My theory of zone offense contains five very important principles.

1. Overload one side of the court.
2. Fill the high and low posts as much as possible.
3. Station a wing wide on the weak side.
4. Reverse the ball from side to side.
5. Use inner rotation of the post men.

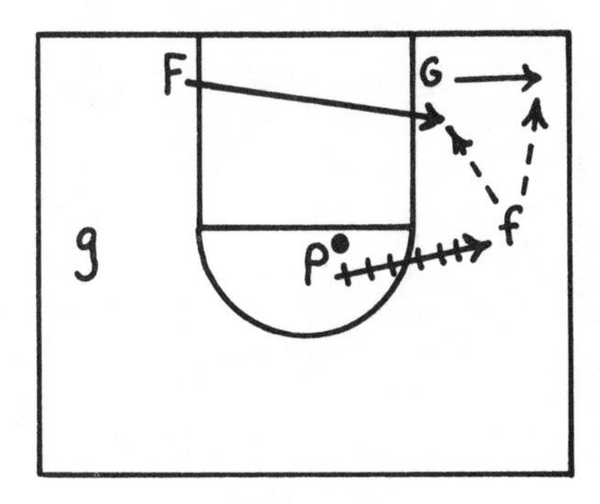

Diagram 7-3A.
High Post to Right Wing

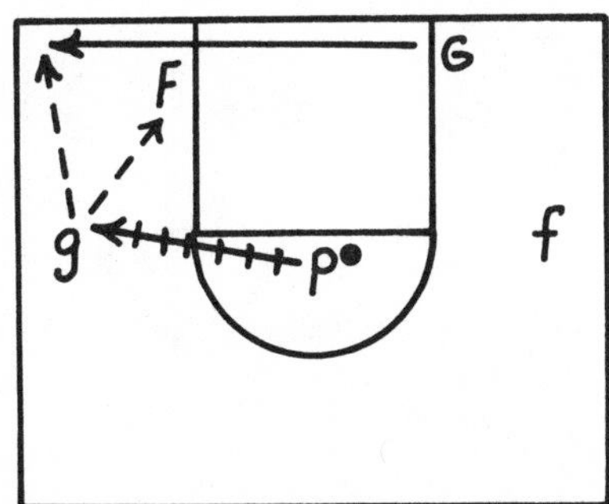

Diagram 7-3B.
High Post to Left Wing

ESTABLISHING THE INTERNAL ATTACK

The first two principles have already been illustrated. The last three are the keys to getting the ball inside and establishing an internal attack.

The weak-side wing must stay wide to keep the zone shift legitimate. If all players congregate on one side of the floor, the zone can easily cover the offensive men. An offensive player on the weak side forces the defense to spread out and respect the cross-court pass. This spread enables perimeter men to pass inside much easier.

The weak-side man also enables the offense to reverse the ball quickly and effectively. Changing sides of attack forces the zone defenders to move and adjust to a new situation. If a defensive mistake occurs due to confusion or slow reaction, then a feed inside is almost assured. Diagram 7-4 illustrates a change of sides from a typical overload.

Note how -P- might have to break to a very high post. This is sometimes necessary in ball reversals and should be encouraged if the middle is jammed. The threat of dumping the ball into the low post is still possible from the top of the key. The important thing is to spread the defense.

The fifth point of emphasis is inner rotation of the two big men. In order to keep the zone from keying on the man at the low post, the big men must exchange positions from time to time. When the low post is jammed and the player cannot receive a direct pass, he must vacate the area and move to the weak-side low post. This causes three helpful consequences:

1. The low post man is relocated in the best offensive rebounding spot, should a perimeter man shoot.
2. The high post is free to slide into the empty low post.
3. The zone must readjust and find a new way to stop the internal game.

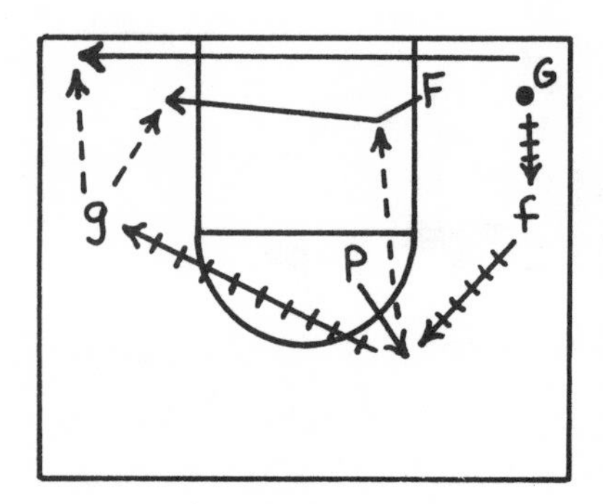

Diagram 7-4.
Change of Sides—
"Ball Reversal"

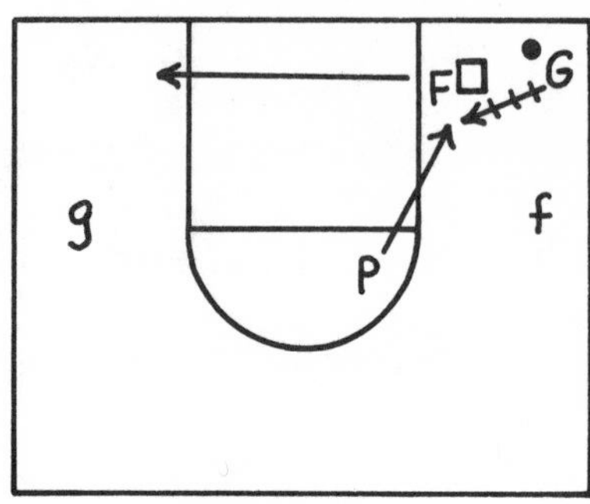

Diagram 7-5.
Inner Rotation

Diagram 7-5 shows a big man leaving the low post because he is fronted and cannot get a pass. The high post moves low to an open passing lane.

The two big men initially line up in the stack to take full advantage of the best low post area. It also enables one or both of them to break to new attack positions much easier. The high post man can charge up to the free throw line whenever he sees an opening. Because all defenders have their backs to the stack, the high post man has a distinct advantage of getting the ball.

When the initial attack starts on the left side, the big forward -F- pops out to receive a pass on the wing. He should try to catch the ball within range of a short bank shot, if possible. Since all big men are schooled in the fine art of bank shooting, this shot can get the offense a quick two points.

As the forward receives the ball, he should take a quick look to his partner at the low post. It the zone is not adjusted quickly, a short pass to the post man is a ticket to an easy basket inside.

Diagram 7-6 illustrates my favorite way to utilize the stack for a quick power basket. Notice that -5- will have a very difficult time fronting -P- when the ball is moved in this manner.

Diagram 7-7 shows the right side attack with no high post required. Remember: -P- only breaks to the high post if there is an opening or if the guards are being pressured.

After passing to the wing -f-, the floater -G- goes to the low post looking for a return pass in the key area. If covered, -G- goes to the corner and allows the post -P- to break low to the ball. The big forward -F- goes to the opening at the high post, and the point -g- moves to the weak side for balance.

Whether the offense attacks the high post, right wing, or left wing, the five principles of zone attack should be met. That is: (1) overload, (2) fill the high a low posts, (3) establish the weak-side threat, (4) reverse the ball, and (5) rotate the posts inside.

Beating zones inside can be done with any zone offense, provided your team looks to go to the posts. Whether you use "The Stack" or your own

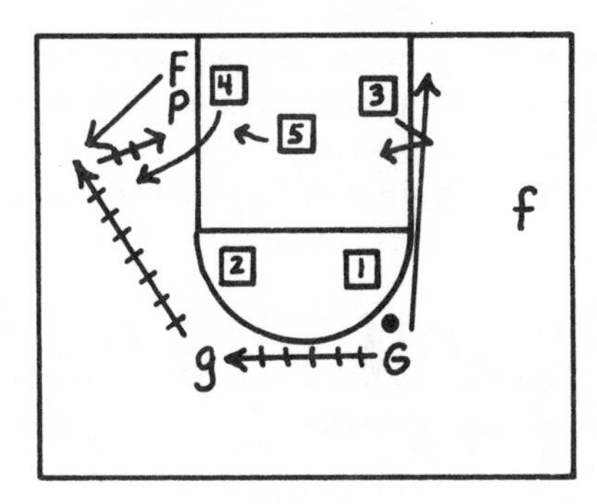

Diagram 7-6.
Left-Side Attack

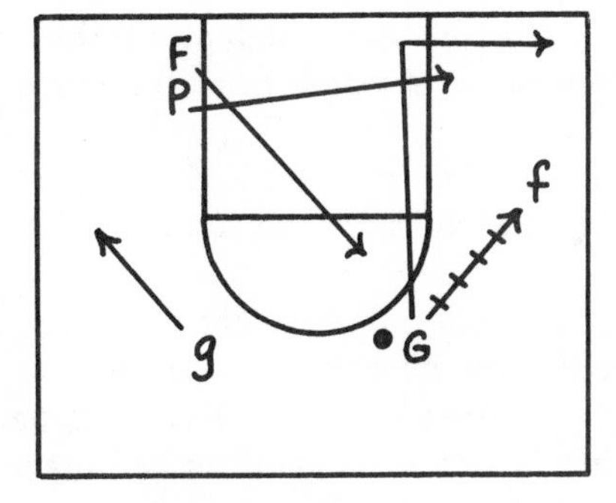

Diagram 7-7.
Right-Side Attack

setup, follow the "five principles" for beating zones and get high percentage shots.

MATCH-UP ZONES

Match-up zones are a more complex version of straight zones. Some coaches favor the matchups because they allow more individual pressure on the shooter.

Rules are developed for challenging the ball and any offensive movement. The defenders guard an opponent in their specific assigned area, but release the responsibility when the offensive man moves to a new area. If no man is in the defender's assigned area, he plays a regular zone and sags to the ball as a helper. In other words, matchups attempt to utilize as much man-to-man as possible and still stay in a zone defense.

Matchups provide excellent pressure against outside shooting teams, especially those who do not pass the ball much. They also protect the defenders from using the extra energy required to play good man-to-man defense. But probably the single most positive factor of matchups is the panic it throws into opposing coaches. Having faced many match-up zones in my coaching career, I can humbly agree that they do present problems uncommon to facing straight zone or man-to-man.

Establishing a third offense to attack matchups is not recommended. The time required to properly teach it to your team will likely never offset the results. Besides, your players have enough to remember when learning their man and zone attacks. One of these two offenses should be used against the matchup. Free-lance opportunities will need to be emphasized, but the inside attack can be the saver.

In recent years, I have always used the "Stack Offense" against the match-up defense. The corner shot is often shut off, but I want the ball inside anyway. If the defense elects to pull itself out to stop the outside shot, then it is easier to find passing lanes to the high and low posts.

Remember, the high post is the best feeding area against any defense. If the post breaks high from the stack, he usually can receive a quick feed against the matchup. By pivoting to the hoop, he immediately has two great options. They are: hit the flashing low post or dump it to the cutting guard. Diagram 7-8 shows the problem match-up defenders face on the high post feed.

Defender -3- is caught defending both -G- and -f-. Each time the ball is passed, the offensive men are moving. This causes the defense to shift and adjust correspondingly. By being patient and reversing the ball once or twice, a very good shot can be obtained.

I have found the matchup to be even weaker inside than straight zones. Once the offense gets the ball to the low post, the defender is usually caught in a half-zone half-man situation. A quick offensive move to the hoop will often prevent the defense from recovering and reacting properly.

Teams that do not front the low post are dead when matching up. Just get the ball inside as soon as possible and let your big men do the work. If they front, use internal rotation, overload, reverse, and keep looking inside until the defense allows a passing lane.

Coaches using zone offenses showing little movement may find the matchup quite trying. Especially in early season when not all phases of attack have been covered, teams are vulnerable to the simplest matchups. In these situations, instructing your team to run its man offense is a smart adjustment. The players are familiar with the pattern, it usually supplies the needed cutting and penetration, plus the bonus of movement. A standing team will beat few defenses, especially the match-up zone.

The One-Four Offense is a very popular method of attacking matchups. The initial alignment presents a problem to the defense immediately. Two players are stationed at the powerful high post positions. The setup forces the defense to bring its big men up to the high posts, thus leaving the baseline and low post areas vulnerable. (Diagram 7-9.)

Four possible passing angles are open to the point man -g-. Diagrams 7-10A and B illustrate options open to the players in the One-Four Offense. A pass to the wing allows the weak-side high post man to cut to the low post. This move attacks the vulnerable strong-side baseline area. If the second pass can be made, the post man should be free to go one-on-one. Diagram 7-10B shows some of the many options open to the receiver of a high post pass. The other post cuts diagonally to the hoop while the wings stay wide, but can move to any opening on the baseline.

Reversing the ball around the perimeter keys internal movement of the posts. The high post cuts diagonally low, while the low post moves to any opening at the new strong-side high post. (Diagram 7-11.)

The One-Four supplies the keys to defeating zones quite well. The high and low posts are filled, there is internal movement, the weak side remains wide, and overloads develop.

Attack the matchups internally, but remember: movement is the key!

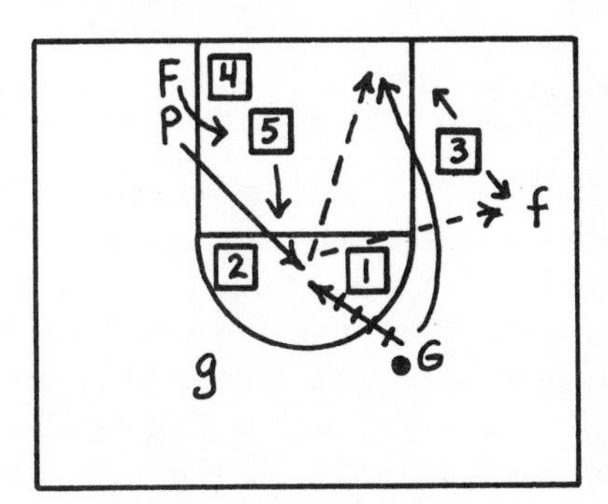

Diagram 7-8.
Attacking the Matchup from the High Post

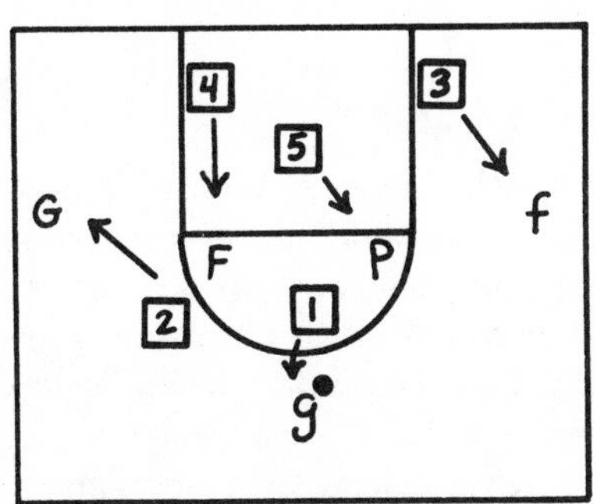

Diagram 7-9.
The One-Four Versus Matchup

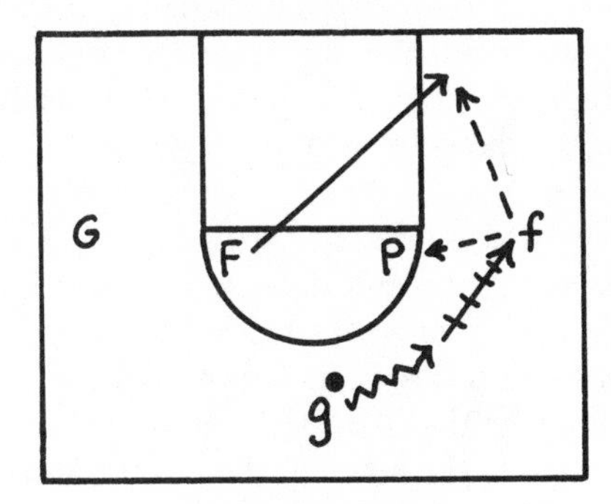

Diagram 7-10A.
Pass to the Wing of One-Four

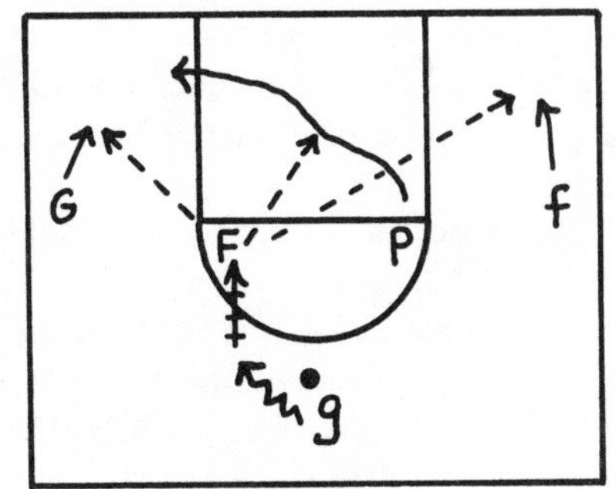

Diagram 7-10B.
Pass to the High Post of One-Four

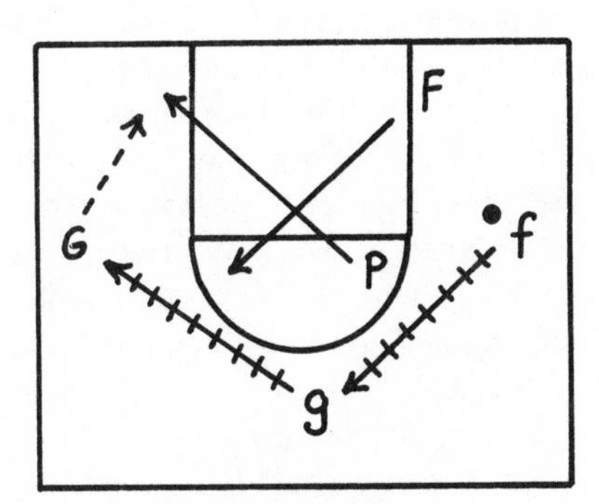

Diagram 7-11.
Reversing the One-Four

DELAY GAME

Another form of internal attack against zones is the delay game. The delay game should not be confused with the stall. It is a tactic used to bring the defense out, spread them apart, and then attack internally. It can be used at any point in the game, provided the score is tied or your team is ahead. I have used the zone delay to kill time when protecting a lead or a star player who is in early foul trouble. It also serves well as a momentum breaker, by slowing the pace of an opponent making a run at your team. The "zone delay" is also effective when an opponent goes to a zone defense after we have successfully beaten their man-to-man defense. The purpose is to force them back into the man coverage.

I first used the "zone delay" in my initial season as varsity coach at Jesuit High School. That year my ball club was led by 6′10″ Mark Wehrle at the post, as you may recall from earlier chapters. Early in the season we faced a very tall and talented Rio Americano High School of Sacramento. Their team featured a fine center named Steve Smith, who later starred at Loyola of Los Angeles.

Rio Americano employed a sticky 1-3-1 zone defense against every opponent. With their physical size, it was a very difficult defense to attack. In this particular game, we took an early first quarter lead due to Wehrle's inside scoring. Unfortunately, Mark picked up three quick fouls and had to leave the contest with seven minutes to go in the first half. Knowing that a five point lead would not last very long against the now taller Rio Americano club, I ordered the "zone delay."

The fans booed and the opponents got upset, but we continued to pass the ball around the outside. The officials ordered Rio Americano to come out and challenge us or face the mandatory technical foul. As soon as the defense spread, we hit the high post and relayed to a cutter for a lay up.

The confused opponents started to gamble more on defense, but they fouled and gave up more easy points. In a situation where I would have gladly settled for a close score at half time, we had completely unnerved the opponent and outscored them by eleven points. It was indeed nice to start the second half with a well-rested Mark Wehrle and a 16 point lead. Rio Americano stayed with their zone is the second half, but we easily won 61-41. Without the "zone delay," momentum could have been reversed and the outcome entirely different.

The "zone delay" alignment is similar to the Stack Offense, only the perimeter men set up near the mid-court line. (See Diagram 7-12.) A guard dribbles the ball over the mid-court line and holds it until the defense comes out or is ordered out.

The forwards are free to move to the wings once the defense moves out to the ball. The high post man breaks up when he sees an opening or a threat of trouble on the perimeter. The goal is to draw three defenders above the

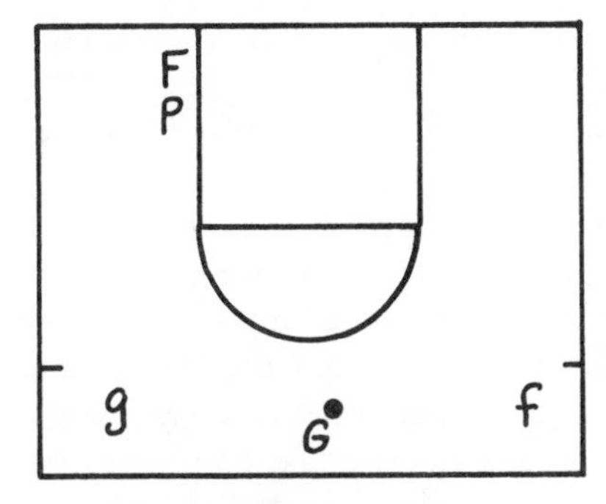

Diagram 7-12.
Zone Delay Alignment

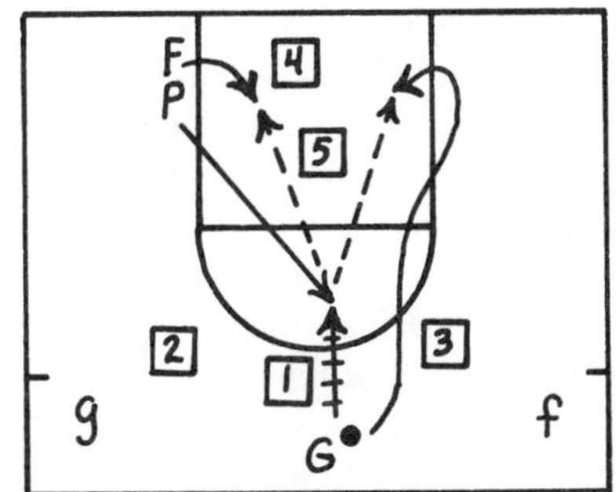

Diagram 7-13.
Zone Delay Attack

top of the key and out of zone coverage. This opens the internal game and allows easy shots. (See Diagram 7-13.)

If no passing lane is open from the high post to the low posts, then the ball should be returned to the two remaining perimeter men. Nothing is lost but time on the clock, and this only hurts the opponents.

The only shots allowed are lay ups and muscle shots inside. The opponent must pay the price for using a zone. He must either switch to a man-to-man defense or face the consequences of the clock running out. The "zone delay" puts pressure on the opponents, especially when they trail on the scoreboard. They are forced to go after the ball, use extra energy, and open the possibilities of reckless fouling. When they finally do get the ball back, the need to score is magnified greatly. If no points are registered, it may be a while before they see the ball again.

Some tips to remember when using the "zone delay" are:

1. Do not dribble or pass needlessly. Hold the ball until the defense comes out and forces movement.
2. Accept only high percentage, inside shot attempts.
3. Protect the ball. Do not force passes into congested areas. Be patient and control momentum.
4. Move to help a teammate who is in trouble. Cut to the ball or to an open area.
5. Use the dribble as a last resort. The worst thing a player can do is use his dribble immediately. This leaves no outlet from a defensive two-time other than a pass.
6. Stay alert so as not to get caught in any "five second violations."

COMBINATION DEFENSES

If your team features one or two outstanding scorers, you may eventually face a combination defense. The most common are the "box-and-one" and the "triangle-and-two." These combination defenses allow opponents to pressure your stars man-to-man while zoning your weaker players. When the combination defense denies the passing lanes to your "Aces," the opponents can cause your team a lot of trouble.

As in match-up zone defenses, the greatest threat of combination defenses is the psychological effect it can have on coach and team. Many times in my career I have heard the anxious words of one of my better players exclaim, "Coach, they are box-and-one on me; what do I do?" If the coach appears upset or panicky in this situation, the opponents gain a psychological edge immediately. A box-and-one is no reason to panic or change your normal game plan. A special offense is again a waste of time, but freedom to use free-lance opportunities must be emphasized.

The regular zone offense should be good enough to attack either the "triangle-and-two" or the "box-and-one." These defenses will have weaknesses that become evident to patient and observant teams.

The "box-and-one" is four man zone, with a fifth player assigned to dog a star player. The chaser should try denying your star any pass, keeping him from becoming a part of the offensive attack.

By creating offensive balance early in the season, you prepare the perfect counter-attack to the "box-and-one." The four teammates take up the early scoring load and render the chaser useless. This can easily happen when the attack centers away from the star. Your ace can set up on the weak side of the court and his teammates can then work the offense against a four man zone. It is hard for four men to cover a good zone offense, so openings will develop.

The "box-and-one" on a post man is not really effective, since the defensive post man usually defends the big man anyway. Most combination defenses key on a star perimeter player. By running your normal zone offense and getting your star to sacrifice himself early, you can pull most teams out of combination defenses. Be patient, look to score internally, and follow the keys to beating regular zone defenses. Moving the ball and sticking to the original game plan will help your team adjust much easier. The defense will eventually break down and good shots will be possible. Any team that bases its attack on the inside will not be denied by a fancy "box-and-one." The opponents might stop one player, but the other players flashing to the posts will have a field day scoring.

A true star player will find a way to beat the opponent, even when chased in a "box-and-one." If he is a frontliner, he can crash the offensive boards for points. As a guard, the star can work harder on the fastbreak, or penetrate and pass to teammates cutting to the basket.

The "triangle-and-two" should never hurt an inside oriented team. Two chasers must follow their men all around the court; so it is not difficult to open up the internal zone.

If the two chasers are covering your double posts, keep the offense moving and follow the normal rules. The defenders have a tiring job of fronting your posts. Eventually the defense will break down and the passing lane inside will open up. A tired defender is foul prone and less effective over the course of a game.

Do not let combination and trick defenses confuse your team. Be patient and stick to the basics. Fundamentals and simplicity win games, not trickery. The only trick you need is the use of the post men!

HALF-COURT PRESSES

The 1-3-1 half-court trapping press is one of the toughest short term defenses my teams have faced. I call it short term because most teams do not have the ability and energy to play this defense for more than a few minutes.

The defense attempts to lure the offense into a corner trap at midcourt. The trap is initiated only when the ball crosses the center court line. Some teams even continue their trapping into the baseline corners. A quick and hustling team can cause a lot of problems to poorly prepared opponents.

Following are some key points to remember when attacking a half-court press:

1. Keep the offensive attack spread.
2. Attack with a two guard front.
3. Station or break a player to the middle of the court—high post.
4. Use short and sharp passes as much as possible.
5. Hit the man in the high post area whenever feasible.
6. High post must quickly cut low if the ball goes to a wing.
7. Attack the press to score, not just to cross midcourt.

Diagram 7-14 illustrates a 1-3-1 half-court press and the recommended setup to attack it. Notice points #1, #2, and #3 above are satisfied with this offensive alignment.

If the guard bringing the ball up can pass to the high post man, he should do so. It is best to relay the ball to the vulnerable middle court area before dribbling across the midcourt line. This will eliminate the two-times that the defense initially looks for. The post man must meet all passes aggressively, as -5- will attempt to cut in for a steal.

One key rule for the guards concerns crossing the center line. The dribbler must be able to penetrate to the five-second marks or else not cross midcourt. Guards must avoid killing their dribble immediately after crossing the center line. This allows the defense to two-time the ball and force a lob or weak bounce pass. Since the defense wants the guard to cross midcourt and terminate the dribble, the offense should avoid this maneuver. If the dribbler can penetrate ten feet or more into the forecourt, then the press is less effective. Short passes to all corners and the high post are possible. A cutter can even move behind the man with the ball, if needed.

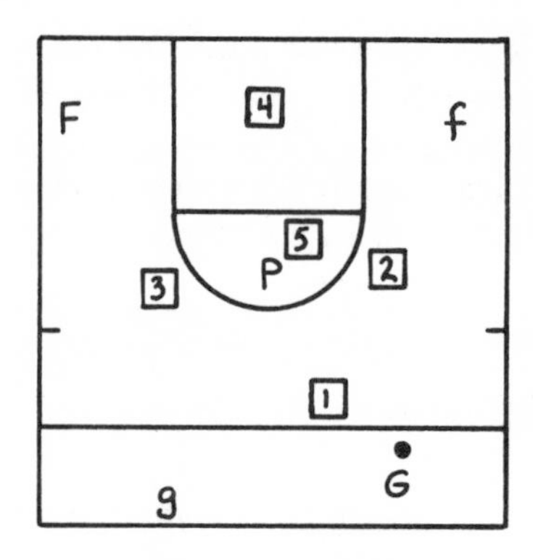

Diagram 7-14.
The Half-Court Press Offense

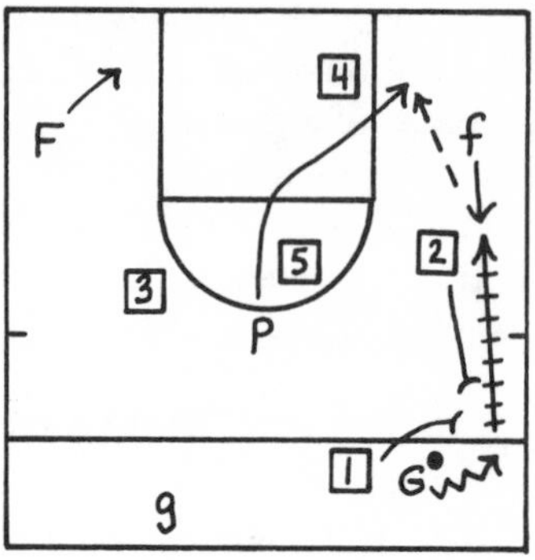

Diagram 7-15.
Challenging the Strong Side

By stationing a forward in the corner and a post man in the center of the court, the defensive wing -2- is required to cover a lot of area. The forward -f- should maintain a position of about fifteen feet behind -2-. This makes him a threat to receive a pass from the attacking guard at any time. The defender -2- now has to choose between trapping the dribbler or stopping the short pass to the wing. (See Diagram 7-15.) If -2- stays back, -G- can easily penetrate to the five-second mark and attack the defense.

Any time the ball goes to a wing, the high post should cut low and look for a quick feed. Since a concentration of defenders is initially around midcourt, the basket is often left unattended or poorly protected. The offense should never be satisfied with just getting the ball into the forecourt, but rather seek to score against the overcommitted defense. The best way to stop the opponents from pressing is to score a few easy baskets. They will soon look to another method of defending your team.

The half-court press is always vulnerable on the weak side, that is, away from the initial attacking side. If the defense stacks the strong side, a quick reversal will find the defenders outnumbered. An easy score will result if the offense looks to pass the ball immediately. Diagram 7-16 shows a quick reversal against an overcompensated defense. The offensive team must be able to read the shifts in the press and adjust to attacking the weaknesses. The coach's job is to make sure his players are aware of the many attacking options.

The weak-side guard always trails the ball slightly in anticipation of the reversal. Upon receiving a back-pass, the guard -g- should look to the high post -p- and the wing -F-. He also has the choice of dribbling the ball over the midcourt line, as he will receive very little resistance from the overcommitted defenders.

The best attacking area is, of course, the high post. Most half-court presses will defend the middle quite well in the beginning. After getting beat in the corners a few times, the defenders will spread out slightly and

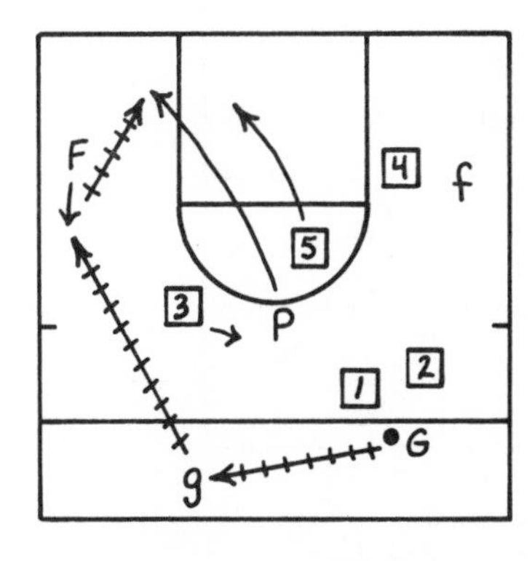

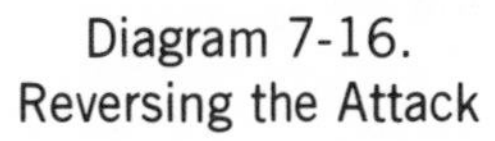

Diagram 7-16.
Reversing the Attack

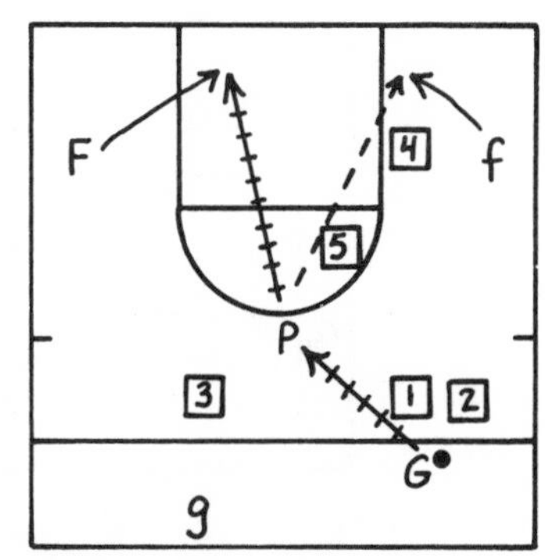

Diagram 7-17.
Attacking the High Post

anticipate the sideline passes. It is important that the guards remain conscious of the high post man at all times, because he will eventually be open. Forcing the ball through compensating wing defenders will lead to turnovers. The guards must read the defense and use the high post feed whenever it becomes available. (See Diagram 7-17.)

The high post man should immediately face the basket and look for the forwards cutting to the basket. Again, the lack of deep defenders makes the half-court press susceptible to backdoor plays.

The internal game and use of post players are very important in attacking half-court pressure, just as they are against all defenses. The use of a tall player in the middle of the court is a key. He is an easy target, he can see over the swarming defenders and spot open cutters, and he can cut to the low post for a quick pass from a wing.

When no shot is available through initial attacking options, the secondary phase of attack should be instigated. The offense must be ready for one of two defensive actions when setting up. First, the defense may continue to two-time the ball. This form of pressure is best handled by keeping the court spread and moving the ball to open areas. A 2-1-2 offensive alignment is best, with the posts breaking low as they did in the original half-court press offense.

The second form of defense seen after a half-court press is a regular zone. If the offense cannot get a good shot from the press offense, they should set up in their normal zone offense.

While it certainly is important to attack the press with scoring in mind, a forced or poor percentage shot is discouraged. The offense must keep their heads against pressure defense and play their normal style.

FULL-COURT PRESSES

Unprepared ball clubs are an easy target for full-court pressing teams.

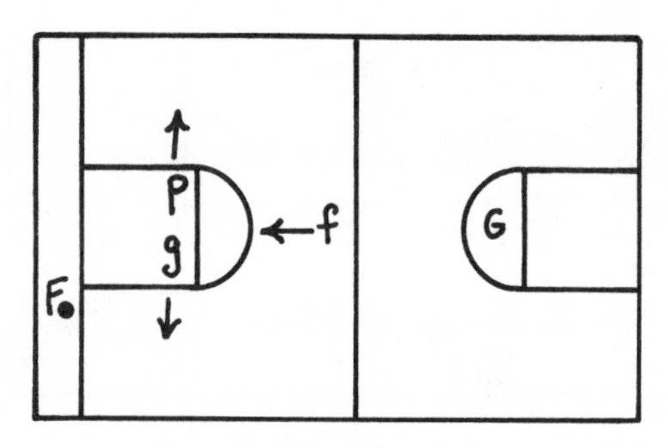

Diagram 7-18.
Full-Court Press Offense

Many games have been turned around in the closing minutes because the trailing team went to full-court pressure and gained a few quick turnovers. Handled properly though, the full-court press can be burnt for easy baskets and assure victory.

Many coaches feel the big man is a burden when facing full-court pressure. They will clear him out of the way and let the guards handle the press, or even go so far as to bench the tall post man. Used properly, the big man can be a valuable weapon in dealing with full-court pressure. Diagram 7-18 shows the basic alignment I use against all full-court pressure. You will notice the similarity between this setup and the "secondary break" outlined in chapter 6. Again, keeping the offenses and attacks similar makes it easier for your team to perform its assignments.

The original setup should force the defenders to cover the whole court. It is a serious mistake to bring all five offensive players into the backcourt for the purpose of getting the ball inbounds. This jams the inlet area and allows the defense to gamble even more. The defenders have less territory to cover and are thus more effective. The offense has no immediate threat to score, so the defense has plenty of time to retreat if the ball is successfully inbounded. Remember the first rule of attacking zone pressure: "Keep the offense spread."

I like to put my best shooter in the deep forecourt when facing presses. Generally this is a guard, (-G- in Diagram 7-18) but it can be a ball-handling forward. The goal of the other four team members is to get the ball to -G- as soon as possible. He will often be one-on-one against a lone safety man. His choices are inviting.

1. He can penetrate and try for a lay up or foul.
2. He can drive the middle and look to feed trailing cutters.
3. He can wait for his temmates to set up the offense.
4. He can shoot the open outside shot immediately.

Choice #4 is very effective when you have a good open-court shooter. While some coaches may argue that a 15 to 20 foot jump shot against the press is poor philosophy, they are usually the same guys who work an offense for two minutes and set *400 screens* to get the same shot! It must be noted that -G- is a good outside shooter, he is wide open, and he is set and waiting for the ball. As far as offensive rebound position, your hustling players will have an equal if not better chance to get any rebound. The defenders are scrambling to get back and do not have assigned block-out areas. Any rebound is up for grabs, so the ball will consistently go to the hungriest team.

During one season I was fortunate enough to coach a great press breaker, John Shepherd. John loved the deep spot, and his eyes lit up whenever the opponents went into full-court pressure. Shepherd could consistently hit the 20 foot shot all night. Because he was only 5′9″, John was not a great scorer when defended one-on-one. But put him at the deep end of a press offense and he could "rain them in." Many times during that season, opponents would see a two point deficit turn into a ten point spread while they were pressing. Shepherd was not the only player I coached who made this attack go. Almost every year I have had at least one shooter who could give the opposition something to think about when they pressed.

As in attacking the half-court press, the key is looking to score right away. Do not be satisfied with merely getting the ball across half court.

Since this is a book on use of the post man, I should now explain how the big boys make this press offense go. I use my big men in the backcourt for five very good reasons.

1. They can see over the defensive pressure of shorter guards and spot open passing lanes.
2. They are easier to pass into because of their reach. Big men can often grab erratic passes that might otherwise become turnovers.
3. Post men are not as apt to dribble immediately upon receiving a pass. They get the ball high above the pressure and look, unlike most guards who like to dribble then look.
4. With the big men in the backcourt helping to bring the ball up, it frees good shooters and penetrators to set up in the forecourt.
5. If the ball is turned over against the press, the big boys are already back to defend and rebound. This may seem like a minor point, but a plus none the less.

It is important to designate one player to always take the ball out of bounds. He must be a good passer and calm under pressure. He should always use a two-handed pass and avoid slow-moving bounced or lob passes. I normally use the slower of two post men, or the big forward -F-.

The two primary inlet men are the post man -P- and the point guard -g-. The ball is in most cases given to the guard because he is the better ball handler. The post man is used as a secondary inlet in case the guard is covered.

The two inlet men set up around the free throw line. To get open they can screen for one another, cross paths, or move straight out. They must try to avoid getting the ball near the endline or in the corners. Passes into the corners will lead to easy trapping situations for the defense and spell turnover for your team. The closer to the free throw line the inlet is made, the harder it is for the zone press to set up an effective trap.

So, the basis for a sound press attack has been established. The big men use their height to pass over the pressure, while the quicker perimeter players use their speed and ball-handling skills to organize a fastbreak. Because the majority of the defenders are concentrated in the backcourt, the safety man on the press is often faced with 3 on 2 and 2 on 1 attacks. It is better to attack with your perimeter men than the posts because of their speed and playmaking abilities.

Diagram 7-19 shows the sideline attack against the 1-2-1-1 full-court press.

The guard -g- must look immediately to the sideline upon receiving the inlet. Two more quick passes will get the ball to your key scorer -G-. If the midcourt man -f- is covered, the guard -g- must look to reverse the ball by one of the two methods illustrated in Diagram 7-20.

The deep guard -G- always waits until the ball is near midcourt before committing himself to a side. He always goes to the side of the ball so he can receive the shortest possible pass.

Attacking the 2-2-1 Zone Press calls for only a slight adjustment on the part of the offense. The midcourt man -f- stays in the center of the court. The middle is the only immediate open area against this press, so station a man there to force a defensive adjustment. The deep man must move to the inlet side of the offense as a strong-side threat. (Diagram 7-21.)

Since most 2-2-1 presses do not immediately two-time the inbounds pass, the guard -g- can look the defense over well before committing himself to passing or dribbling. He should look to the middle for a pass to -f-, or long to -P- or -G-. If no one is open, the guard must dribble up the sideline and challenge -4-, thus freeing -G-. (See Diagram 7-22.)

-F- serves as a safety in case a reversal is needed or a turnover occurs. If the ball is passed back to -F-, -P- moves back to receive a shorter pass. -G- moves to the opposite side of the court to take the feed from -P-. (See Diagram 7-23.)

Any time the ball goes to the middle man -f-, he should face his basket and look to feed one of the cutting wings. If there is daylight between him and the basket, -f- can drive toward the free throw line. He must be conscious of retreating defenders who will attempt to knock the dribble loose from behind. The key, as always, is for -f- to get the ball to -G-.

Some additional thoughts I have on attacking full-court pressure follow.

1. Do not panic! Keep the attack under control and at your tempo.
2. Ten seconds is a long time, so do not rush passes or dribble reck-

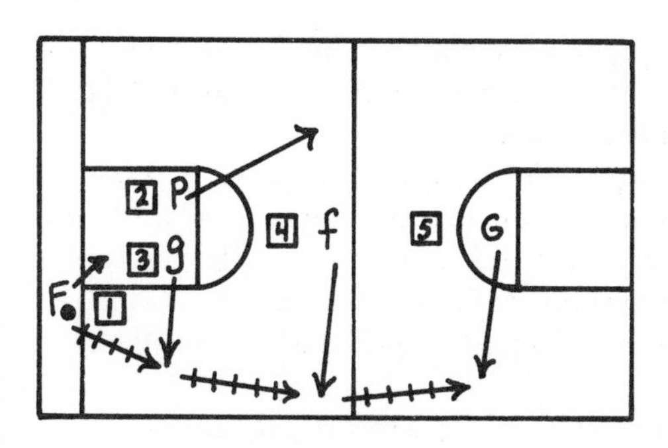

Diagram 7-19.
Attacking the 1-2-1-1 Press

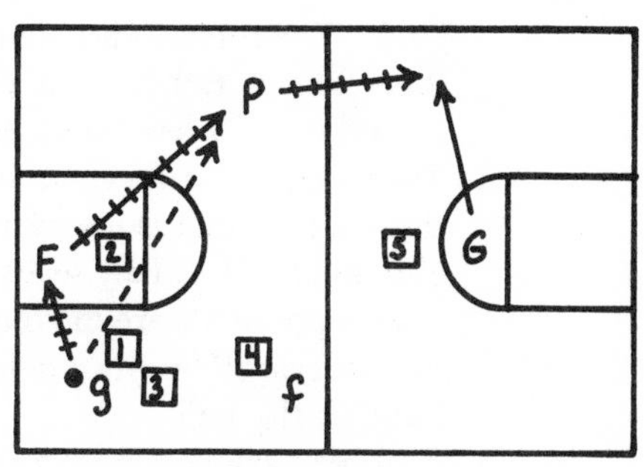

Diagram 7-20.
Reversing Against
the 1-2-1-1

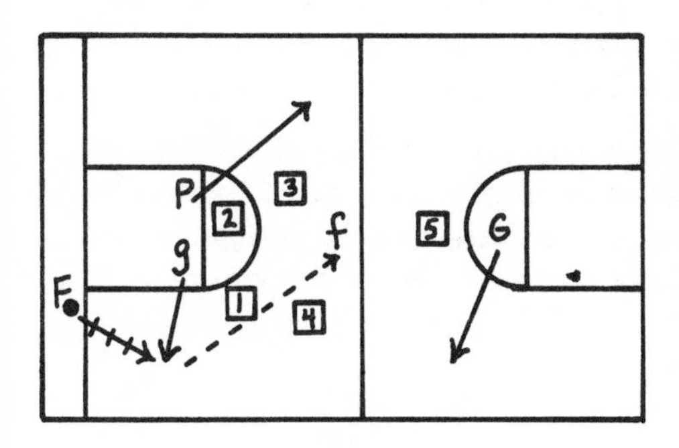

Diagram 7-21.
Attacking the 2-2-1

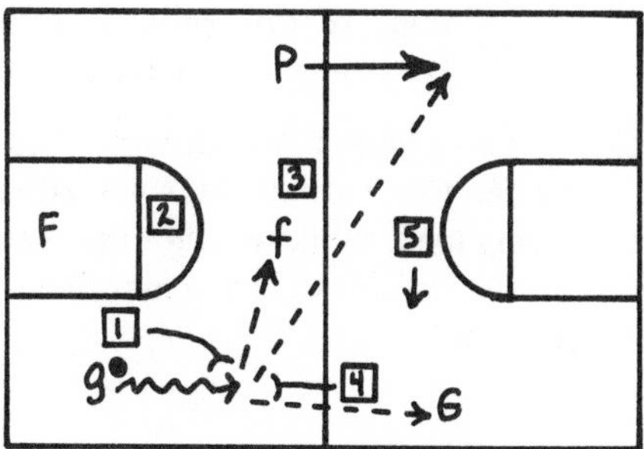

Diagram 7-22.
Forcing the 2-2-1 Press

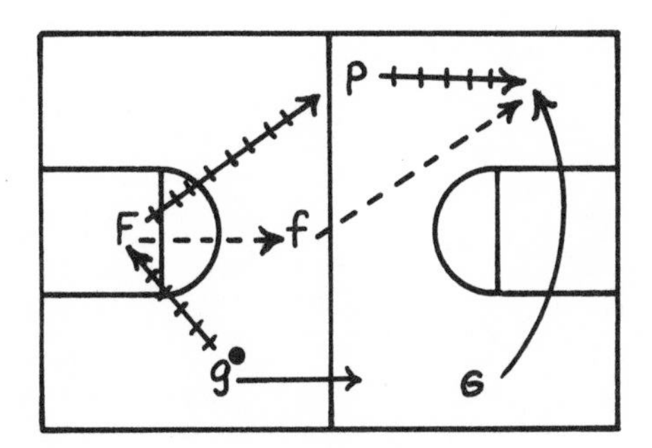

Diagram 7-23.
Reversing the 2-2-1

lessly. The referees are more apt to give eleven or twelve seconds to the offense, rather than eight or nine seconds. The ball can be passed quite a few times in ten seconds.

3. Take a ten-second violation before throwing a "hope pass." A poorly thrown pass that is intercepted creates "instant momentum" for the opponents. It usually leads to a fastbreak and easy score because so many opponents are in your backcourt. Taking the ten-second violation at least allows your defense a chance to regroup while the official handles the ball.
4. Dribble against zone pressure only as a last resort. Always look to pass upon first receiving the ball. If no one is open, the dribble can get you out of a tight situation. If two-timed, fake a high pass to get the defenders off balance, then dribble by them.
5. In most cases, post men should not dribble the ball unless no one is within twenty feet of them. The big men can see over most traps, so they will be able to spot the open teammate. There may be exceptions to this rule, as some big men handle the ball quite well. However, dribbling is best left to the guards on most teams.

This chapter has attempted to show how the posts can be used against any defensive attack. In some situations the big boys are asked to carry the scoring load, while at other times they are used to set up the perimeter men. You should always strive for offensive balance, but the game begins from the inside out.

8

COACHING THE DOUBLE AND TRIPLE POST

The influx of more and more tall players in modern basketball has often led today's coaches into adopting double or triple post offenses. This strategy provides coaches a chance to use more than one player inside. While a single post setup allows four quicker players to work off of one big man, the multi-post offenses offer two and three-man inside power attacks. In order to use available size, coaches would do well to adopt a multi-post offense. Rather than benching one of the big men or playing him out of position on a wing, a double or triple post attack seems more appropriate.

A big man is usually too slow to play outside as a forward. He is valuable around the basket and can be a very effective scorer from the low post. Tall players should always operate around the hoop; so if two big men play at the same time, a double post offense is advised.

THE DOUBLE POST

There are three types of teams in which a double post offense is recommended.

1. A playing unit that consistently uses two extra tall players at the same time.
2. A playing unit that consistently uses one tall player and one average sized, but strong, inside player. The average-sized post man would be slow, and therefore not a potential wing man. He would be a good offensive rebounder and inside scorer.
3. A playing unit that uses two average-sized inside players. They would both be too slow for the wings, but they would like to muscle around the basket, crash the offensive boards, and score from the inside.

In general, the potential double post men are more valuable around the basket than outside. They have size that is an advantage to the post player, but lack the ball handling and outside shooting abilities of good wing men.

If you coach two average-sized front liners who cannot shoot or move well outside, you should consider a double post attack. You will be adopting an offense to fit your personnel, rather than fitting the personnel to an offense. While many coaches would feel uncomfortable with such a philosophy, they should remember that flexibility is a good trait to possess.

Using a double post also provides flexibility in the use of perimeter players. You can use the following combinations.

1. **Two post men, two forwards, and a guard.** This combination is advised if you wish to put four tall men on the court at the same time. One point guard is responsible for all ball handling and playmaking.
2. **Two post men and three guards.** This combination can be used when you want speed along with height. The two post men are responsible for most of the defensive rebounding, while the three guards concentrate on initiating a fast break attack. This offers the best type of double post "speed attack."
3. **Two post men, one forward, and two guards.** This is the standard type of double post attack. The two guards are responsible for the playmaking and ball handling. The forward is a versatile type who serves as a front liner on the boards, yet he possesses the speed traits of a guard. His quickness can be utilized on defense and on fast break opportunities.

As can easily be seen, double post attacks can offer a variety of combinations to fit your philosophy. You can use a combination of players that will fast break, run a controlled game, or play various defenses.

There are basically three types of double post alignments: (1) The High-Low Post, (2) The Double Low Post, and (3) The Double High Post.

THE HIGH-LOW POST

The high-low post offense is generally incorporated in a 1-3-1 alignment. (See Diagram 8-1.) One of the post men is stationed around the free throw line and serves as a high post. The other post man is stationed at the low post or floats underneath the basket.

The high post should be able to shoot jump shots from 18 feet on in, drive to the hoop if given the opening, and pass to open players. He must be eager enough to go to the offensive boards on every shot attempt, even when he is aggressively blocked out. The high post is often used as a screener for the wings or the low post man. Since he must screen and his position is relatively stationary, the slower and heavier post man is generally used at the high post.

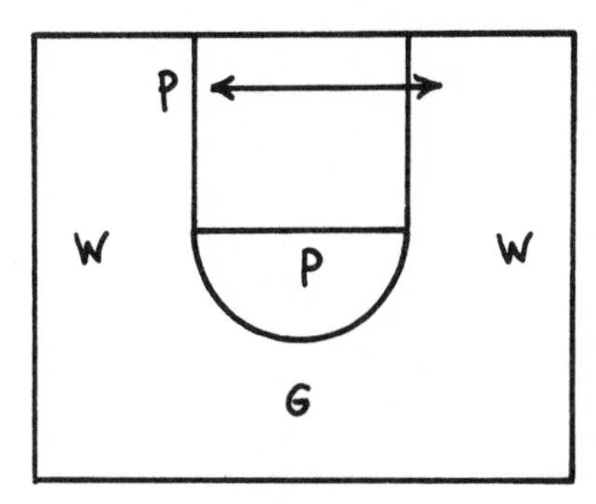

Diagram 8-1.
The High-Low Post, or
1-3-1 Offense

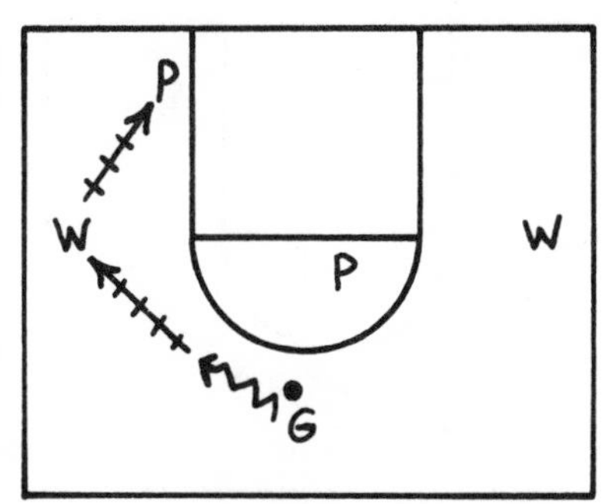

Diagram 8-2.
To Left Wing, to
Low Left

The low post man should be the player who can score best from that position. He has good post moves and the height to aid in getting shots off. The low post is usually the tallest post man, and he knows how to use his height. He can choose a position or float back and forth across the lane, but he must be careful not to be too far under the basket. The area above the rectangle on the lane is the best place to operate, as mentioned in chapter 2. The low post man will have numerous opportunities to tip in missed shots and to get offensive rebounds. He must stay alert and have his hands ready at all times.

A pass to either wing offers an excellent opportunity to pass to the low post. (See Diagrams 8-2 and 8-3.)

The high-low post offense presents more opportunities for a two-man game than other double post alignments. The two posts should work together at all times. They must be aware of each other's position, look to pass to their partner before any other team member, and together cover the two key rebounding areas mentioned in chapter 5.

When the high post receives the ball, he must pivot immediately and face the basket. He should be looking for the low post out of the corner of his eye, and pass inside if he is open. If a shot or drive situation is apparent, the high post man must be ready to react. (See Diagram 8-4.)

If the high post cannot hit low, drive, or shoot, he should look to one of the wing men. A quick pass to the outside forces the defense on low post men to adjust very quickly. Failure to cut off the newly created passing lanes will leave excellent chances to score. (See Diagram 8-5.)

The high post can pick the low post man and open up two new scoring opportunities. He must be alert to the three-second lane and not get caught inside. After the pick, the high post should look for a possible high lob pass in case both defenders go to the low post man. He then moves to a rebounding position outside the lane. (See Diagram 8-6.)

Before cutting across the key to set the pick, the high post should slide

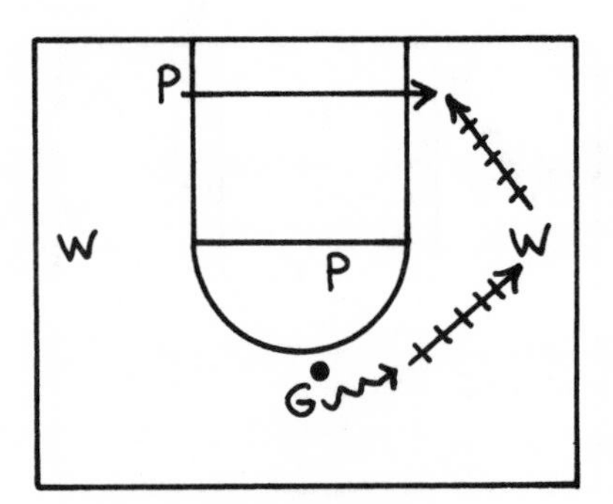

Diagram 8-3.
To Right Wing, to
Low Right

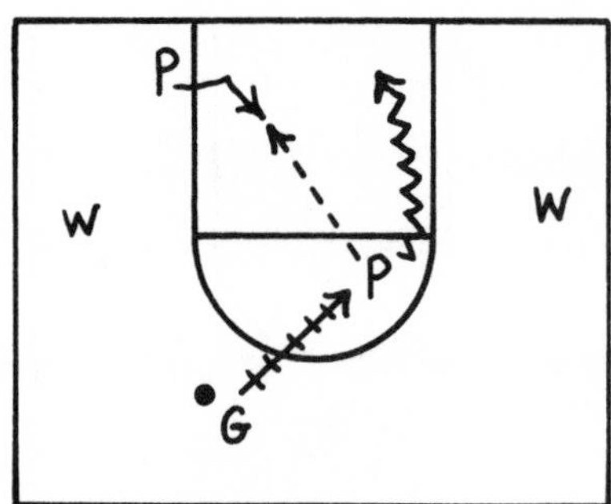

Diagram 8-4.
Look for Other Post

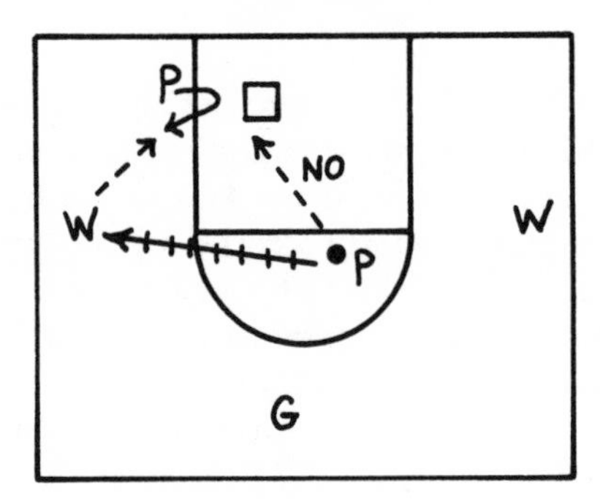

Diagram 8-5.
Changing the Passing
Angle

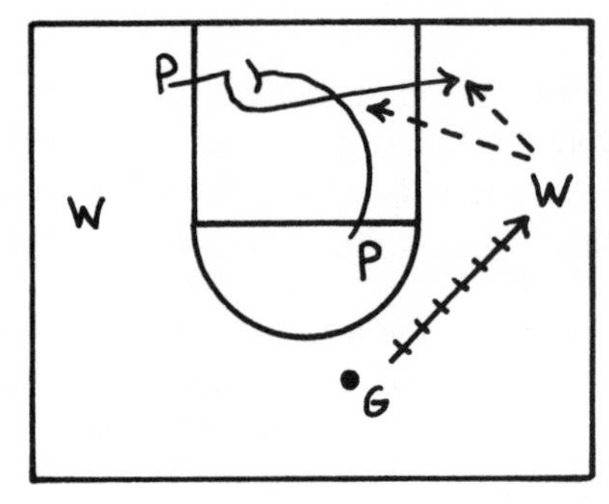

Diagram 8-6.
Pick for Low Post

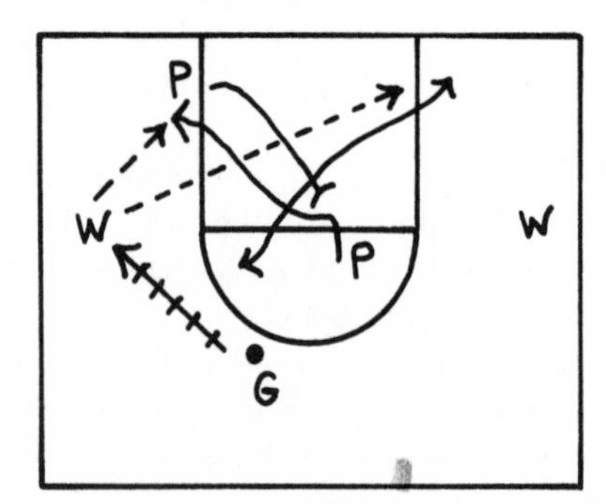

Diagram 8-7.
Pick for High Post

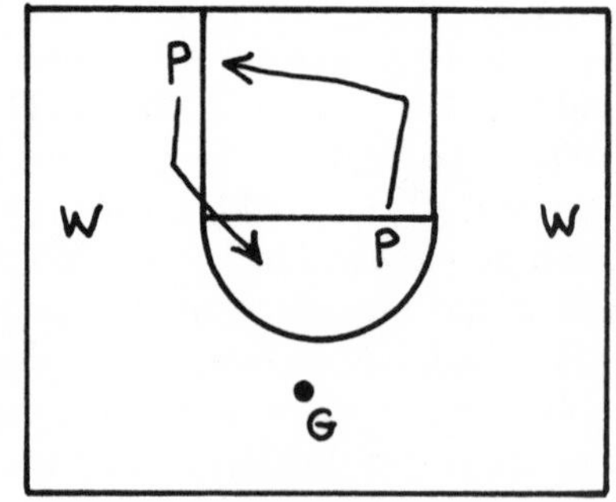

Diagram 8-8.
Interchange of Posts

down the lane for a possible pass. Often the defense may be caught sleeping, and the high post man can score in the low post area.

The low post man can pick for the high post man and allow him to move into the internal zone. After the pick, the low post man can roll to the opposite low post area. This allows him to receive a lob pass should the defense make a mistake in switching; and it also puts the low post man in a good rebounding position. Another option the picking low post has is to step above the free throw line. Sometimes both post defenders will follow the man going low, leaving the high post area open. Free throw line jump shots are often obtained on this simple pick-interchange. (See Diagram 8-7.)

Once in a while the situation dictates an interchange of the high and low post players. This is easily accomplished by the low post sliding up and the high post breaking down into the vacated low post area. (See Diagram 8-8.) By doing so, the post men can take advantage of one particularly weak low post defender. It also allows the post men to bring a big defender away from the basket. This can eliminate an intimidator or great shot blocker. Players must avoid each other when interchanging to guard against defensive switches.

If the high post defender is in foul trouble, you may wish to interchange your posts and work on him. He will either foul out or play cautious defense. Whichever he chooses, your team will benefit.

THE DOUBLE LOW POST

The double low post offense is usually integrated into a 1-2-2 setup. (See Diagram 8-9.) Both big men are stationed at the low post with one on each side of the lane. Very little movement is required from the post men, so it is a great offensive alignment for young teams. It is highly recommended for inexperienced post men because they are not required to move very much to get a pass. They provide an immediate threat to the defense, even without the ball.

I had great success with this offense as a sophomore coach at the high school level. It was simple to teach, and the alignment placed two big men in key rebounding and scoring positions. Inexperienced defenders had to play good defense, or easy baskets resulted. The guards were forced to look for passes into the low posts, and the posts always received the ball in excellent shooting range. This gave them a chance to develop the "basic three" post moves without the added task of locating relative position. All they had to concern themselves with was getting open, scoring, or rebounding. I highly recommend this offense for teaching the inside game.

When the ball is passed to a low post man, the guards should keep their defensive men busy so they will not sag and bother the posts. The "split" works well to accomplish this, and it provides good scoring opportunities for the guards. The wing who hits the post sets a pick for the point guard, and the two players actually exchange positions. (See Diagram 8-10.)

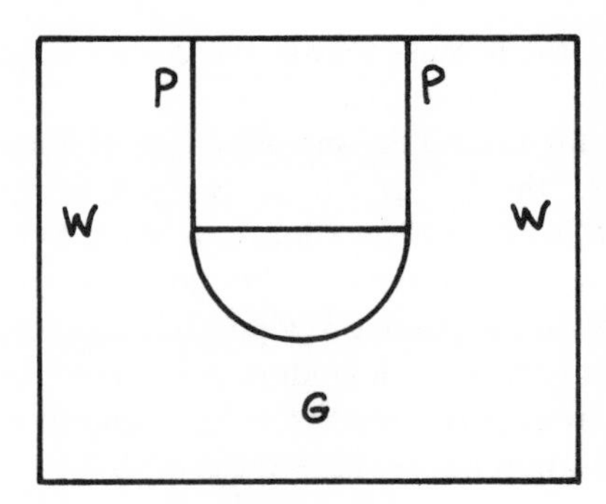

Diagram 8-9.
Double Low Post,
or 1-2-2

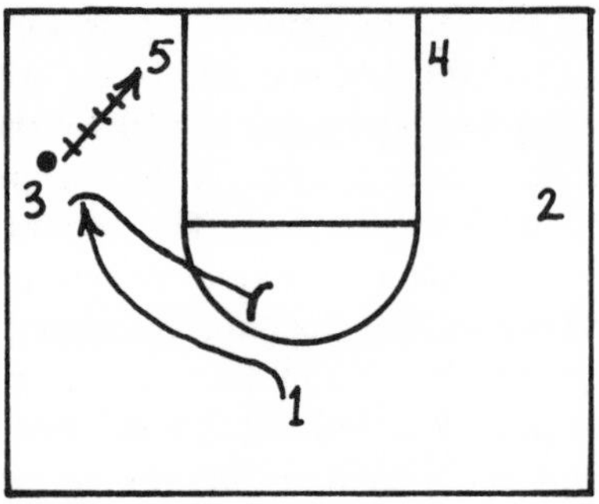

Diagram 8-10.
Guards Split on Pass
to Low Post

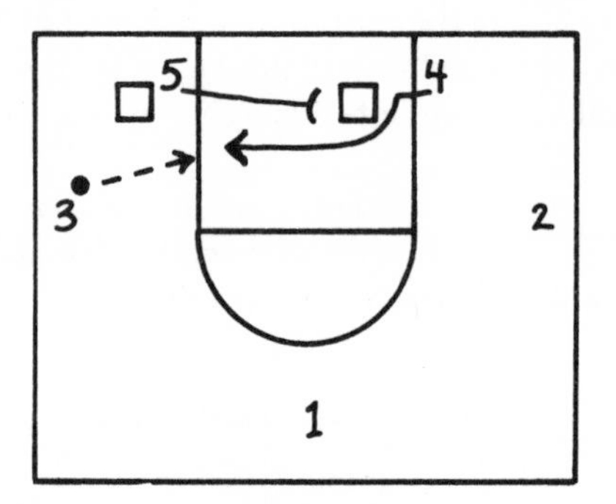

Diagram 8-11.
Pick and Exchange of
Low Posts

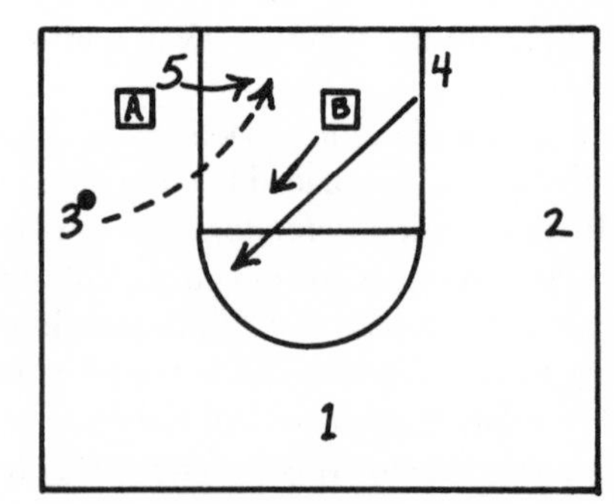

Diagram 8-12A.
Beating the Fronting and
Switching Tactics

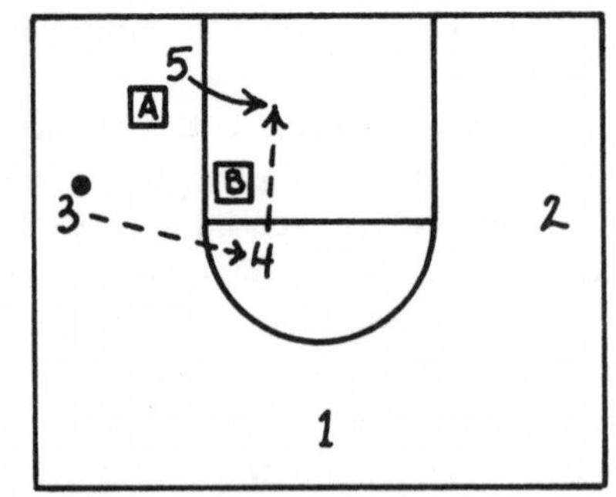

Diagram 8-12B.
Beating the Fronting Tactic

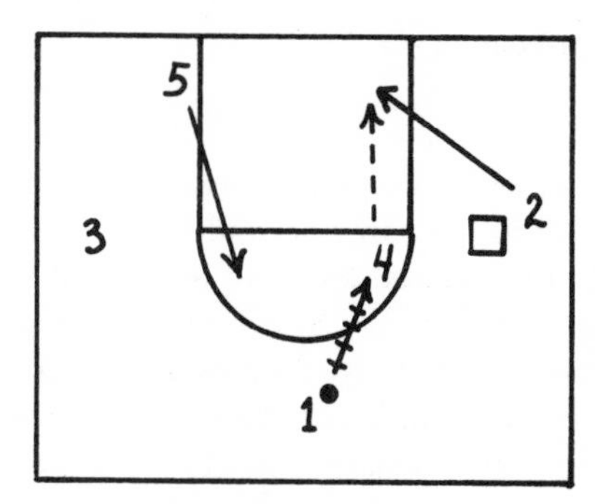

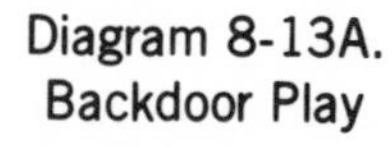
Diagram 8-13A.
Backdoor Play

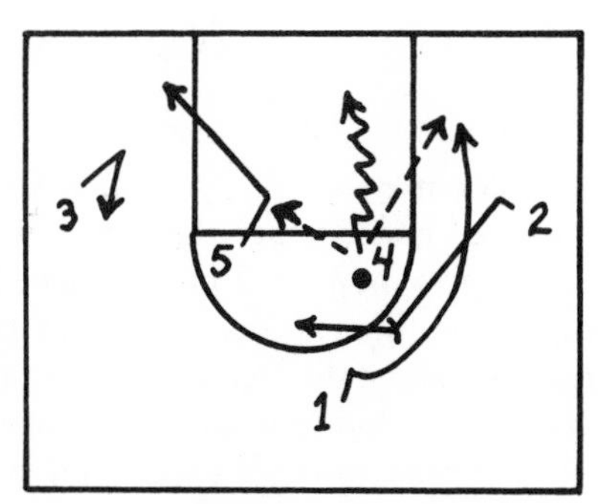

Diagram 8-13B.
Continuation of
Backdoor

If the low post man is covered so he cannot receive a pass, he must immediately pick for the other post man. This brings a new man into the low post area who should now be open. The post who originally picked should look for a high lob pass, in case both defenders go to the strong side post man. Also, after a pick, the weak side post man must get out of the lane to avoid a three-second violation. He then re-establishes a post position and is alert to rebound any shot attempts. (See Diagram 8-11.)

Sometimes the opposition will use zone principles and switches on each pick your post men set for each other. Consequently, your posts will always be fronted and cannot receive direct passes. Diagrams 8-12 A and B illustrate the proper method of defeating such tactics. The opposite post man -4- breaks to the high post and receives a pass. The strong side low post man -5- crosses and looks for a quick pass inside for an easy shot. I found this maneuver worked very well on teams that front and switch against the double-low setup. Fronting the low post leaves the defense at a disadvantage, when the passing angle is changed to the high post. Many easy lay ups will result when this simple move is performed.

As 4 comes to the high post, the wing should be alert to a possible lob pass over A to 5. This can also result in an easy score and added confusion to the defense.

If the point man has trouble getting the ball to a wing, the low post men should break up to a high post. As the ball is received, the post man looks for the wing who breaks "backdoor." This play is designed to take advantage of a defender overplaying a wing. He will often be beaten by the backdoor pass and the wing will score an easy lay in. (See Diagram 8-13A.)

If the backdoor pass cannot be made, the wing man should come back and pick for the point man. This split action will often free one of the guards and lead to a lay up or jump shot. The post is also free to go one-on-one, since the helping defense will be involved in the split action. The other post man -5- should keep his man occupied by flashing into the key or dropping low post. (See Diagram 8-13B.)

THE DOUBLE HIGH POST

The double high post offense usually is represented by a 1-4 alignment. (See Diagram 8-14.) The post men are positioned on each corner of the free throw line, making sure they are not within the three-second lane.

The post men must move to get to the desired low post areas, but the setup helps them to out-maneuver the defense. Because four players are spread out along the free throw line, this alignment works well against zone defenses. The internal zone defensive players can be drawn out and movement will reposition offensive men in the open inside areas. The 1-4 is also valuable against match-up zone defenses because it forces the defenders into man-to-man coverage. Simple movement will again open key scoring areas.

When you possess two experienced and versatile post men, the 1-4 is a very effective offense. The potential to use all of the plays from the double low and high-low offenses is possible in the double-high attack. Simply by sliding down to the low post, new dimensions are added to the 1-4 attack.

Another method of establishing a double-high setup is to have the posts low, then break up to the high post as the ball arrives at the top of the key. (See Diagram 8-15.) This adds an extra bit of movement that can often open up passing lanes and good scoring opportunities.

A pass to a wing tells the strong side high post to pick for his partner, the weak-side high post. The weak-side post then cuts to the basket and looks for a return pass and easy score. If he is covered, he sets up at the low post and again tries to receive a pass. The picker rolls to the weak-side low post, but he keeps alert to the possibility of a lob pass near the rim. (See Diagram 8-16A.) The picker will also be able to roll high (near the free throw line), when both post defenders sag. This allows the offense to take on the appearance and principles of the "High-Low Attack." (See Diagram 8-16B.)

If the man-to-man defenders are consistently switching on the high post pick and roll, then a roll to the strong side is a good counter move. The strong-side post picks and then rolls immediately to the strong-side low post. The weak-side post comes off of the pick and looks for a pass and shot from the strong-side high post. This movement offers an overloaded 1-3-1 attack. (See Diagram 8-17.)

A pass to the high post from the wing dictates a high-low rule. The high post man must face the basket immediately and look to pass to the low post, drive, or shoot. The low post man -4- clears to the other side of the key to open a driving lane for 5. (See Diagram 8-18.)

When the point man passes to the high post, the backdoor play discussed in the double low offense can be keyed. Another possibility is for the post to use a drop-step pivot and turn to the middle of the key. (See Diagram 8-19.) This allows the other post man to cut diagonally across the lane, looking for a quick pass. He should have his hands up as he moves toward the strong-side low post. The strong-side wing should look to go backdoor, then split with the point man. This movement serves quite well to keep the

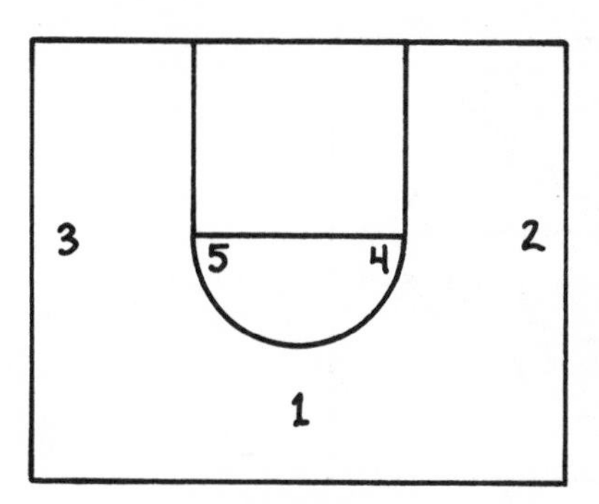

Diagram 8-14.
The Double High Post,
or 1-4

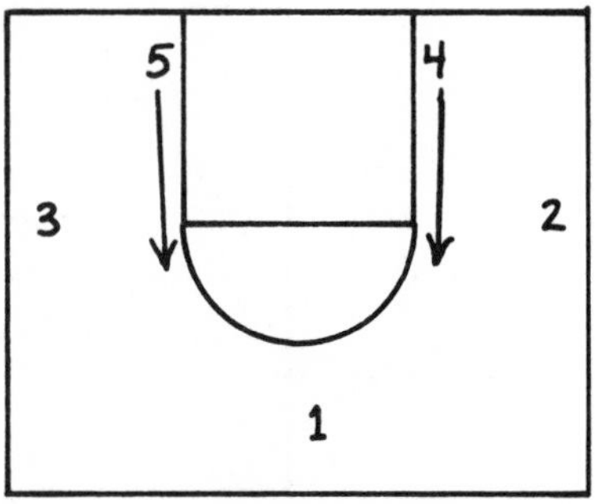

Diagram 8-15.
Double Low to Double
High

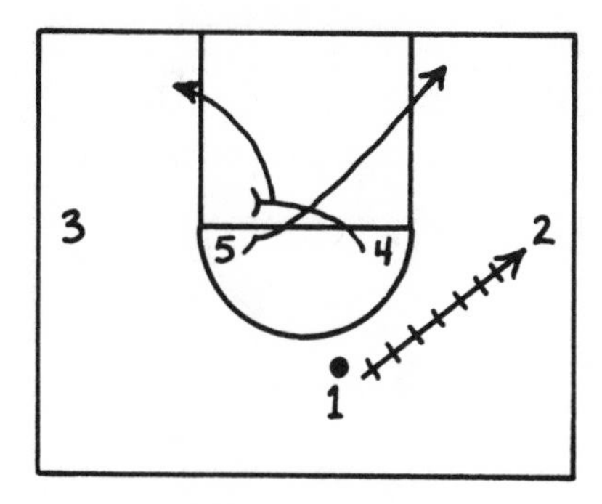

Diagram 8-16A.
Pick-and-Roll to
Low Post

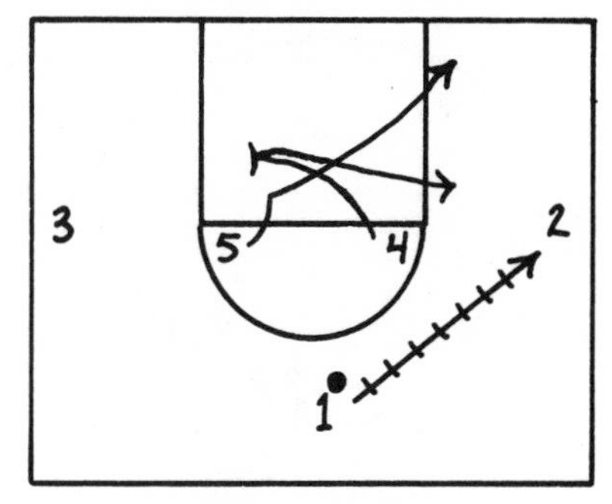

Diagram 8-16B.
Pick-and-Roll to
High Post

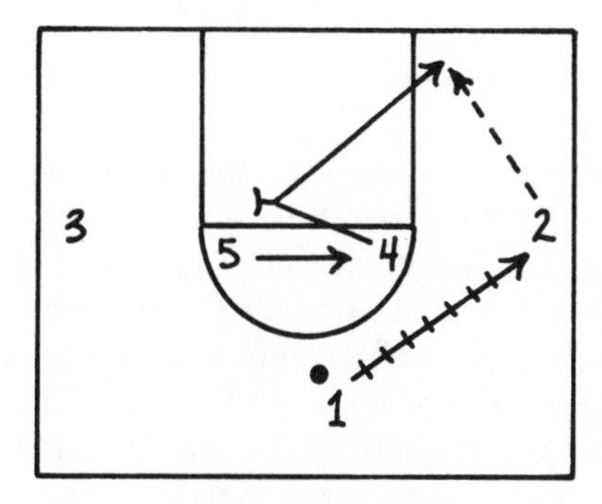

Diagram 8-17.
Pick-and-Roll versus
a Switch

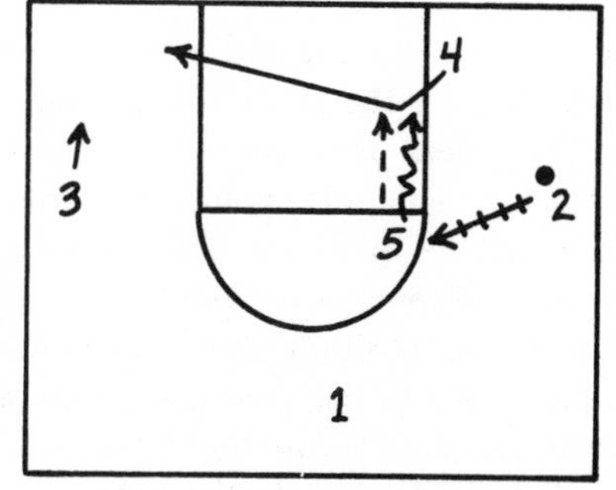

Diagram 8-18.
Pass to High Post—
Overload

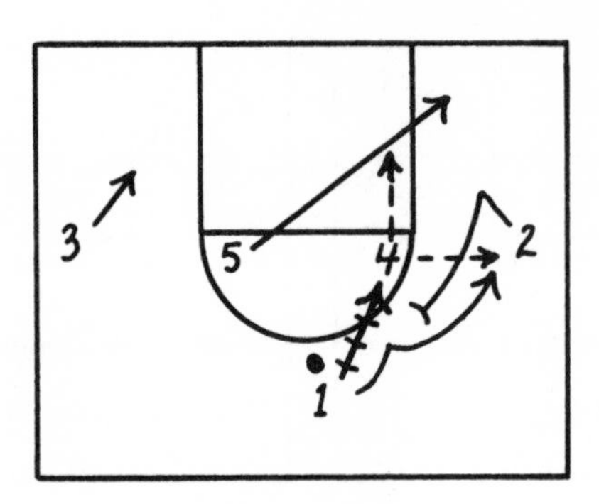

Diagram 8-19.
Point Passes to
High Post

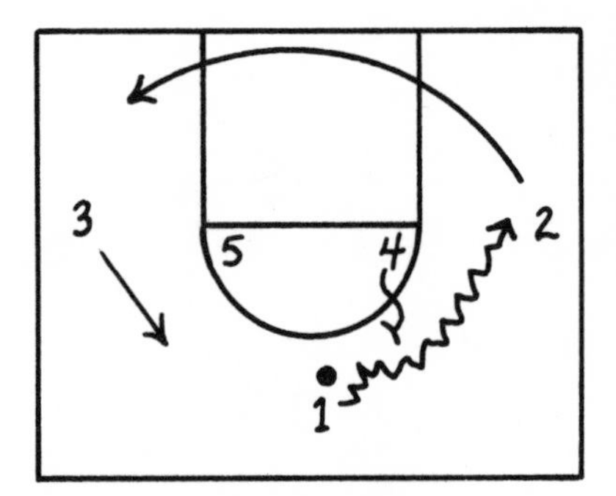

Diagram 8-20A.
Clear Play and
Rub Out

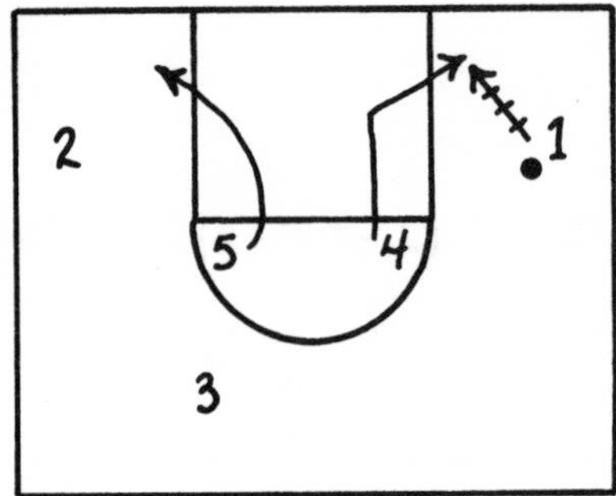

Diagram 8-20B.
Roll and Pass
Low

defense from sagging and jamming up the post men. Good open shots often materialize for the guards if sagging occurs.

The "clear play" can also be used very effectively with the double high post setup. The point man clears one of the wing men through to the opposite side. This opens one side of the court and sets up the blind pick by a high post man. If the guard cannot drive all the way for a lay in, he should dribble out to a wing position. (See Diagram 8-20A.) This allows him to have a good passing angle to the post man, who should roll to a low post position. The offense can now follow the rules of a double low post alignment. (See Diagram 8-20B.) The "clear play" can be a valuable weapon late in tight games. It allows the coach to get to the strength of the post offense quickly, involving chosen personnel, and a minimum of passes. In essence, the "clear play" becomes a three-man game: the two posts and one guard.

All plays diagrammed can be run to either side of the court. A coach should try to stress a balanced attack for a game plan. This includes running plays equally on each side of the court, and mixing up the plays used. In crucial situations, the team should be aware of its own strengths and work to these areas. Some suggestions include:

1. Working the ball to the left low post, provided both of your post men are right handers. (See chapter 2, Choosing a Side.)
2. Working the ball to a player who is defended by a man in foul trouble.
3. Running the clear play on the right side if you think the right-handed point man can go all the way.
4. Working the ball to a post man who has a shorter defender or a very weak defender.
5. Running the backdoor play automatically when the defense pressures the wings.

Double post offenses provide simple, yet powerful scoring opportunities for teams that have two big men. The "big boys" are kept around the low post areas where they can use various post moves to score easy baskets. Traditional plays such as the backdoor, pick and roll, and splits can be added to the inside game. This incorporates the guards into the offense and prevents the defenders from collapsing on your post players.

The two post men must learn to work together, as they will have numerous opportunities to play two-man basketball. This includes picking for one another, passing to one another, and filling the open rebound areas. When the two post men work together, they actually become an offense within an offense.

Combinations of the three basic double post alignments can be incorporated into an advanced offense offering plenty of challenges to any defense. If you want to make sure your team will "put pressure on the hoop," then consider a double post attack.

THE TRIPLE POST

You may desire to play three tall players consistently as a unit. One possible type of attack would be a triple post offense. I have never actually seen an offense featuring three players each stationed at a separate post position. However, there are a few offenses that have three different players at various post areas from time to time.

If you want to establish a *true* triple post setup, you would probably have to use one player at the high post, and one at each of the two low posts. You can easily imagine the congestion within the key if a team used such a stationary alignment. There would be at least six players bunched together within a small area: three offensive and three defensive men. The congestion would limit the freedom each post man needs in order to score from his particular post area. For this reason, coaches generally alternate their three front liners at one of the post positions.

The most feasible triple post alignment would be a 2-3 setup. (See

Diagram 8-21.) P1 could be at a low post, as shown in the diagram, or at a high post. The three post men would alternate at the P1 position, depending on the following factors.

1. One of the post men may be a superior player having a good scoring night.
2. One of the post men may have a short defensive forward on him. This defender would have trouble stopping low post moves.
3. One of the post men may have a defensive player who is in foul trouble.
4. One of the post men may have a very poor defensive player guarding him. Easy baskets will result if you work on weak defenders.
5. You may wish to change player positions so the defense will have to adjust. This adds variety to the triple post attack.
6. You may wish to bring the opponent's tallest defender out to the wing. This hinders a big defender in his attempts to intimidate and dominate on defense. It also pulls him away from the rebounding area.
7. A post man can go out to the wing and use his speed to drive by a slower defender.

When using a triple post offense, remember to keep the attack simple and direct. The use of three tall players at one time does not require any fancy patterns or intricate plays. Size and power become the name of the game. Your front line will probably be slow and awkward on offense, but they will be devastating around the basket. Do not expect them to drive to the hoop. Design plays with minimal movement that will get one or two big boys open at the low posts. Let the guards drive, ball handle, and set up the offense.

I will briefly explain some of the triple post plays that can be used.

The high post power move is keyed by a pass to the high post. The two wings break to the basket, looking for a pass. (See Diagram 8-22A.) If the initial cut is stopped, then P2 and P3 will flash into the lane briefly. If P2 or P3 receive the ball inside, a quick power move should result in two points.

When the low posts are covered, the high post passes to a guard who has moved to a wing. This will provide a new passing angle to the low post by way of the baseline. P1 vacates the high post area by moving to the weak side, and P3 flashes to the high post if the pass is prevented to P2. This opens up the potential lob pass to P2, if he is being fronted. (See Diagram 8-22B.)

When the ball goes to P3 at the high post, he must immediately look to shoot or pass to a cutting P2. A quick pass to P1 opens a new passing angle to P2 at the right low post. (See Diagram 8-22C.) When the cuts and passes are timed properly, P2 will always get the ball inside. It is assumed that low post men know what to do once they get the ball around the basket.

A pass from a guard to wing keys a quick cut by the high post—P1. (See Diagram 8-23A.) If P1 beats his defender to the low post, a baseline pass will

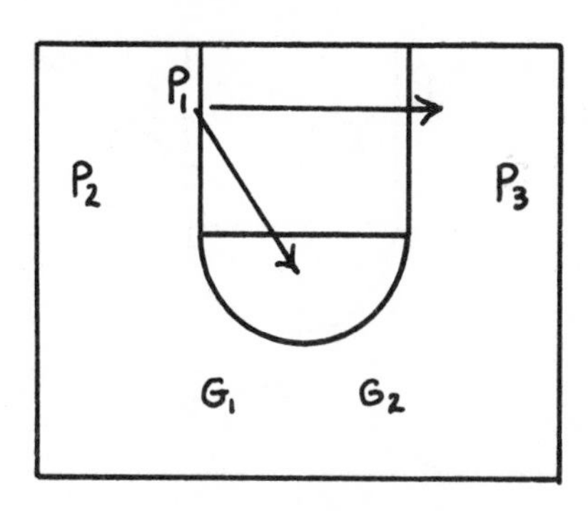

Diagram 8-21.
The 2-3 Triple Post
Alignment

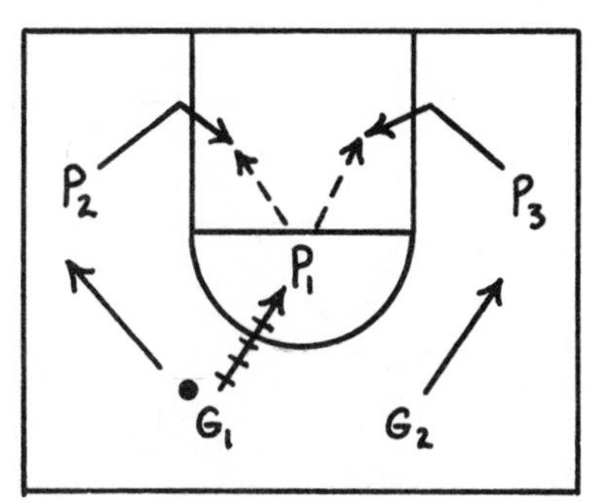

Diagram 8-22A.
High Post Power
Move

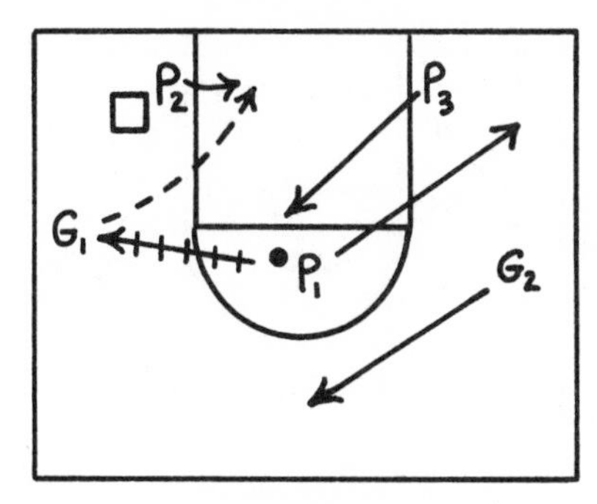

Diagram 8-22B.
Second Option—
High Post to Wing

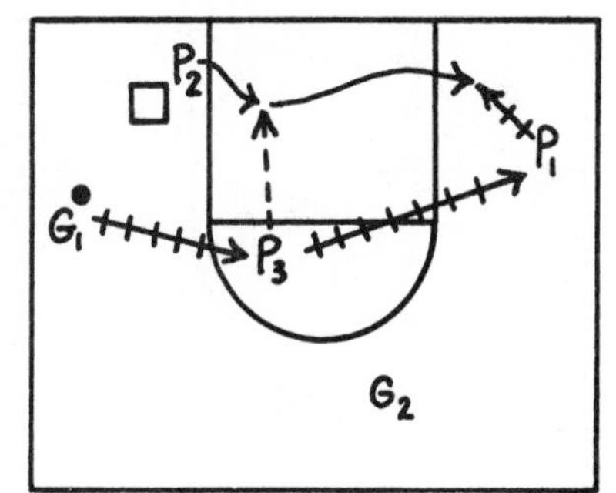

Diagram 8-22C.
Third Option—
Weak Side Attack

result in a good inside scoring opportunity. G1 cuts away from the ball and moves to the weak side.

If Pl is fronted and cannot get the ball, P3 breaks to the high post looking for a pass. Again, the same pattern is followed as discussed in the high post plays. (See Diagram 8-23B.)

The 2-3 setup has changed to a 1-3-1, with the original high post -P1- posting underneath. P3 must move to the weak side after passing from the high post position. This allows P2 to flash into the key area. The weak side defense is kept occupied, the lob pass to Pl is possible, and new passing lanes are opened.

When the guard -G2- dribbles at the side post man, P3 cuts to the low post. If he has the advantage, P3 will receive a pass and perform a low post move. (See Diagram 8-24A.) Pl vacates the high post to take the defensive help away from P3.

If P3 is fronted, P2 breaks to the high post to open up the lob pass possibility. G2 can hit P2 and then around to Pl as in earlier diagrams. If P2

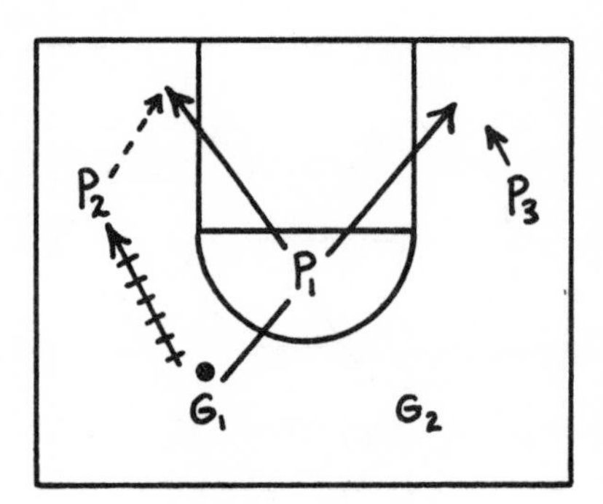

Diagram 8-23A.
Pass to the Wing

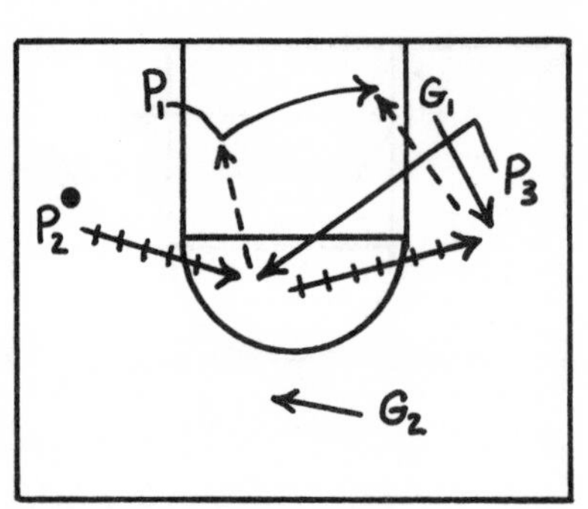

Diagram 8-23B.
New High Post
Moves In

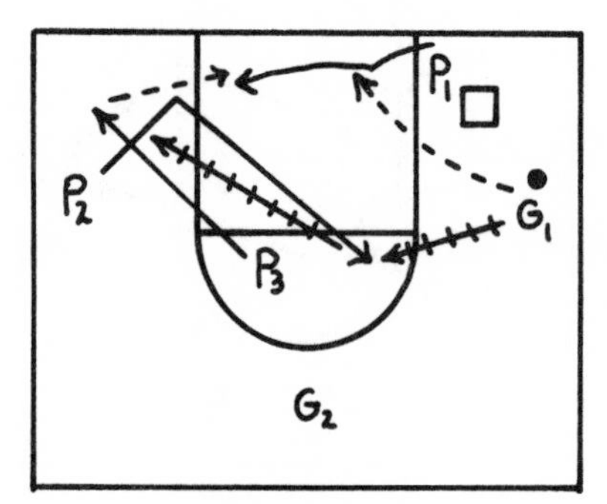

Diagram 8-23C.
Reversing the
Triple Post

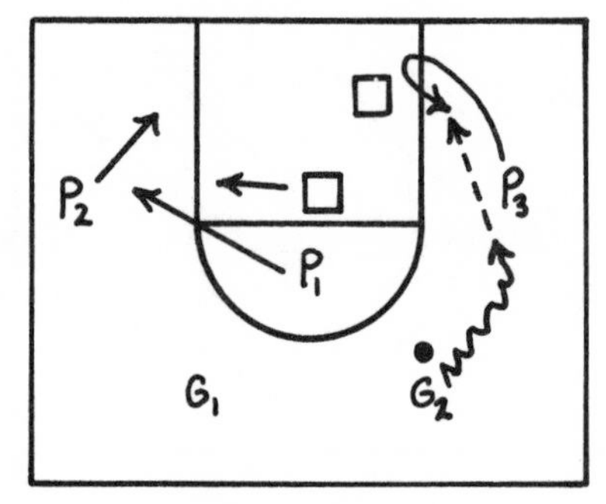

Diagram 8-24A.
Dribble to Wing

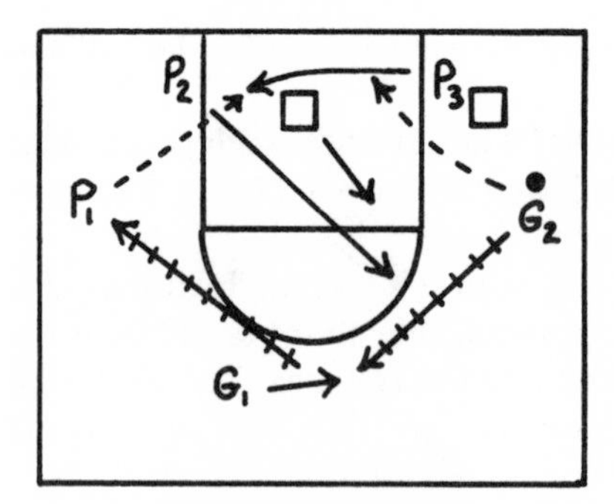

Diagram 8-24B.
Around the Top Weak
Side Attack

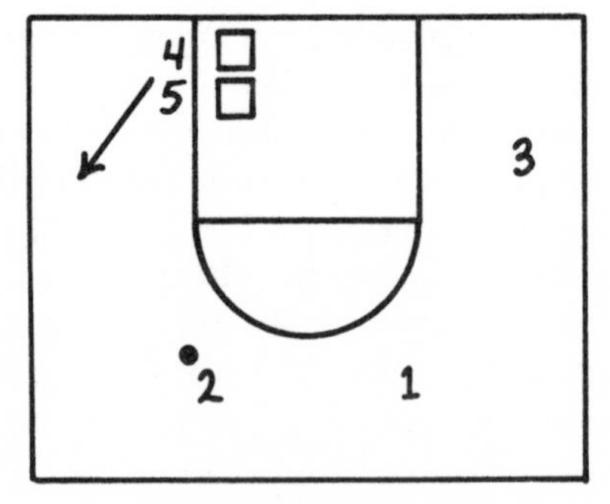

Diagram 8-25.
Stack Offense

is jammed and cannot receive a pass, then G2 will hit G1, who can swing the ball around to P1. The offense again takes the 1-3-1 formation with P3 remaining low. Naturally, the "dribble play" can work to either side. If G1 had dribbled to P2's side, then P2 would have floated the low post area.

These are but a few of the potential plays that can be executed by a triple post ball club. Your imagination will allow you to devise plays that fit the personnel on your team. I did not include any plays for the guards, but you can readily add some. Just remember that the key to a triple post offense is simplicity. Get the ball to the low post as quickly and easily as possible. Use your size advantage inside.

Tex Winter has written a book, *The Triple-Post Offense*, which presents his very successful post attack. The offense is based upon a single post setup, but allows all three front liners to rotate into the low post. The guard attack is also well incorporated into the offense. Many coaches may develop some ideas to fit their guard-orientated philosophies after reading this book.

THE STACK OFFENSE

The stack offense is a versatile post attack gaining popularity among many coaches. Depending upon your personnel, it can involve double or triple post options.

Since most basketball players are right handed, the stack offense is generally set up on the left side. This takes advantage of the good bankboard angle for the pop-out man and a strong low post is already established. The diagram below illustrates a good right hander's stack setup. (See Diagram 8-25.) Players 4 and 5 are the post men, or the 3 and 4 men can switch spots. The 5 man should remain at the left low post in most instances because he would be the biggest and least mobile player.

Either man in the stack can pop out to the wing position, leaving the other player at the low post area. Generally, the bottom man -4- on the stack will use the top man -5- as a screen, and do most of the popping out. The pop man should immediately look to shoot a bank shot or pass in to the low post. The guard cuts to the weak-side low post after passing to the wing. (See Diagram 8-26A.)

If 5 is covered, the ball swings around to 2 who pops out from 3's pick. 2 can shoot or hit 3 for his low post move. If covered, 3 crosses the key and joins 5 to form a double pick for 4. 3 and 5 form a new stack on the left side. If 4 is stopped, the ball can be swung again to the left side stack. This pattern can continue until the desired shot is obtained.

The stack offense can easily be used as a triple post attack involving the three front line players. The stack may be initiated on either side, depending on the position of the ball. If the ball is brought up the right side, then the 4 man simply slides around the pick of 3. (See Diagram 8-27.)

If the passing lane to the pop-out man is pressured, then the low post

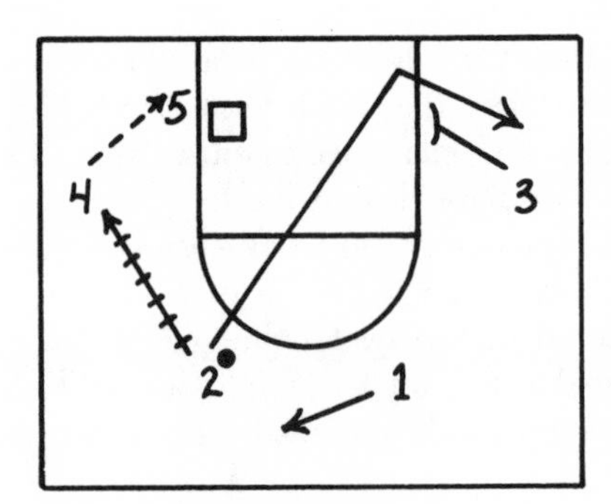

Diagram 8-26A.
Basic Movement—
Left Side Attack

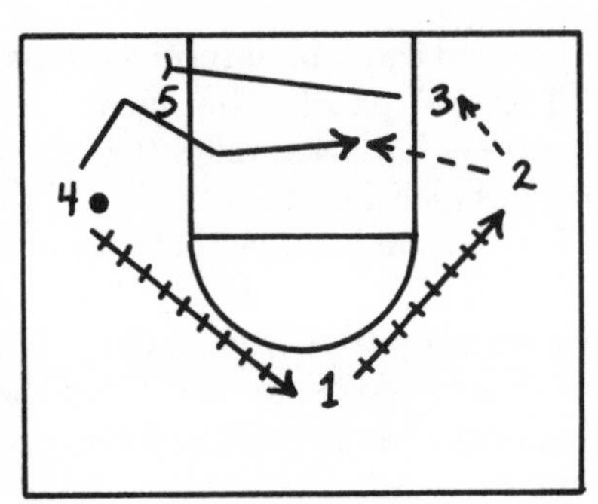

Diagram 8-26B.
Stack Continued

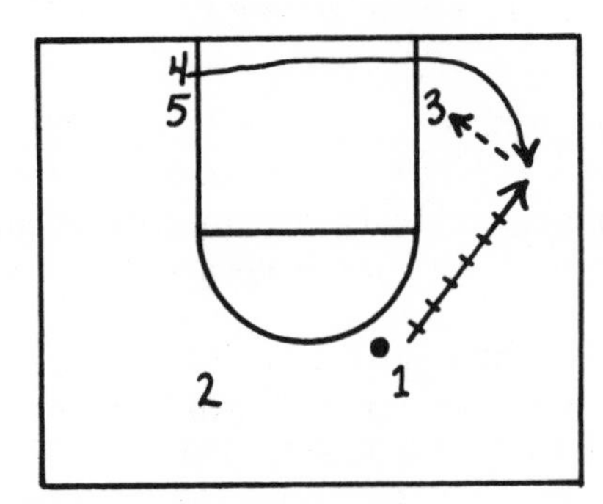

Diagram 8-27.
Swinging the Stack

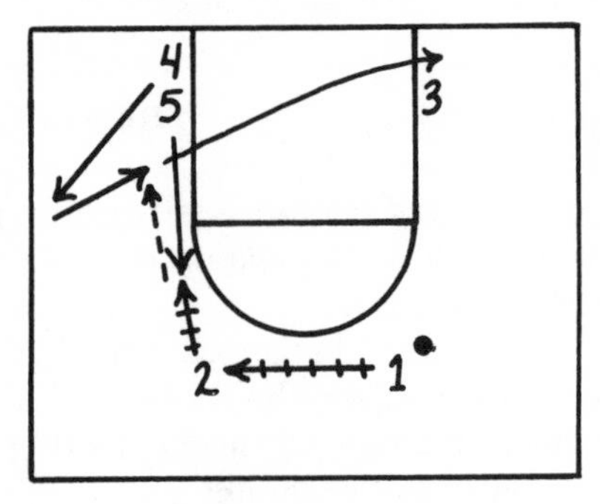

Diagram 8-28A.
Backdoor from the Stack
Set Up

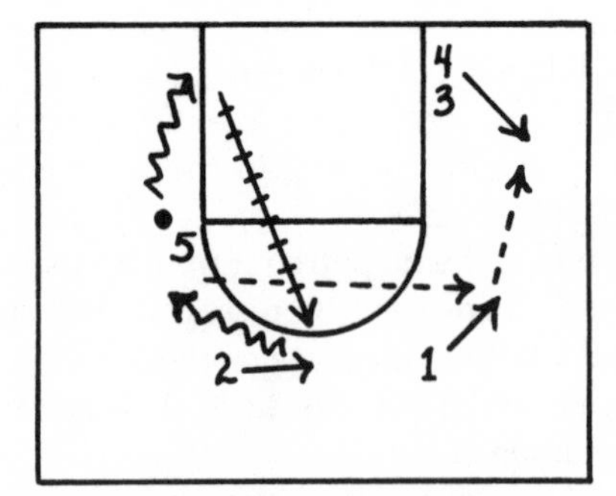

Diagram 8-28B.
Backdoor Continued

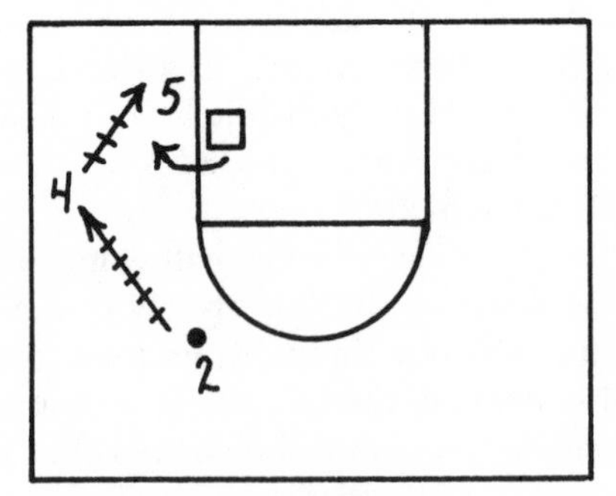

Diagram 8-29.
The Feed Inside

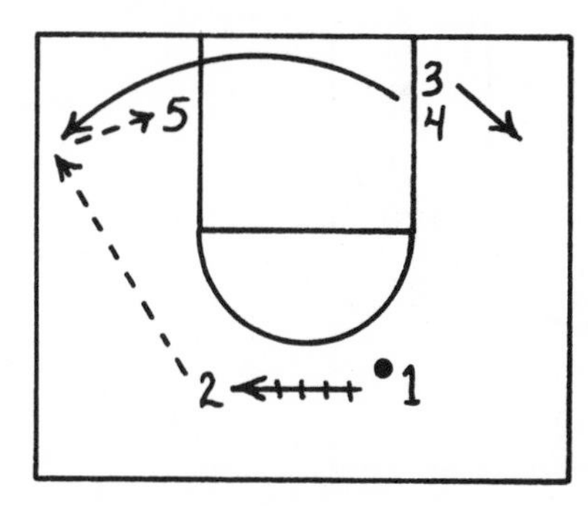

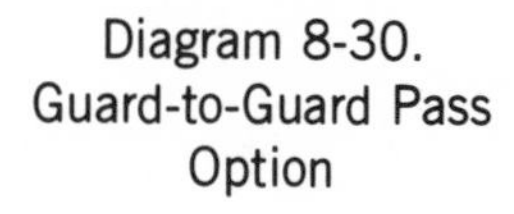
Diagram 8-30.
Guard-to-Guard Pass
Option

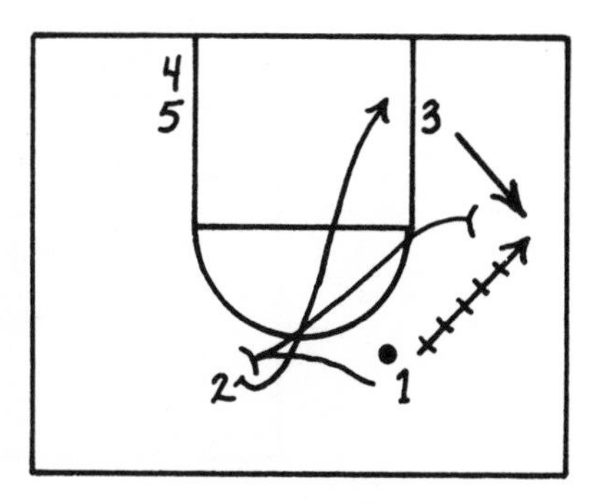

Diagram 8-31A.
Two Pick Play

should break up to the free throw line for a backdoor play. (See Diagram 8-28A.)

After 4 clears, he forms a weak-side stack with 3. 5 looks to drive or hits 2 for a pick and roll. If 2 decides to swing the ball to 1, then the right side stack initiates the continuous pattern diagrammed earlier.

The success of the stack offense lies in the problems it causes the defense at the low post. As one post man pops out to a wing and receives a pass, the defense on the low post must change his position. The offensive man merely positions himself at the low post and anxiously awaits the feed inside. The defense often is forced to leave the baseline open, allowing the muscle shot. (See Diagram 8-29.)

A guard-to-guard pass away from the stack keys the swing action of the stack men. (See Diagram 8-30.) Again, any pop man receiving a pass at the wing must immediately look to the low post.

When the weak-side guard (guard away from stack) initiates the offense, it is generally a good idea to have a play involving the players away from the stack. To balance the stack offense, the diagram below suggests a play for the guards. (See Diagram 8-31A.) Player 1 passes to 3 and picks for 2, who cuts for the basket. Player 1 then reverse pivots and sets a second pick for 3 to drive off. This action can get excellent shots for the guards, plus it occupies the weak-side defense on the posts. The pop man often gets an easy bank shot or feeds the low post after 3 passes to him. (See Diagram 8-31B.)

The stack attack uses the "two-pick play" well when the posts are immobile and inexperienced. If your posts are still learning and your better talent is in the guard and forward positions, then the stationary stack would serve you best. The basic movement on the left side, the two-pick on the right side, and a backdoor play make a good stack offense. The swing plays can be added as the team gains experience, or if a triple post is desired.

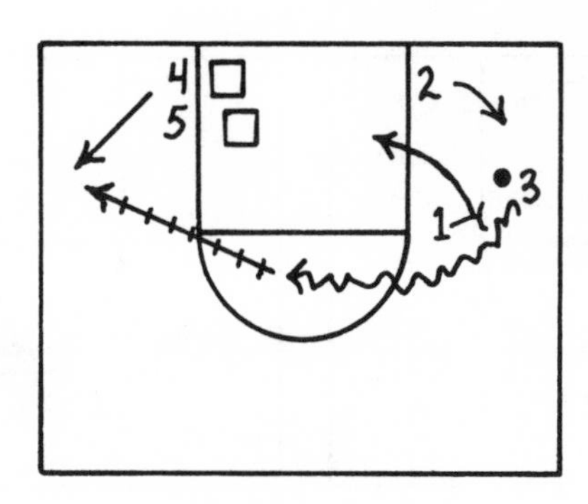

Diagram 8-31B.
Weak Side Pop Action

Whether you have two big men or three, the multiple-post offenses can serve you well. The plays should be kept simple, allowing the post men to hang around the basket for scoring and rebounding purposes. However, movement is needed to keep the defense honest. If the "big boys" stand around too much, the defenders will be able to double-team, sag, and help stop the inside attack.

Take advantage of your height and your opponent's weak defenders. Seldom do teams have two good inside defensive players. If a mismatch is evident, work the ball to the low post man with the advantage.

Keep the "big boys" near the basket and use them as much as possible. You will be rewarded with more victories and championships if you use your height.

9

HOW TO EFFECTIVELY USE ANY PLAYER AT THE POST

The introduction to this book emphasized that post play is for any size player. You may wait for years and still never be blessed with a tall player who can dominate the post area. Rather than abandoning the inside attack and using a perimeter offense, develop what talent you have by adjusting your offensive philosophy.

I mentioned earlier that I teach the "basic three" post moves to my entire squad. I expect each member of the team to be able to maneuver from the low post and score when needed. My offense is designed so it is possible to move a guard or forward to the low post, as well as the pivot man. This is important for four significant reasons.

1. To take advantage of a talented player, regardless of what his natural position might be.
2. To exploit weak defenders that the opponents attempt to hide.
3. To capitalize on a height advantage at any position.
4. To pressure a defender who is in foul trouble.

Face it! Winning a basketball game is a tough job, and we, as coaches, need all the advantages we can find. Being able to post any player on the squad is a plus. The high percentage shot and ability to draw fouls makes the low post attractive for any player of any size.

THE SHORT OR INEXPERIENCED POST MAN

A team that has no player above average height is certainly at a disadvantage. Selecting a post man with a short squad often becomes a process of elimination for the coach.

"Joe and Fred can handle the ball and shoot outside well, so they will play guard. Bob and Pete hustle and shoot fair, so they are forwards. Now that leaves Ol' Herman for the center spot."

Unfortunately, Ol' Herman is more of a liability than a help to the team. Thus, the key spot on this short squad is manned by the least-talented player.

I cannot buy that theory. The important position of post man must be filled by a good athlete. He does not have to be tall to be a threat. Aggressiveness, hustle, jumping ability, quickness, and intelligence are other traits that can more than make up for a lack of height.

The short post man should learn all of the post moves, just as a tall player would. The hook shot and jump hook are very valuable to the short post man, especially when his defender is much taller. These shots are hardest to block and can be developed for a high shot percentage.

A short post man with good quick moves can create a lot of problems for opponents with slow, tall centers. The quickness enables the smaller player to maneuver easily for a feed inside. Once he has received the ball, the shorter man can again use his quickness to get by the slower opponent. This will frustrate the bigger defender and can eventually get him into foul trouble.

Aggressiveness is another important trait of any post player. Even when faced with an extreme height disadvantage, a good post man must accept the challenge and go at the defender. By reading the defense, reacting with the proper move, and challenging the opponent, a small post man can *play big*! When two or three shots are rejected by the taller defender, he will eventually make mistakes and foul. The fouls lead to free throws and force the big man to be less aggressive during the game. That is when the short post man suddenly becomes the *biggest man on the floor*!

The young and inexperienced tall player creates a totally different problem for the coach. That is, how can he be used and allowed to develop without getting in the way of the better players? This problem often arises at the high school level where a 6′6″ lanky sophomore plays with four talented juniors and seniors. The coach wants to use the big man's natural talents, but cannot afford to sacrifice the teamwork of the four veterans. With the recent adoption of the N.C.A.A.'s "freshman eligible rule," more college coaches now face this problem.

The answer again is simplicity. Take the pressure off of the young and developing big kid by giving him simple assignments. Keep him out of fancy offensive patterns. Put him at the low post and let him operate from there. Make the "big boy" work to get open at his best low post area, and instruct him to pursue all shot attempts. This is an easy assignment, but it takes the pressure off of your inexperienced player and puts it all on the opponents. They have to contend with a big man under the basket who is posting up, tipping missed shots, and causing havoc.

This nondemanding approach allows the inexperienced big man to gain much-needed confidence. As he learns his way around the court and masters the inside moves, more responsibility can be placed on his shoulders. It is important to keep the young big man confident, because experience will make him all the better. Do not overload a young player with responsibility. If he is allowed to grow naturally, the coach and team will eventually be rewarded by his dominating play.

The young post man should be encouraged and praised for his efforts. Persuade him to use his post moves when he gets the ball inside. He will never learn to score if he passes it back to the perimeter after receiving a feed at the low post. A word of praise for any attempted post move, whether successful or not, does a lot to inspire a young player. Once big men learn how simple it is to use the "basic three," they will not be easily discouraged.

POSTING FORWARDS

There are times when posting one of the forwards can be an advantage to the offensive team. A double post is actually a way to automatically post a forward, because few teams use more than one post themselves. This forces one of the opponent's forwards to defend a post man.

A tall lanky forward can be a strong weapon when used inside. The coach must also be willing to take advantage of forwards who are physical, jump well, or are very talented. Utilizing these types of players at the low post can spell the difference between victory and defeat.

There are three primary ways to get a forward set up at the low post area.

1. Station the forward at the low post initially. The double post is an example of a stationary setup.
2. Have the forward move to the low post from the ball side of the offense. He can be involved in some sort of pick or just move low and post himself.
3. Let the forward flash across the key from the weak side and look for a quick feed inside. This can be off of a pick or a free-lance cut.

Chapter 8 dealt with many ways of posting forwards through double and triple post alignments. Most of these options are also available to single-post offenses. The two quickest ways to shift a forward to the low post are shown in Diagrams 9-1 and 9-2.

The "Passing Game Offense" offers many opportunities to sneak a forward into the low post area. Because of the freedom of movement allowed in this offense, a hungry forward can post himself at any time. If a situation arises where you want a specific forward to get the ball at the low post, then the team can be instructed to move and pass until the key player gets open. The movement of the "Passing Game" will present a difficult task for the defense; therefore, a quick flash post will usually result in two points.

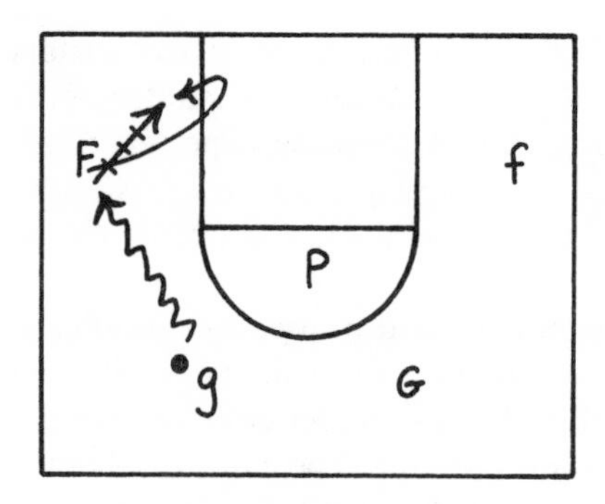

Diagram 9-1.
Strong Side
Forward Low

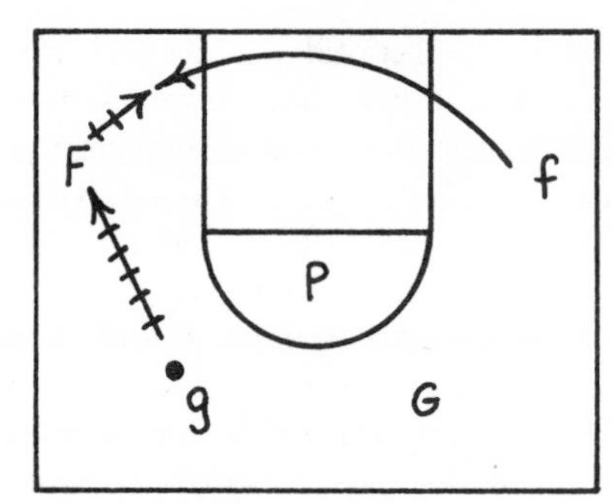

Diagram 9-2.
Weak Side
Flash Post

Since many forwards are aggressive, posting them inside takes advantage of a key trait. The added characteristics of physical size, jumping ability, and quickness can make some forwards even tougher than post men.

A very talented forward should operate inside whenever possible. The inside shot is a higher percentage for him, plus he can put extra pressure on the defense. Because his moves are hard to defend, the gifted forward will draw a lot of fouls around the basket. As in post theory, attacking the opponents inside is smart basketball. The outside bomber forward can be stopped much easier than a posting and driving frontliner.

POSTING GUARDS

A tall guard or a strong guard is another asset that the smart coach can use to an advantage. Due to the unfamiliarity of playing post defense, opposing guards have a very difficult time defending inside. An offensive guard that has learned to read the defense and has mastered the post moves will find the low post to his liking.

To take advantage of the four situations listed at the beginning of this chapter, have a special play or two for low posting your guards. If a team has a particularly tall and aggressive guard, then consideration should be given to incorporating low post plays for guards in the regular offense. A 6′3″ guard defended by a 5′11″ opponent can be used to an advantage, just as a 6′8″ post man can be used against a 6′4″ opponent. Rather than shooting uncontested twenty foot jump shots, the big guard can use his height advantage to shoot uncontested five foot bank shots or easy muscle shots.

The power cut has always been a favorite of mine to move a guard into the low post. He can rub off of the high post and sometimes get a wide open lay up. As the defense catches on, posting up inside can still be an effective way to take advantage of a mismatch. (See Diagram 9-3.)

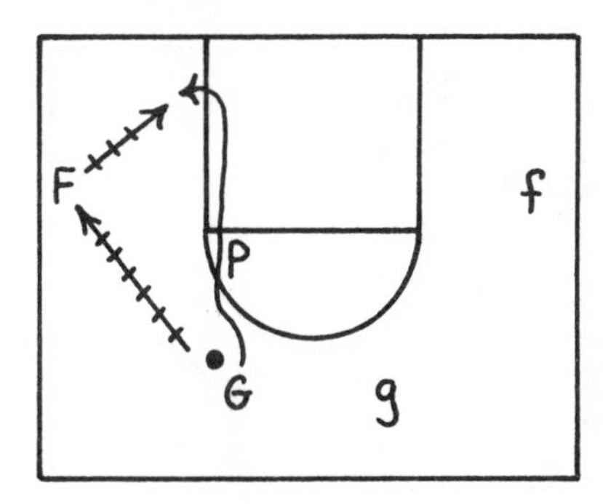

Diagram 9-3.
The Power Cut
for Guards

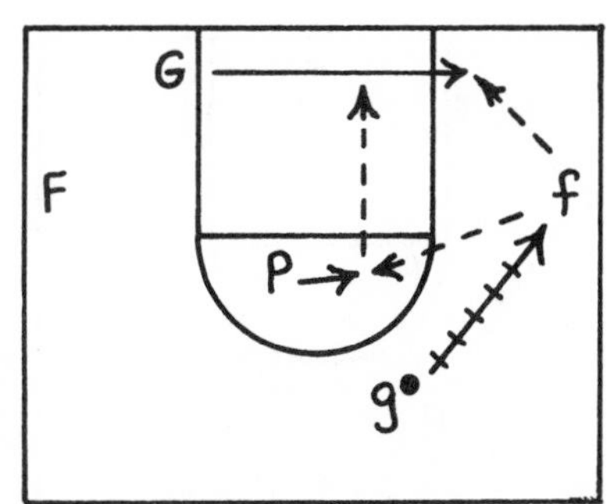

Diagram 9-4.
1-3-1 For Big Guard

Guards should always attack the baseline from the low post. The muscle shot or bank shot will receive minimal resistance from the defensive help of a tall post defender. The hook shot can be effective if the move is made quickly. However, attacking the middle will be more difficult for all but the tallest and strongest of guards.

The shuffle cut or weak-side guard cut is another way to post a guard. The guard passes the ball to the forward, while the weak-side guard cuts to the low post. The cutter can attempt to rub his defender out on a high post player, or just flash-cut to the post area.

If a situation arises where the offensive guard has an obvious mismatch, you may wish to call for a 1-3-1 setup. (See Diagram 9-4.) From this alignment the guard works to get open inside against the inferior opponent, while his teammates work to get the ball to him.

You do not have to have a tall guard to be effective inside. Just as in post play, aggressiveness, jumping ability, and good moves will make any guard tough at the low post. More than any other position, the offensive guard can dominate his defender inside. The lack of practice time spent on guards defending the low post and the unfamiliarity of the position to defensive guards, makes this a vulnerable area of attack. The speed, quickness, and desire of many little men make them pesty challenges for opponents defending the internal area.

The power split combines the possibilities of guards and forwards posting on the same play. This is an excellent pattern to use when your better talent plays the perimeter. (See Diagrams 9-5A and B.)

If the power cut is covered, the forward -F- hits -P- and sets a pick on the guard -G-. The post has the option to hit the guard -G- coming off of the pick, or -F- rolling under the basket. When the ball goes to -G-, he can shoot or pass into -F- at the low post. This play and other options for posting guards and forwards are incorporated into my "Power Post Offense," contained in the next chapter.

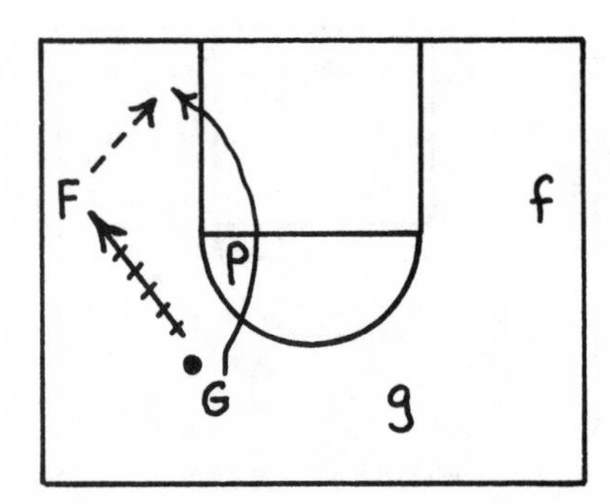

Diagram 9-5A.
Power Split

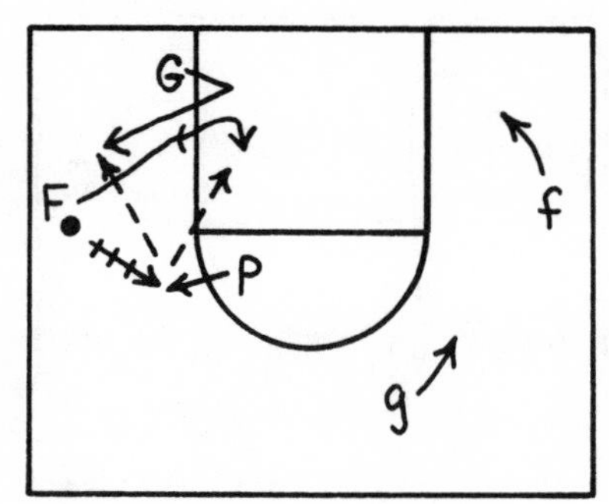

Diagram 9-5B.
Power Split Continued

10

WINNING WITH THE POWER POST OFFENSE

"Power Basketball" is a style of play that demands offensive attack in the internal zone. The offense should shoot 75 per cent of its shots within twelve feet of the basket and draw an average of 25 or more free throws per game. With these goals in mind, I developed the "Power Post Offense" for use against man-to-man defenses.

The "Power Post Offense" can be adjusted to fit yearly changes in personnel. Since I often have been blessed with good big men, I normally use the 1-3-1 alignment. If the squad lacks a tall post man, the plays work well from a 2-1-2 setup.

The offense consists of three primary plays which provide low post opportunities for a guard, forward, and the post man. Four secondary plays can be added to take advantage of talented players and sagging defenses. I do not attempt to add the secondary plays until the team has some game experience with the primary offense. The primary plays are enough offense for most teams, especially young and inexperienced ones. I sometimes add the secondary plays after the nonleague schedule is completed. They serve to stimulate the players and add a new dimension to the team.

The initial alignment for a team with a tall, right-handed post man is illustrated in Diagram 10-1. The big man is stationed at the best low post spot. Players shift to the 1-3-1 after the guard -G- gets to the top of the key.

Selecting players to fit each of the spots in the offense is usually quite easy for the average squad. Following is the guide I use when evaluating future as well as present personnel.

-P- **The Low Post Player.** The player with the best low post moves or best potential to develop low post moves. He should be one of the tallest players on the team so he can go to the hoop, present a big pass target, and gather offensive rebounds.

-F- **The High Post Player.** The least mobile forward or the post man

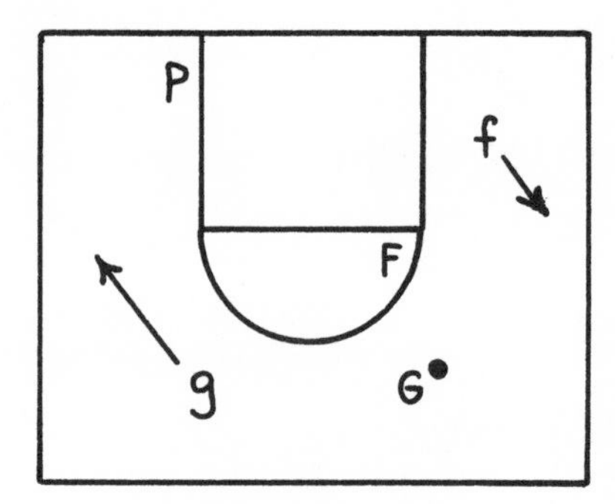

Diagram 10-1.
The Power Post
1-3-1 Alignment

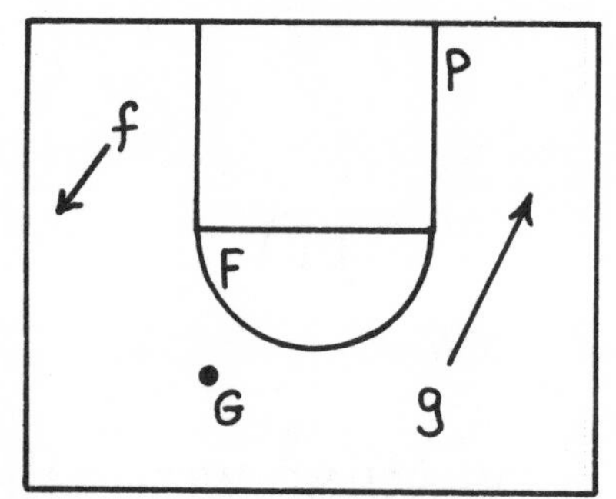

Diagram 10-2.
The Left-Handed
Post Alignment

with the poorer inside moves. This spot can have a lot of latitude to it. A slow, wide forward may be used as a picker, feeder, and rebounder. A short but quick forward can be a driver, shooter, and pesty rebounder. If the squad has two good low post men, they can alternate between the high and the low posts. The high post has many chances to feed the low post areas, so he must be a good passer.

-f- **The Right Wing.** The best outside shooting forward. He must be able to get open for passes, so quickness is desirable. The shortest forward usually plays this spot. He should be able to shoot the twenty footer if his defender sags off. The ability to penetrate, post up inside, and crash the offensive boards are pluses. A left-handed player is a natural for this position. He can drive off of the high post with his strong hand, or post low on his best side. I have been fortunate enough to have coached three very good left-handed forwards who scored well from this spot. Right handers have done well too, I might add.

-g- **The Short Guard.** The best outside shooting guard. Since he plays the wing, he must be able to draw his defender out with the threat of his outside shot. A poor shooter will find his defender sagging into the low post and congesting the internal area. This guard needs to be a good penetrator and passer, so he can position himself to feed inside.

-G- **The Big Guard.** The best posting guard. Usually he is the tallest or most physical guard on the team. He will need to cut underneath a lot and post the defensive guard, so he needs strong post move potential. A short guard will work here, but he must be scrappy and willing to challenge the defenders inside.

When the low post player is left handed, the initial offensive alignment should be reversed. (See Diagram 10-2.) The post man sets up on his best spot, which is the right low post position. The high post man -F- moves to the left side, the wing -f- goes to the left side, and the guards switch sides. If you are lucky enough to coach a squad with a left-handed post man and four right-handed perimeter players, the offense will fit everyone perfectly. "Power Basketball" will then be fulfilled to its maximum.

Since most teams are geared to all right-handed squads, I will present my version of the right-hander's "Power Post Offense." If you desire versatility, have the squad set up left side one time and right side another time. This will help offset some defensive stacking and open the internal zone. It can also aid in posting a particular player at his strong side in key situations. As the options are explained, this will become clearer.

Parts of this offense were presented in chapter 8 on double and triple posting. Because the "Power Post Offense" attempts to post from three to five players, there is a connection with multiple post offenses.

THE THREE PRIMARY PLAYS

The "Power Post Offense" is made up of three primary plays.

1. The Power Play
2. The Power Rub Out
3. The High Post Split

1. The Power Play

The Power Play is the keystone to building the offense. It is a simple and direct way to attack the internal zone with your best post man. If the opponents cannot effectively defend the big man, this play will score many easy baskets. It is a quick attack option that puts immediate pressure on the internal defenders. Unless the opposition has an intimidating center, your club can run this play about half of the time you set up. Diagram 10-3A illustrates the Power Play with early options.

The point guard -G- can pass to the wing -g-, or the wing guard -g- can dribble the ball to the left wing area. Of course, the low post must station himself above the red square. The wing guard should locate himself at a good passing angle to the low post. This is about half way between the red square and the free throw line, and half way between the key and the sideline. A direct feed or a lob pass is easier to make from this angle.

The two forwards exchange positions to keep their defenders from sagging into the low post man. This opens the internal zone for the lob, or provides a new option pass to -f-.

If -g- cannot get the ball to -P-, he can hit -f- for a quick shot or feed inside to -P-. Reversing the ball to -F- will sometimes catch the low post defender lagging and result in an easy feed to -P-. Diagram 10-3B shows -P- cutting to the ball after it has been reversed to -F-.

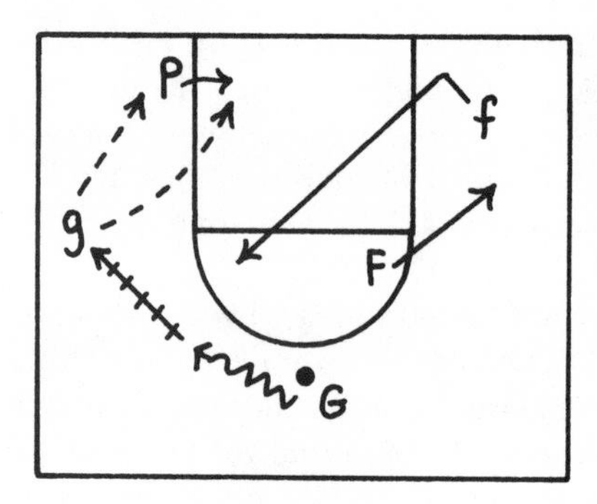

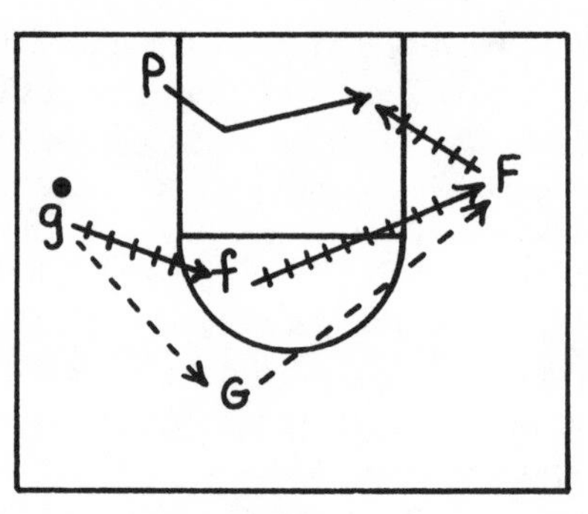

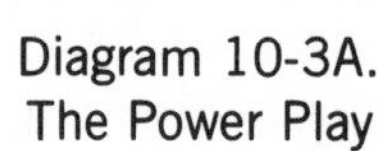
Diagram 10-3A.
The Power Play

Diagram 10-3B.
Power Play Reversal

Two quick passes will get the ball to the opposite side of the court and present an entirely different picture to the offensive players. Player -F- might have an open bank shot if his defender sags too much on -P-. If the defender on -G- sags to stop the pass to -f-, player -g- can reverse the ball around the top of the key. The reversal provides the same 1-3-1 alignment, only now -P- is breaking to the ball. The movement usually gets -P- open for a post move.

The key to making the Power Play work is the determination of the perimeter men to get the ball to the low post. If the guard can hit the post initially, then he must do it until the defense adjusts and stops all passing lanes. This will make the reversal work for an even better shot.

2. The Power Rub Out

The second play in the offense is the Power Rub Out for the big guard. This play is keyed with a pass to the short forward -f- by the point man. The wing -f- must time his breakout from the low post so -G- can hit him on the move. Timing between the two is very important or needless turnovers result. After the point man -G- hits the wing -f-, the guard attempts to rub his defender out on the high post -F-. (See diagram 10-4A.) If the guard's defender is slowed even momentarily, -G- will be free for a return pass and lay up.

This is a play where quick guards can beat their defenders on the initial pass and can cut for easy lay ups. Bigger and slower guards can post their defenders inside and work their low post moves.

After the guard -G- rubs out on the high post, -F- turns inside and diagonally picks for the low post man -P-. This occupies the defensive big men so they will not help out on the posting guard. It also frees -P- at the high post to receive a pass from -f-, thus initiating the second option of the Power Rub Out. (See Diagram 10-4B.)

When -f- cannot hit -G-, he looks for -P- breaking to the high post. A

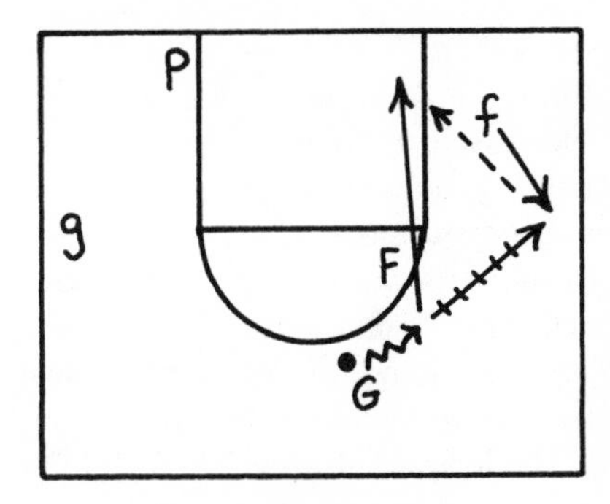

Diagram 10-4A.
The Power Rub Out

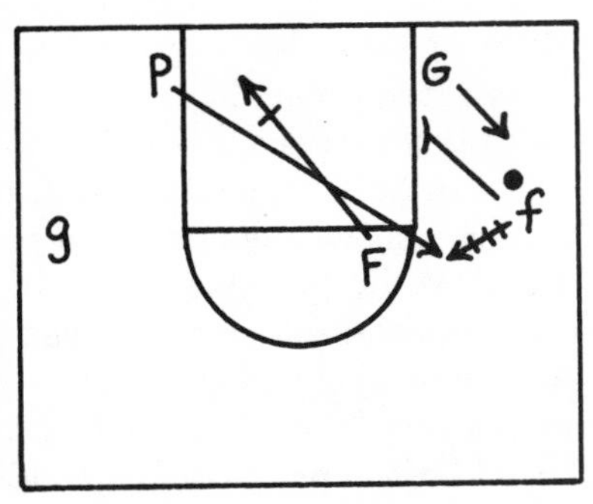

Diagram 10-4B.
The Power Split

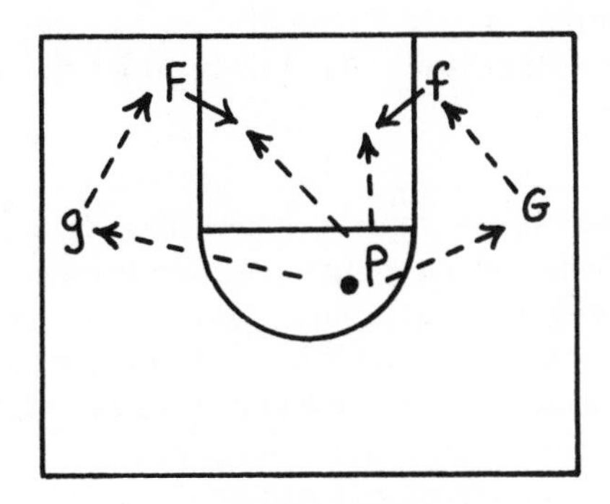

Diagram 10-4C.
Post Man's Options

pass to -P- keys the Power Split where -f- picks for -G-. -P- then has five very good options, as illustrated in Diagram 10-4C.

1. He can pass to -f- rolling to the basket after the pick on -G-.
2. He can hit -G- popping outside off of the pick by -f-.
3. He can feed -F- flashing into the key from the weak-side low post.
4. He can reverse the ball to -g-, who may shoot or feed -F- posting inside.
5. He can shoot or drive if given the opportunity.

The Power Rub Out provides most of the essentials for good Power Basketball. Both low posts are being filled by moving and screening players, the high post keys five attacking directions, and a reversal is possible if the defense sags to the strong side. But the real power punch is that a guard, a forward, and a post man all get to move to the low posts. This puts the pressure right where you want it—on the opponent's defense!

The wing -f-, must be sure to save his dribble when he first receives the ball. If the passing lanes to the low post and high post are blocked, the dribble can save a jump ball call. Remember, a man in possession of the ball who is closely guarded has only five seconds to dribble, shoot, or pass. Killing the dribble immediately after receiving the ball eliminates the drive potential and allows the defense to pressure even more.

The drive by the wing -f- can be turned into various counter plays. I favor the pick-and-roll off of the high post. (See Diagram 10-5.)

As I mentioned earlier in the chapter, a left-handed player at this position can be very tough. He may fake to the baseline and use his strong hand to go off of -P- and penetrate the middle. The forward -f- then has many fine options. He can pull up and hit the jump shot, continue to drive for a lay up, feed the rolling post man -P- on a defensive switch, or pass off to any other open teammate. A good helping defense will sag and stop the inside attack initially, but often a pass out to the wing -g- will open a new attacking area. This is the Power Option or feed to the left low post -F-.

Another forward option is explained later under the Secondary Plays.

3. The High Post Split

The third member of the three primary plays is the High Post Split. Unlike conventional splits off of the high post, my version is a split under the basket. This play serves as a counter to the Power Rub Out Play. If the pass cannot be made to the wing -f-, the High Post Split becomes automatic.

Opponents will sometimes attempt to overplay the forward -f- and stop the Power Rub Out. In order to relieve some of the pressure, the point guard -G- must hit the high post and initiate the split. The first option is a backdoor cut by the wing -f-. (See Diagram 10-6A.) If the defense is slow to react or the defender turns his back to the ball, then a lay up will result. The next time down the court the defender will probably loosen up and allow the pass to -f-.

When the defense is able to stop the backdoor option, the split under the basket is next. The wing -f- crosses under the hoop and sets a pick on the low post defender. (See Diagram 10-6B.) A good pick will open the post man -P- for a quick feed and a short hook shot or lay up.

After passing to the high post, the point man should immediately cut to the open corner on the right side. This discourages his defender from attacking the ball at the high post and positions -G- at a good feeding angle.

The high post -F- has the familiar options outlined earlier. (See Diagram 10-6C.) Player -P- crosses over to the right low post, while -f- posts up on the left side. Quick feeds are possible inside, or a pass to the wing can open new passing lanes.

Having diagrammed and explained the three primary options of the Power Post Offense, some of its strong points are now obvious.

1. There is a lot of similarity between this man-to-man offense and the zone offense in Chapter 7.

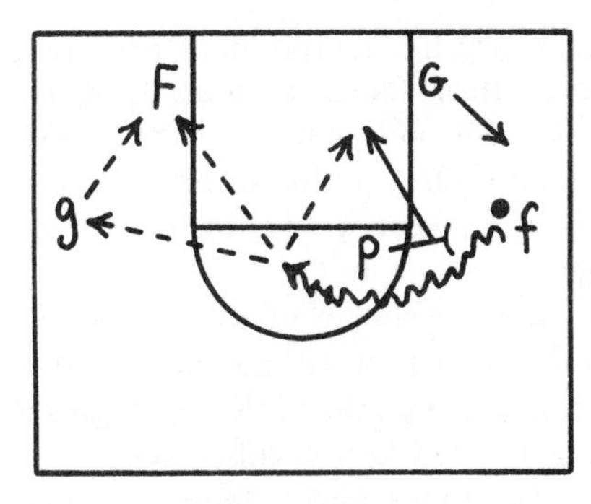

Diagram 10-5.
The Pick-and-Roll Option

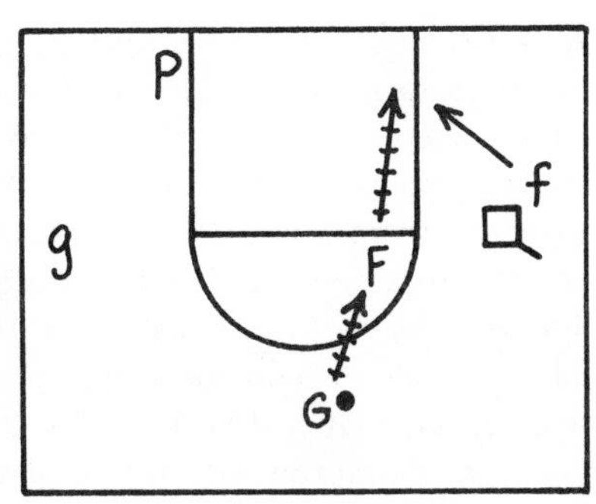

Diagram 10-6A.
The High Post Split—
Backdoor

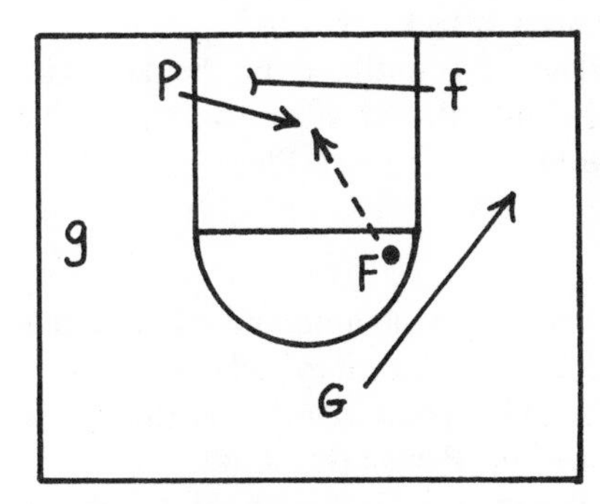

Diagram 10-6B.
The Split to the
Big Man

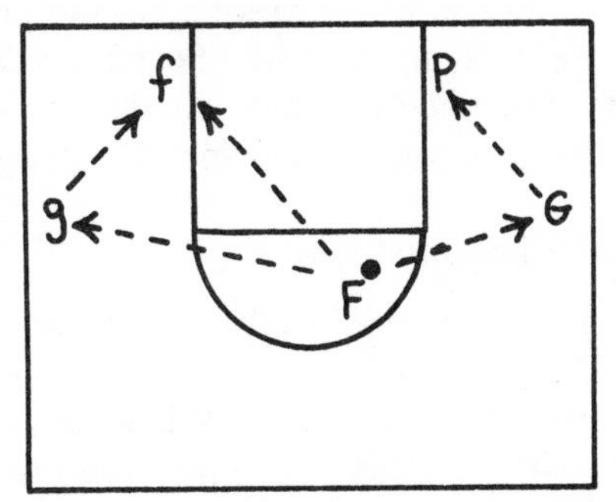

Diagram 10-6C.
High Post Split Posting

2. The guards quickly move to the wings where they are in good shooting or feeding position.
3. A big man centers the offense from the high post area.
4. Both low post spots are usually filled with good inside scorers.
5. All five players move to good scoring areas immediately.

The offense provides three principle shooting areas. Besides the low post, these include the high post and wings. This allows the players to work on spot shots, thus developing confidence and accuracy. Wing shots can be bank shots, if desired. The high post corresponds to free throw distance, and the low posts offer high percentage shots at all times.

THE SECONDARY PLAYS

"Secondary Plays" may be added to the "Power Post Offense" as the situation dictates. Once the players become familiar and comfortable with the three primary plays, new options can easily be incorporated. I use secondary plays to present new looks in our attack. Serious scouting by the opponents allows them to stack their defense and slow our attack. Key players may get two-timed or jammed inside. One or two secondary plays will give the team a change of pace, open the best scorers for shots, and confuse the opponent's defensive strategy.

Special plays are also necessary to take advantage of the changes in annual talent. When your best player is the short forward, you may want to devise a specific play just for him. The following year, the high post might be your all star. A different secondary play is needed to free this player.

"Secondary Plays" are just that: secondary to the main offense. You may wish to devise your own to fit your needs. Guard against introducing too many extra options, however; because this will get away from the desired simplicity. Stick to a couple of plays that will aid your squad in tight situations, but continue to rely upon the primary attack.

Four of my favorite "Secondary Plays" are outlined in the following pages. Remember, they should only be introduced after the squad has gained game experience and confidence in the "Primary Plays."

1. The Diagonal Play

I first devised this play as a means of posting a talented and tall high post man. It also serves as an extra option for the point guard who is not very effective at posting inside. When your squad has short guards and the opposing guards are taller, this play can replace the Power Rub Out.

The play starts out the same as the Power Rub Out, with the point man -G- passing to the wing -f-. Instead of cutting to the low post, -G- makes a diagonal cut to the weak side of the court. This keys the high post man to cut to the low post area. The wing looks to get the ball to -F-, if possible. (See Diagram 10-7A.)

If -F- is fronted at the low post, -P- should break up to the strong side high post. This opens the over-top lob pass possibility to -F-. Player -P- is now free to receive a pass from -f-. He can then shoot, feed -F- from the new angle, or reverse the ball to -G- on the weak side. (See Diagram 10-7B.)

Player -g- moves to the top of the key to serve as the safety man. If -P- is covered at the high post, -f- can hit -g- and the ball may still be reversed. When -G- does receive the ball, he will often find a flashing -F- open for an easy muscle shot. (See Diagram 10-7C.)

You have undoubtedly noticed the similarity between the "Diagonal Play" and "The Power Play." Actually, this is what the Diagonal Play is meant to be: a Power Play for the high post man -F-. The play takes advantage of your talented high post man or the opponent's weak defender on -F-. It gets the guards moving, but keeps the internal zone open for the big boys. Finally, the "Diagonal" presents a different look to a basic play.

Reversing the ball is very important to the success of any power play. A stacked defense will front and double up on your low post men, but the

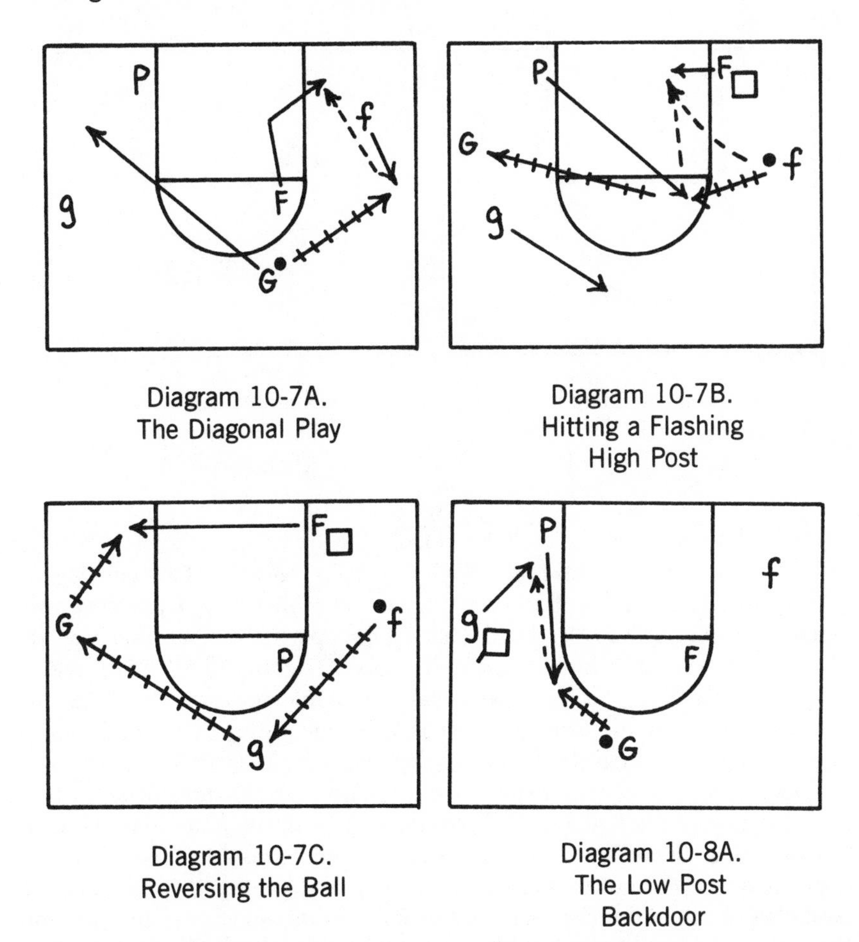

Diagram 10-7A.
The Diagonal Play

Diagram 10-7B.
Hitting a Flashing
High Post

Diagram 10-7C.
Reversing the Ball

Diagram 10-8A.
The Low Post
Backdoor

reversal opens new avenues to scoring. To make the Power Play or Diagonal Play work effectively, the coach must insist his perimeter men look to reverse against sagging defenses. Three quick passes will get the desired inside shot and leave the defense frustrated and beaten.

2. The Backdoor Play

When the low post "Power Play" is effectively run, it becomes a powerful scoring maneuver. Opponents will counter by overplaying the left wing man -g- and attempt to turn the attack to the right side. The Backdoor Play can be introduced to assure the big man of getting the ball.

Defenders who overplay must be made to pay the price by the use of backdoor options. This special secondary play will keep the offense balanced and allow your team to use the big man when they wish.

The low post man automatically keys the backdoor by breaking to the high post. When -P- sees -g- being pressured on the wing, he should quickly cut high and look for a feed from -G-. (See Diagram 10-8A.) The wing -g-

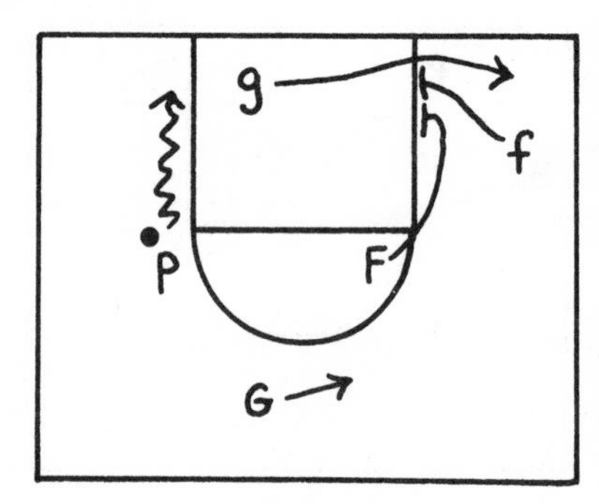

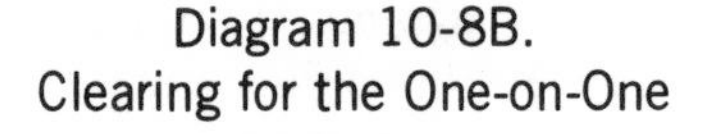
Diagram 10-8B.
Clearing for the One-on-One

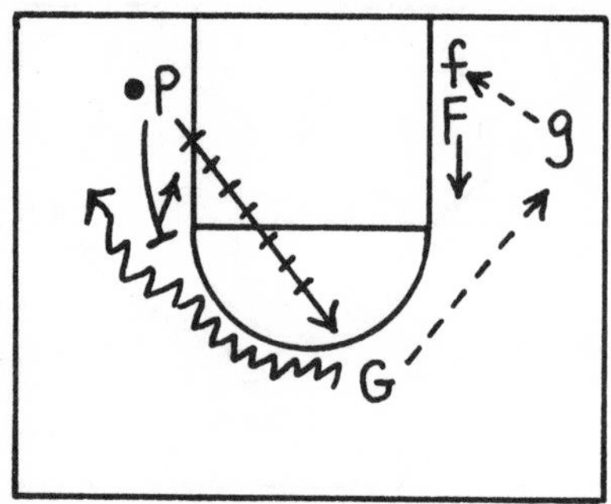

Diagram 10-8C.
The Reverse or
Pick-and-Roll

immediately sprints to the basket and looks for the backdoor feed. When the defender is slow to react, as in the High Post Split, -g- will get an open lay up.

Up to this point, the Backdoor Play is the same as the High Post Split. When -g- is properly covered and does not get open on the backdoor cut, the similarity to the primary version ends. (See Diagram 10-8B.) The play is designed to use -P- and his inside talents. While -g- clears out, the two forwards form a double pick on the weak side. The post man is now free to go one-on-one, or reverse the ball to -g- behind the pick.

The post man -P- can drive for the lay up, muscle shot, or short bank shot. If he cannot get off a high percentage attempt, the point man -G- is his release valve. Some teams will sag and attempt to double time -P- on his drive. A quick pass out to -G- will allow the guard to hit any open teammate on the weak side. Often, -g- will be free for a short bank shot or jumper from the corner. He might also be able to feed the ball to the forwards -f- or -F- at the low post. (See Diagram 10-8C.)

If -g- is sufficiently covered, the point man -G- can choose to run a pick-and-roll off of -P-. A driving lay up or feed to the low post is possible, depending upon the reaction of the defenders. Should the play break down, -F- can move back to the high post, -g- to the point, and the offense is ready to start over.

3. The Double Back Option Play

The Power Rub Out Play offers an excellent secondary option for the short forward -f- called the Double Back Option Play. When the cutting guard is covered, -f- may choose to drive off of the high post player. Since most defensive teams like to jam the key, a double back to the strong side can catch the opponents off guard. This play is great for sneaking a quick two pointer or for posting the short forward inside.

After driving to the top of the key and finding no room to penetrate, -f- may reverse pivot and pass to the guard -G- popping out. (Diagram 10-9A.)

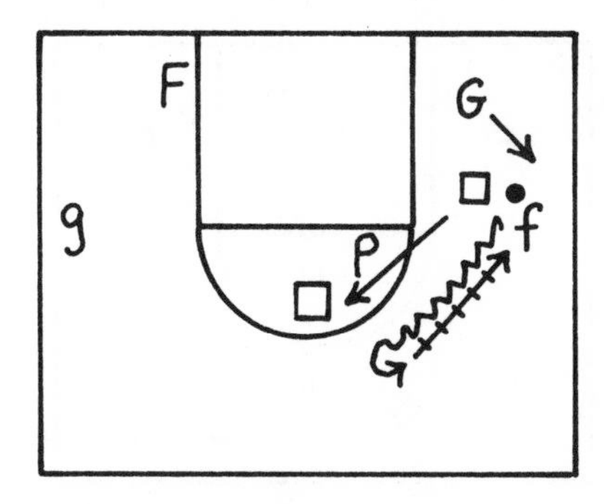

Diagram 10-9A.
The Double Back

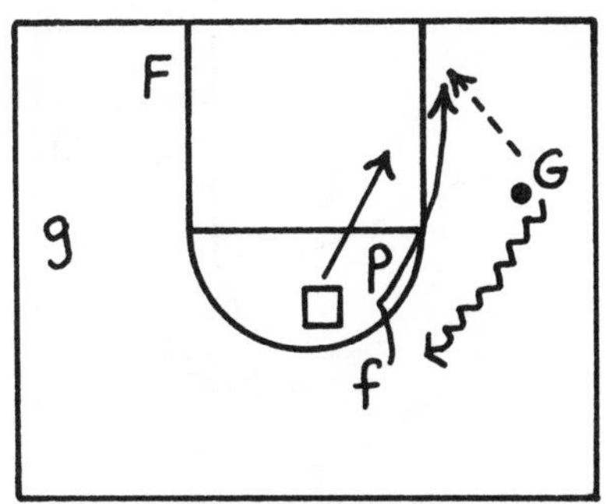

Diagram 10-9B.
The Forward Rub Out

The defender on -f- will usually get trapped behind the high post, thus leaving the cutter open for a return pass and lay up. (See Diagram 10-9B.) If the defense adjusts and covers -f- properly, -G- can feed the high or low posts, or dribble to the top of the key to start a new series.

4. The Dribble-At Play

An outstanding forward who can score inside as well as from the wing requires a special power play. There are times when it is advantageous to post the short forward inside, as mentioned in chapter 9. The Dribble-At Play is a power play for -f-. By dribbling to the right wing, -G- can force a shift in the offensive alignment, as shown in Diagram 10-10. This will allow the short forward to post inside, just as -P- does on the Power Play.

The high post moves weak side, allowing the low post man to break high. A reverse can be worked to free -f- on the opposite low post side.

The Power Post Offense gives your team a chance to post every player with four basic plays. Either guard can play the point and run a Rub Out Play. The posts can alternate between high and low positions to provide versatility. Through secondary plays, the short forward can be moved to the low post.

As mentioned earlier, I sometimes have the team set up backwards. This is the left-handed post man alignment illustrated in Diagram 10-2. This can throw the opponents off and allow two or three quick baskets. Besides presenting a different look, the backwards alignment enables the guard to post on his best side. This makes the Rub Out more effective and puts the Dribble-At on a more comfortable side. Even the Power Play for -P- gains some advantage when the post man moves back to his strong side on the reverse.

On a team with no big man, the 2-1-2 initial setup might be preferred to the 1-3-1 alignment. Where the 1-3-1 attempts to key on the big post man under the basket, the 2-1-2 presents balance to the offense. (See Diagram 10-11.)

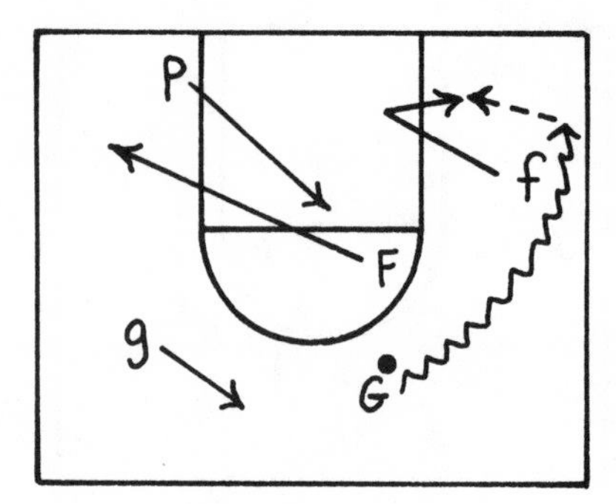

Diagram 10-10.
The Dribble-At Play

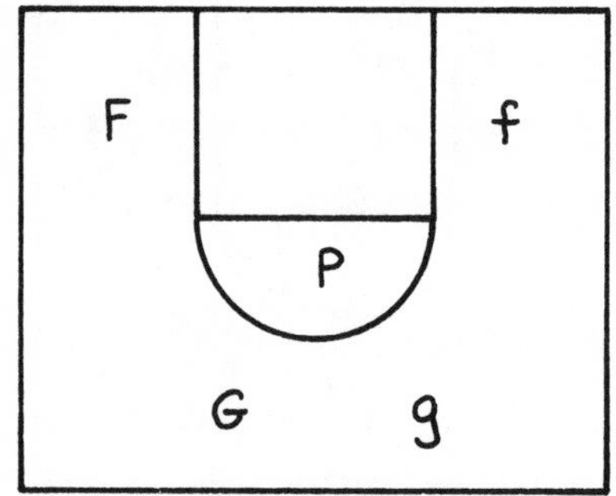

Diagram 10-11.
The Power Post
2-1-2 Alignment

To run a Power Play, a guard dribbles to the wing and shifts the attack to a 1-3-1. A pass to the wing keys the Power Rub Out or Diagonal Series. Feeding the high post calls for the High Post Split Play and its many options.

Because of the balance to the 2-1-2, your team can search out a weakness in the opponent and then continually attack it. The only real difference between the 2-1-2 and 1-3-1 alignment is that the latter allows the big man to always set up at the low post.

Defensive safety responsibility falls on -g-, who must rotate back on every shot attempt. The other guard -G- can be flexible in this attack. If you want a fourth offensive rebounder, the big guard -G- is the man. Against quick breaking teams, -G- can be used as a second safety to stop the fast break.

In closing, I would like to present some short reminders and tips for running a successful Power Offense.

1. All players must learn post moves and post shots; included is the muscle shot, bank shot, and hook shot.
2. Perimeter players should always look to pass to open teammates in the "Internal Zone" before attempting long shots.
3. Any player possessing the ball in the internal zone must attempt to score. The exception would be if a pass were possible to a more open teammate in the "Internal Zone."
4. Players should never fall away from the hoop or defensive players. "Put Pressure on the Hoop" and on the defense. Three-point plays are an integral part of Power Basketball.
5. Outside shots (15 feet or more) should only be taken when the defense is sagging off enough to allow unmolested attempts. No rushed or forced outside shots are permitted.

11

DEVELOPING SOUND POST DEFENSE

A defensive team can only be as good as the defensive abilities of the individuals who play. The post man must be well schooled in defensive principles. He is not only the key offensive player, but also the corner-stone of solid team defense.

The most effective offensive attacks attempt to penetrate the internal zone and get high percentage shots. The post defender is often the determining factor as to the type of shot that will be allowed. He must contain the opponent's pivot man, and he also has the potential to help teammates stop penetration. An active and intelligent post man is a necessity in making an excellent defensive team.

A good defensive team is hard to beat because it is the most consistent. While ball clubs may experience off nights or cold streaks on offense, the defense remains uniform. Good defensive teams are stingy with the type of shots they give up. Poor defensive clubs can be exploited for weaknesses and large point totals.

Since the post man is the hub of a tough defense, pay particular attention to his development. The big man is often the most uncoordinated and inexperienced player on a team. His mere presence may intimidate many penetrating opponents, but his clumsiness can lead to senseless fouls. The post man must be taught to analyze and think ahead when on defense.

Many teams are now employing offenses that allow various players to play the low and high post positions. Guards and forwards must also learn to play sound post defense. As stated earlier, I try to develop a whole team of good post players. This includes the defensive end of the court as well as the offensive.

DEVELOPING INDIVIDUAL DEFENSIVE TRAITS

The post man is expected to develop all of his defensive skills, just as the guards and forwards do. He may be required to guard a man who plays the perimeter, an opponent involved in a movement offense, or even help in the back court during a pressing situation. The post man must learn to be a versatile defensive player, if the team expects to have a strong and adaptable defense.

Physical Traits

Following are listed some physical traits that post men must work on. Through drill and instruction, a ball player can learn to use his physical tools more effectively. The awareness of this need for development rests with you.

1. Quickness

The quick defender can cover up a lot of mistakes because he recovers rapidly. Once he has learned proper defensive fundamentals, the quick player can cut off, contain, and confuse his opponent.

There are two types of quickness that you must watch for: (1) hand quickness, and (2) quickness of feet. They do not necessarily go together in ball players. Quite often you will find slow moving big men with the uncanny ability to steal passes or knock the ball loose. Their quick hands can make them more valuable to the defense then the quick runners.

The age-old question then arises: Can quickness be learned? It can be improved through repetition, drill, and awareness. Any game or skill involving the feet or hands will increase the effectiveness of these important tools. Experience and education will also make the player quicker, because he will become more alert. He can then anticipate certain offensive moves and capitalize on the knowledge. Again, you are responsible for teaching the post man to think quicker.

2. Footwork and Positioning

Defensive players must not be allowed to cross their feet except when chasing an opponent from behind. Good defensive footwork calls for sliding the feet, with the trailing leg never approaching closer than six inches to the lead leg. Short, choppy steps are desirable for quicker reaction to dribblers and other opponents with the ball. Keeping the feet in contact with the floor while moving is a key to good defensive footwork. Loping, galloping, and bouncing should be eliminated. The defensive player cannot change direction and speed as easily when his feet are too far off of the floor.

General rules of positioning include staying between your man and the basket when he has the ball, and staying between the ball and your man when he does not have the ball. Overplaying a strong hand is advisable on opponents who prefer to always drive in one direction.

Floor position relative to weak-side help, defending the post area, and influencing the dribbler are governed by your philosophy and teaching. If no instruction is given pertaining to positioning, the post man misses out on a very important aspect of team defensive play. Situations should be discussed and reviewed on the court periodically throughout the season.

3. Body Balance

The post man is often a young man who has grown at a tremendous rate. He may lack coordination and have difficulty staying on his feet during the fast pace of a basketball game. You should recognize that teaching body balance to the awkward player is necessary before success at advanced skills can be realized.

The player's feet should be spread about shoulder width with the weight evenly distributed. The knees must be slightly bent so that the hips are lowered. The back remains straight and the head should be kept directly above the midpoint of the feet. A bent back and hanging head throw the center of gravity in front of the feet. This leads to slower reactions and awkwardness.

Good body balance is important both offensively and defensively. The same basic positions of balance can be followed at both ends of the court.

4. Arms and Hands

A long-armed player of modest stature can be more effective defensively than a short-armed tall man. His extra reach will enable him to cover more of the passing lanes much to the surprise of unsuspecting opponents.

The post man generally has the longest arms on the team, so he must keep them in a ready position on defense. When the ball is away, the big man should keep his hands in front of his shoulders. From this position, a defender can react to any pass, shot, or loose ball which enters his area.

5. Eyes

Defensive post men must be reminded that basketball is played with a ball, so they should never let it out of their sight. The post man should develop his peripheral vision and positioning so he can see the ball and his man at all times. If movement forces the post to choose between seeing the ball or his man, he must choose the ball. When you keep your eye on the ball, you keep track of the game and play team defense.

The defender who loses sight of his assigned man is expected to retreat until he again sees "man and ball." Remember: "You cannot defend something you cannot see." See the ball always! It is the only thing that counts as two points when it goes in the hoop.

6. Voice

Communication is vital to good team defense. The post man is usually defending in a position where he can see a lot of action—the key area. Unlike his teammates playing guard or forward, he can watch all the other nine players in most situations. The post must warn his teammates of potential picks, double screens, clear-out situations, or open opponents. His talking also serves as encouragement to keep his teammates alert.

In essence, the psychological aspects of communication distract opponents and establish a team's dedication to stopping an attack.

7. Size

The tall post man must take advantage of his size when playing defense. Shots can be blocked and shooters intimidated when height is used effectively. However, a big man who overcommits can pick up needless fouls and hurt his team.

A muscular post man should also use his physical size wisely. He can let opponents know who the boss is, wear them out physically, and intimidate them inside. The physical player must also maintain self control, or he will end up on the bench with foul problems.

Size can be very beneficial on defense, but only when the player uses his head and combines the other six traits with his size.

Mental Requirements

It can easily be seen that a post man will not execute the physical requirements of good defense unless he can control the mental aspects. A "thinking player" can even offset some of the physical traits he may lack. Below are listed the four basic mental requirements for good defensive post play.

1. Desire

The big man must want to be a good defensive player. Without the determination it takes to improve, the post will never be the enforcer that the coach wants. It is tedious work to condition and develop into a strong defensive center. The player must be alert and concentrate during all defensive practice situations.

If he is determined, the post player can receive as much satisfaction and praise for his defense as his offense. He can help teammates, intimidate the shorter opponents, and dominate his own man.

Demand hard work from your post men during practice. Praise should accompany any apparent improvement or attempt to work harder.

2. Aggressiveness

The post man must have the initiative to force the play. He should move and react swiftly, but also establish his determination. By playing aggressively, the big man will be hard-nosed. He will dominate his opponents and play a very physical game. The post man must not let others push him around. He must anticipate and battle the opponents for the right to control the flow of play.

Some post men will naturally be aggressive. Their physical makeup or temperament may be cause for aggressiveness in itself. However, the coach more often is faced with the challenge of making a tall, lanky boy tough. This player must build aggressiveness by improving his confidence. The coach can aid by offering a weight program that will improve the psychic and overall strength. Toughness drills which require hard work and physical contact allow the post man to develop a hard-nosed attitude.

Aggressiveness also must be controlled. An overaggressive player will lose control of himself and get into foul trouble.

3. Confidence

The pride established through hard work will lead to confidence in the post man. If he feels at ease with his own ability, the big man will respect but never fear an opponent.

A lack of confidence confuses the mind and slows reaction. When the post man is ready and anxious to defend, he will react quickly and correctly.

A confident player keeps his cool when the other team is beating him. He knows that an adjustment next time will stop the move, or that the opponents will soon "cool off" in their hot shooting. Confidence allows the post man to keep up the hard work that will eventually make his team a winner.

4. Poise

The poised post player keeps his emotions under control and his temper down. He refuses to get rattled or upset in tight situations. Generally, poise comes with experience: the experience of game play, practice situations, and success through participation.

The post man must know when to gamble on defense, when to hustle a "little extra," and when to risk a foul through more physical play. This judgment comes from knowing one's own ability in relation to the ability of the opponents.

DEFENDING THE POST WITHOUT THE BALL

Defense must start before the opponent has the ball in the post area. The job is much easier if the defender is alert, aggressive, and thinking before his man gets the ball. Although it is almost impossible to stop a man from receiving a pass, a good defensive post man can limit the times his opponent gets the ball in the internal zone. This is where the mental requirements can aid the physical traits. Hustle and concentration will make the opponent constantly work to get the ball, then work again to get up a shot.

On the average, the offensive post man has possession of the ball less than any other player. He seldom dribbles or initiates the play, but rather moves around the key looking for a pass. When the post does get the ball, he shoots or feeds off almost immediately. With this in mind, you can easily see that the defensive post man defends a man without the ball at most times. Therefore, the big man must be schooled in helping teammates and preventing his man from getting the ball. The degree to which he should help or prevent depends on the effectiveness of the opponent's center.

By forcing the high-scoring offensive post man to work for the ball, the defender can often coerce him into receiving a pass out of position. Sometimes the offense will ignore a pressured post man and leave him out of the pattern completely. Anything done to get the big man out of his normal game will benefit the defensive club.

The general rule of playing between the man and the ball can be followed by post defenders in most situations. When the offensive man is on the weak side, the defender loosens up and positions himself to see the ball and the man. This position takes the appearance of a flat triangle. (See Diagram 11-1.) The defender should focus his attention half way between the ball and the opponent, using peripheral vision to see both.

When the offensive post sets up away from the ball, the defender must loosen up and move toward the ball for two reasons. First, he jams the key and is in excellent position to stop penetration. The dribbler can be discouraged and cutters will be congested. Secondly, the defender is then ready for any flash post attempt. If the offensive post decides to break across the key toward the ball, he will be picked up and controlled easier. By being off of the weak-side post, the defender will be able to see and react to the opponent's movement.

When defending a weak-side post man, the defender must utilize himself in the internal zone.

Defending the Flash Post

The flash post is a very common move in many offensive attacks. It can be done by guards and forwards as well as post men. The coach must see that all players know how to properly defend the flashing post man.

As a weak-side offensive player attempts to cut across the key, the defender must challenge him immediately. When the opponent was on the weak side, the defensive player was in a help or open position. The attack of the offensive man forces the defender to close his position and challenge the passing lane.

The defender must force his opponent to cut high and away from the dangerous low post area. Under no circumstances should a flash post man be allowed to cut along the baseline. A baseline cutter must be stopped and forced up toward the high post. The defender always contests the passing lane from the baseline side. The offensive post man cannot be allowed to reach a low post position with the defender on his top side. In such a situation, a quick pass could lead to a lay up or muscle shot.

In diagram 11-2, the defender stays between the opponent and the ball, forces his man high, and stops the baseline feed by fronting the low post. Diagram 11-3 illustrates the defender preventing the flash post from cutting along the baseline. This eliminates a quick cut to the strong-side low post.

The defender of a flash post must remember to always keep visual con-

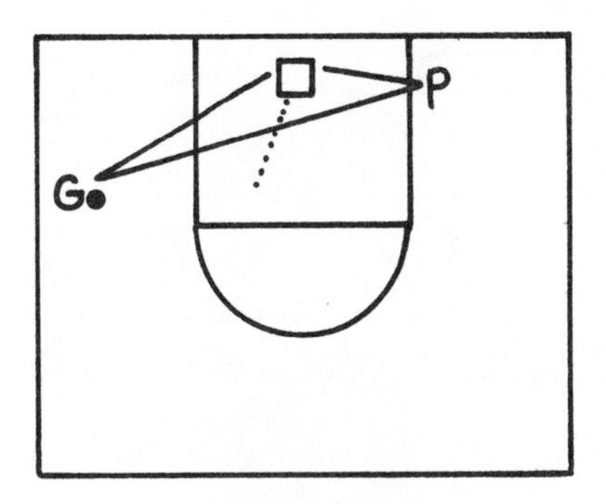

Diagram 11-1.
Defending the Weak Side
Post

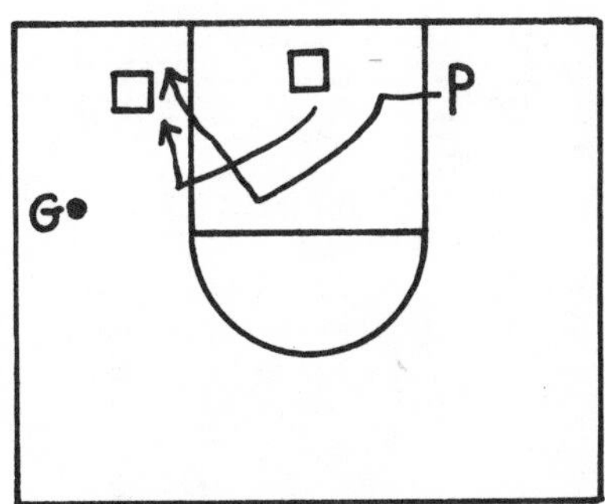

Diagram 11-2.
Stopping the Flash
and Roll Down

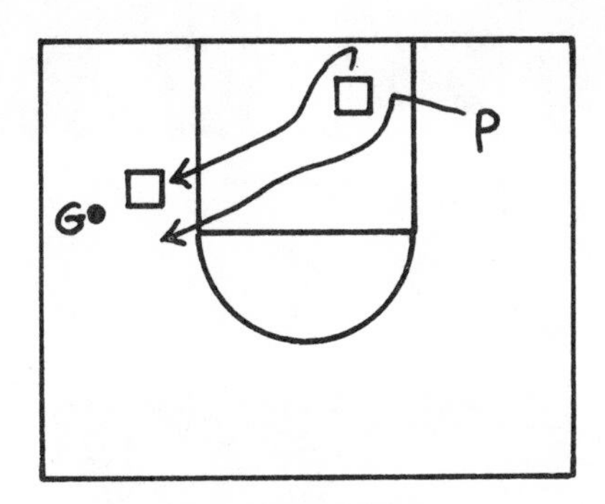

Diagram 11-3.
Stopping the Baseline Cut

tact with the ball. A mistake in footwork and positioning can only be covered if the defensive man can see the ball. It is impossible to stop something you cannot see! Insist that all post men know where the ball is at all times.

As in preventing a pass to the wing from a guard, the flash post defender must keep his lead hand and arm extended in front of the cutter. This helps deny any passing lane and prepares the defensive man for stealing or deflecting attempted passes. (Photo Series 11-1.)

Defending the Low Post

A player stationed at the ball side, low post position can be defended in one of three ways.

1. **Behind.** The passing lanes are left open, as the defender positions himself between the low post man and the basket. (See Photo 11-2A.)
2. **Fronting.** The defender positions himself directly between the low

Photo Series 11-1.
Flash Post Defense

Photo 11-2A.
Playing Behind

Photo 11-2B.
Fronting the Post

Photo 11-2C.
Playing the Side

post player and the ball. This cuts off all direct passing lanes. (See Photo 11-2B.)

3. **The Side.** The defender plays either the top or baseline side of the low post man. A defensive hand and arm are extended into the passing lane, thus narrowing the passing angle. (See Photo 11-2C.)

When the defense plays behind an opponent stationed at the low post, he is admittedly conceding a shot from the internal zone. Since most teams do not send players to the low post unless they can score, playing behind is extremely dangerous. If the opponent is no offensive threat, playing behind him at the low post might be wise. It leaves the defender in a good spot to help teammates, and it also leaves him in a good rebounding position. In most instances, though, playing behind any opponent at the low post is asking for trouble.

Fronting the low post practically eliminates the scoring threat of a stationary player. The only possible feed is the lob pass, which is risky and difficult to handle.

The defender must always keep his attention focused on the ball when fronting. In most cases he will lose visual contact with the opponent, but he must never lose sight of the ball. To assure constant location of the low post man, the defender should maintain body contact. Playing close to the post is advisable in the internal zone. It limits the opponent's freedom of movement and provides the needed physical contact. The defensive man must always keep one hand up and in the passing lane. The other hand can be used to locate the opponent. Once hand contact is made, the defender should take up the slack and front tightly.

The dangers of fronting are quite obvious. The defender is completely out of position to rebound, stop the lob pass, or help teammates. The coach must decide whether the low post player is dangerous enough to risk the gamble of fronting. Obviously, the fronting defender will need plenty of help from his teammates.

The method I prefer is defending from the side, or as I like to call it, "Fronting from the side." The side position combines the best of fronting and playing behind. It requires the most work defensively, but it can give your team an awesome inside defensive attack. I instruct all of my players in low post defense, because they will find themselves in that position from time to time. My teams have had good success on low post defense every year. Using the side method has certainly been a key!

Assuming the ball is at a wing position, the low post defender will have to choose a side to defend. The general rule I use is: "When the ball is below the free throw line extended, play the baseline side. When it is above the free throw line extended, play the top side." If the ball is near mid court, the low post defender is on the top side. Moving the ball near the baseline forces the defense to play on the baseline side. (Diagrams 11-4A and 11-4B.)

Any time the ball moves in such a way that it forces the low post defender to change sides, he must always step in front of the offensive player. The

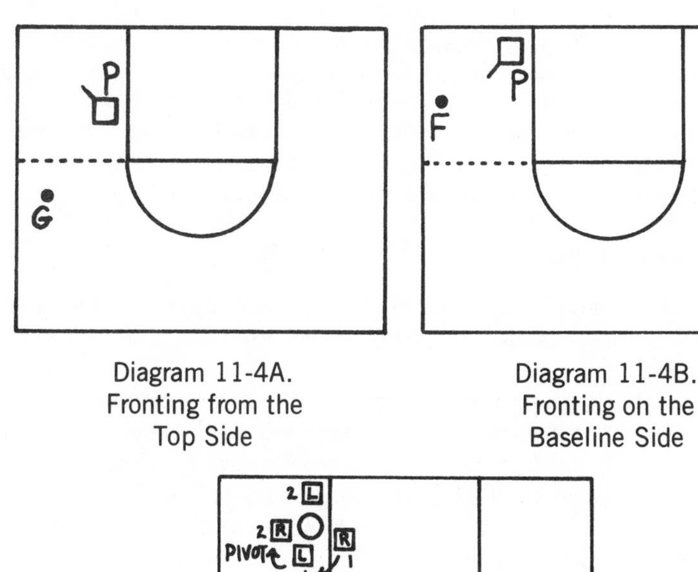

Diagram 11-4A.
Fronting from the
Top Side

Diagram 11-4B.
Fronting on the
Baseline Side

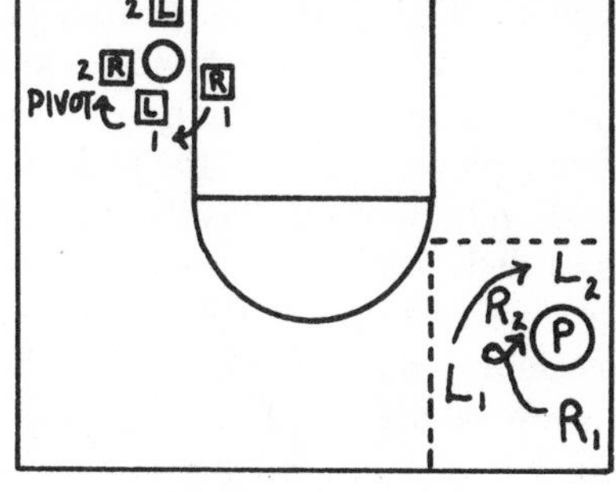

Diagram 11-5.
Switching Sides on
the Low Post

passing lane to the low post must never be exposed. The defender has to maintain a position between his man and the ball.

Defending the post from the side requires good footwork, especially when the defender must switch sides. Consider the left low post position, defense on the top side. (See Diagram 11-5.) The ball is at the left guard position, above the free throw line. The defender should have his left foot and leg in front of the offensive man. The left arm is up and in the passing lane. The right arm is flexed and contacting the low post man. The right foot is back and beside the opponent.

When the ball shifts to a position on the wing below the free throw line, the defender must step in front of his man and switch to a baseline side, defensive position. The right foot crosses in front of the post and is used as a pivot. The left foot is moved behind the right, but in front of the offensive man, and is placed behind and to the side of the opponent. In two easy steps, the defensive man has switched defensive sides without leaving an open passing lane. The baseline position has the right foot up and the right hand in the passing lane.

You must watch for lazy eyes and hands in post defense. The footwork can be fantastic, but passes will get inside if the hand is not in the passing lane. Insist on the lead arm being extended straight up in front of a low post player. This will discourage many potential feeds and cut down the inside game. Do not allow your low post defenders to have drooping arms. Remember, alert defenders can cover up many physical limitations.

Defending the High Post

The high post should also be played from the side, but the defender does not front when changing sides. If the ball moves from one defensive side to another, the defender quickly shifts his feet behind the offensive man. (See Diagram 11-6.) The high post man is stationed fifteen feet or more from the basket. Fronting at that distance would leave too much room for the post man to back door. A quick cut and lob pass would leave the defender totally out of the picture. While the high post is considered a great offensive attacking area, the defense cannot afford to front and leave the key area open.

A defensive hand should be kept in the passing lane to the high post as much as possible. When a player flashes to the high post, the defender must work to maintain a position between the ball and the man. The alert defensive man will be able to deflect a lot of passes if he positions correctly.

If a high post man tries to drop to a low post, the defender will already be in good position to establish himself defensively. The side position should be held if the man cuts toward the ball. If the high post moves away from the ball, the defender must loosen up and prepare for a flash post attempt. (Diagram 11-7.)

In defending a post man, the primary objective is to prevent him from receiving the ball in the internal zone. The defense will not give up too many easy shots if the initial offensive moves are made from the perimeter. The defender must be careful that the opponent does not gradually push him back under the basket. If the defensive man is alert and constantly working to maintain position, then he can control the offensive post man.

When defending the high post, a player must watch for open cutters or penetrating dribblers. He can be very instrumental in helping teammates by protecting against short shots. Any shot attempt by the opposition requires the big man to screen out and check any rebound possibilities of the opposing center.

GUARDING A POST MAN WITH THE BALL

The key to guarding any man with the ball is: "Make him do something that he does not want to do." This rule also holds true for the defensive post man. If the opponent likes to shoot outside jump shots, he should be played tight and forced to drive, pass, or hurry the shot. If he likes to go baseline from the low post, the baseline should be sealed off and the opponent forced

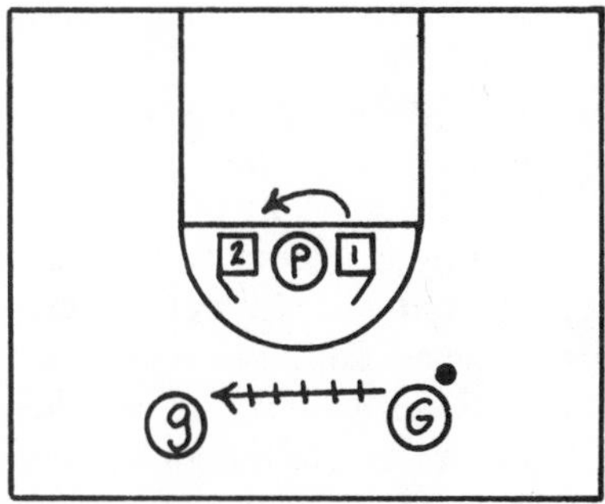

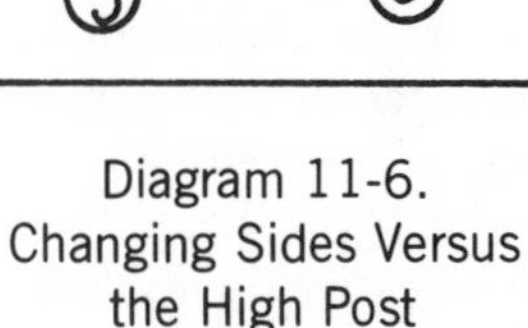

Diagram 11-6.
Changing Sides Versus
the High Post

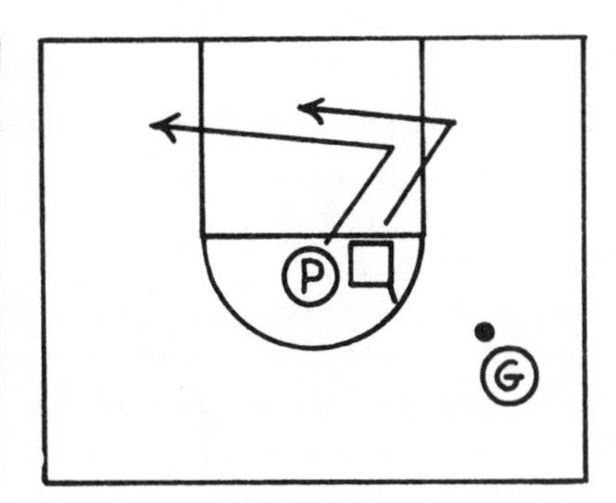

Diagram 11-7.
Defending High Post
Movement

to swing to the middle. If the offensive post man likes to drive right handed, then he should be forced left by overplaying his strong side. Take away an opponent's strong points, and you take control of the game.

Once an offensive post man receives the ball, the defender must follow the general rule of "staying between the ball and the basket." The defensive man should immediately back off of the opponent approximately one arm's length. This will give the defender time to react and prevent a quick drive to the basket. The defender should also move closer to the strong side of the offensive post man. The strong side is determined by the particular move the defense wishes to stop.

The defensive man must keep one hand up, about head high, and the other one down on the most likely driving side. If the man dribbles, both hands are brought down below the waist with the palms pointing up. When the dribble is terminated, the defender should close in and put both hands up. This will discourage any shot attempt and also congest the passing lanes.

At times, mismatches will occur in the post area that require slightly different rules for defending the pivot player. When a shorter man is guarding a very tall opponent, he should play the ball tight and crowd the offensive man. He must use his quickness to prevent penetration, and try to keep the big man as far from the basket as possible.

When a taller defender is guarding a short post player, he should back off another two feet. This puts him in position to prevent a quicker man from beating him to the hoop. The tall defender can afford to play loose because his extra reach will still allow him to contest any shot attempt. He must stop the penetration that a short, quick offensive man will attempt, or face early foul trouble.

When a player receives the ball, there are three things he can attempt to do. These are: pass, dribble, or shoot. The post man must know how to deal with each of these options successfully.

The Potential Pass

A good defender will contest passes and make the post man's job difficult. The high post man will be looking to pass more than the low post player. If a high post player raises the ball above his head, he certainly is in a poor position to drive. The defender can close in and pressure the passing lane or potential shot attempt. Often, the pressured man will step backwards to avoid the defender. Since he is moving away from the hoop, this is beneficial to the defense. If the offensive man is a driving threat, the defensive man should close in on the dangerous side. As soon as the high post man brings the ball back down to a driving position, the defender must quickly bounce back to his original position of one arm's length distance.

At the conclusion of a dribble, the defender again should move in and challenge the passing lanes. Both hands must be extended up, and the eyes should focus on the ball. This pressure will often result in turnovers by the opponents because of deflections, hurried passes, or five-second violations.

To deflect passes, the tall post man should get the maximum use out of his long arms. I teach my players to reach back and out to deflect pass attempts, rather than up and in. If a pass is attempted in the direction of the defender's right hand, he should throw his arm back and out. This motion moves the hand farther from the passer and allows more time to react to the ball. A defender with quick hands can anticipate passes and deflect quite a few of them with this method. While the opponent may be able to easily pass around the defender's body, he now becomes faced with a second line of defense. The hands are working behind the body as well as in front and beside it.

The pass and cut, or "give and go" as it is more commonly known, must be anticipated and controlled. Especially from the high post, a pivot player can pass and cut immediately to the low post. If the defender is caught flat footed, a return pass to the cutter will result in two points. When an opponent makes a pass, the defensive man must retreat one step back and one step in the direction of the ball. This must be done quickly or the cutter will place himself between the defender and the ball. Moving toward the ball allows the defender to form a "flat triangle" and gain visual contact on both man and ball. (See Diagram 11-8.) The only possible cut now is away from the ball, which is the movement desired by the defense.

Defending the Dribble

Post men are not required to dribble very often, so defending the drive can be easy for alert defenders. Usually one dribble is all that is needed for a big man to get from his position to the hoop. The defensive man's job then is to prevent the one dribble or direct the dribbler away from the basket. Since there are few two-way drivers, overplaying the strong hand will usually stop the post man.

The defensive post player must get his center of gravity low if he wants

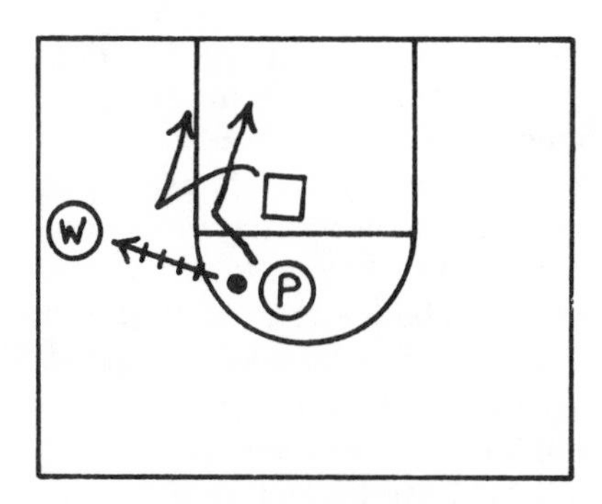

Diagram 11-8.
Pass-Cut Defense

to stop the dribbler. Because of his height, it takes constant reminders and practice to get a big man to use proper footwork and body balance.

Slapping at the dribble should be avoided. Post men are not noted for their quick hands, so the stealing should be left to the guards and fast forwards. Needless fouls from attempted steals by big men are a problem all coaches can do without. Containment and control of direction are the primary duties of the defensive post men.

When a post man drives, the defender should get low and retreat until he can turn the opponent from his intended direction. The defensive man must get his chest in front of the dribbler and avoid any hand contact. Turning the offensive man out of the key and toward the sidelines is the goal. When the dribble is terminated, the defender closes in and raises his hands to block any shot or pass attempts.

Contesting the Shot

The offensive man shoots in two different situations. He will shoot either before dribbling or at the conclusion of a dribble. The defensive strategy is determined by the situation, as each represents unique circumstances.

The player who first receives the ball is a triple threat—pass, shoot, or dribble. He can improve his position with the dribble, so the defender must carefully guard against the drive. Once the offensive man has used his dribble, he can only pass or shoot. The defensive man then can afford to close in, wave his arms, and crowd the potential shooter.

The post defender should always close in on the opponent's strong side. In most cases, the strong driving side is also the same side the offensive man shoots from. An example would be: a right-handed dribbler is usually a right-handed shooter. By contesting the opponent's right side, the defender is also contesting the shooting hand.

When the dribble is still available, the defensive man should stay an arm's length away. One arm is up to distract the shot or pass, and the other hand and arm are down to contest the drive. The defender must be alert for fakes and rocker-step moves. Any overcommitting at this time will allow the opponent to drive to the hoop unobstructed. The weight must remain evenly balanced on the balls of both feet. If the offensive man is a particularly quick driver, the defender can keep his weight on the back foot. This will allow faster retreating and enable the defense to prevent the drive. However, the equal balancing of weight on both feet is the best overall defensive position. Watch for post men who tend to lean forward on defense. They must be instructed in the importance of balance, or they will be left standing on the perimeter while the opponent scores lay ups.

A defender should not leave his feet until the shot is taken. We have all heard this bit of advice many times. But how can it be reasonable against today's fast action and quick jump shots? If you wait for the shooter to leave his feet before you jump to block the shot, the ball will already be half way to the basket.

Contesting the shot consists of three physical efforts: (1) getting a hand up and distracting the shooter, (2) crowding the shooter and forcing him to panic, and (3) jumping up to block the shot or bother the shooter. I want my defenders to perform the first two efforts against every potential shooter. The third effort is required of all inside attempts and versus the shooter who has terminated his dribble. If the opponent has not dribbled, the defender only needs to get a hand in the shooter's face. The defense cannot afford to jump up and down in attempts to block shots, if the threat of a dribble is still present. Keeping the opponent guessing by contesting and crowding will throw off his shooting just enough to give your team the edge. It is more important to stop penetration, avoid unnecessary fouls, and to get rebound position, than to try blocking outside shots.

The defense of inside shots is a different story. It is the same as defending a player who has killed his dribble on the perimeter. An opponent at the low post has nowhere to drive, so the defender can and must play close. Any attempt at shot blocking that requires jumping must be controlled. The defender must jump straight up so he will not float into the shooter and give up a senseless foul. The blocking arm and hand must also be controlled. They should go straight up and never slap down into the shooter. Again, senseless fouls must be avoided.

I encourage my players to yell "Hey" as their man shoots. This is distracting to the shooter and also alerts our players to screen out for a potential rebound.

A driving opponent shooting on the move should be challenged with the nearest hand of the defender. If the leap is parallel to the path of the dribbler, then body contact can be avoided. In most instance, only a player with superior height or leaping ability will be able to block the driving lay up. Contesting and crowding without fouling will sometimes cause the shooter to blow the shot. When this happens, the defender certainly does not want to foul and give the opponent a second chance.

While blocked shots are a sight to see and often cause shifts in momentum, they are risky defensive moves. They should only be done by superior players who have the height, jumping ability, timing, and experience to be successful.

Through proper footwork, positioning, and thinking, the defense can determine the shots it will give up. The keys are keeping the opponents shooting on the perimeter and under pressure, but not allowing free throws.

Defending a post man with the ball is generally a one-on-one game. Seldom do teams pick for their post player. Since the pivot man is expected to feed or score as soon as he gets the ball, the defender must immediately recognize the offensive man's intentions and challenge them.

HELPING TEAMMATES

Because the post man generally defends around the hoop, he is in an excellent position to help his teammates. Having a very tall center is even more beneficial. His shot blocking potential is often enough to convince opponents to stay outside and shoot. Since most teams have only an average-sized post player, for now I will only deal with the types of help any post man can provide.

Conversion

Conversion is a fairly recent term in basketball that has gained importance with coaches each season. The modern, fastbreaking style of play has placed new emphasis on conversion. Conversion simply means changing from offense to defense, or defense to offense with each change of possession. The faster a team can convert, the better chance it has to fastbreak on offense or stop the break defensively.

The post man can be a tremendous help to his team defensively, if he hustles and converts consistently. The loafing or out-of-shape center is of little help in a fast-paced game. Good conversion enables the post man to help his teammates in the following ways:

1. The biggest player and best rebounder is always available to hit the boards.
2. The tallest player and best intimidator is always back to slow the opponents.
3. The opponent's big man is usually the last one up the court, so the defensive post man is an extra defender.

When your post man gets tired, rest him. Do not lose the conversion advantage at the post position. Make sure all players are in top physical condition, especially the underdeveloped young post man. Some teams handle conversion by the platooning of pivot players. One plays for six minutes, goes all out, and then is replaced by a fresh post man who continues the hot pace. I have successfully used this principle on my ball clubs, as you may recall from earlier chapters.

The post position can be a big help to team conversion, and it should be observed and encouraged by the coach. Insist that your post man hustle in order to be one of the first players down the court.

The Pick-and-Roll

The pick-and-roll play can be a very dangerous two-man attack when it involves the post player. The pick can free a guard for a driving lay up or medium-range jump shot. If a switch is used to stop the guard, the roll man may get open going to the basket. A mismatch will develop on the switch which puts the defensive post man on a quick guard, and a short defender on a rolling post player.

The post man should not be required to switch on pick-and-roll plays. He is put at too much of a disadvantage when switched to a perimeter player. The defensive post player is valuable inside as a rebounder and helper. He is practically useless to his team when he gets drawn twenty feet from the basket.

When the post man sees his man moving toward the ball, he is required to call out the potential screen. The phrase, "Watch your right," or "Watch your left," should be used to inform teammates as to the direction of the approaching pick. The post man must then loosen up and prepare to turn the dribbler away from the screen. (See Diagram 11-9.)

The post man must "contain" the dribbler and force him to veer away from the pick. This enables the defensive guard to slide over the top of the pick and recover his man. If the guard is slow to recover, the defensive post player retreats and zones up; thus preventing a quick drive by the offensive guard. In essence, the big man plays one against two until the defensive guard recovers sufficiently enough to guard his man again.

At no time can the post leave his assigned man and switch to another player. This would free a potentially dangerous scorer, with the big man rolling to the basket. The defensive post man must be accountable for his

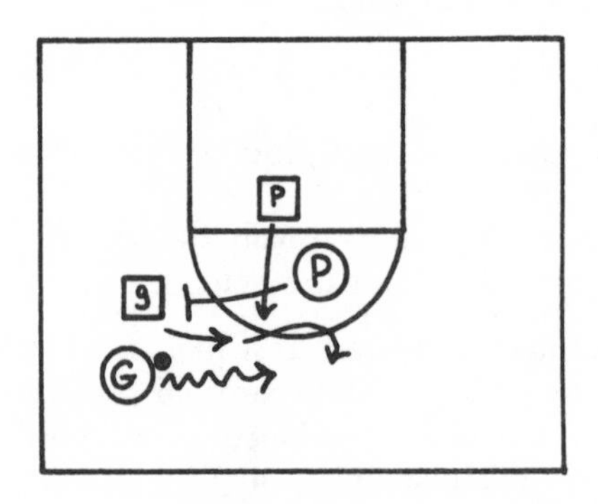

Diagram 11-9.
Defending the Pick-and-Roll

man at all times, so he can recover and contest any efforts to score. (See Photo Series 11-3.)

Photo Series 11-3.
Stopping the Pick-and-Roll

Photo Series 11-3 (cont.)
Stopping the Pick-and-Roll

The guard must always go over the top of picks set within shooting range. He can defend the shot better and will not be sealed off by the rolling offensive player.

The defensive post player recovers to his man after the guard gains control of his original man. The post man must stay between the ball and the man, watching for attempted feeds into the low post.

It should also be noted that other weak-side defenders will be sagging and converging into the ball on pick-and-roll plays. When the defense sags properly, the two-man game of pick-and-roll becomes two against five. Good team defense will help make the pivot man's job easier.

Drawing the Charge

One of the primary objectives of good team defense is to stop penetration of the ball. Since the post man is generally around the basket, he must

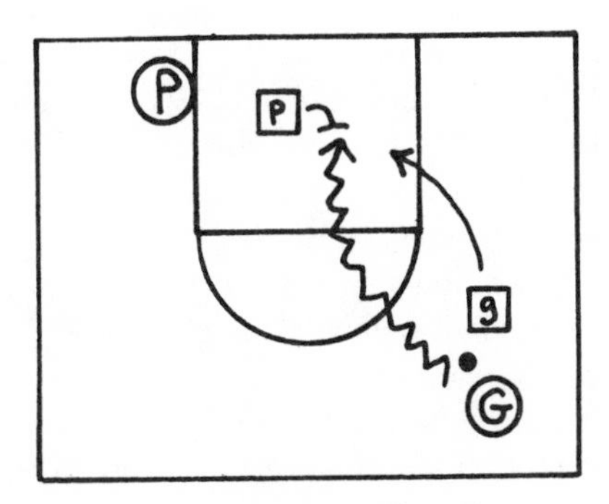

Diagram 11-10.
Helping to Stop
Penetration

be alert to opponents driving the lane. As mentioned earlier, the post man's looming presence may be enough to slow or stop the initial drive by itself. Even the average-sized centers can be strong factors in solid team defense, when they are alert and positioned correctly.

If the ball is in the possession of a driving perimeter player, the big man must loosen up defensively. When the opponent's center is stationed on the weak side, the defender can play off and jam the lane very effectively. (See Diagram 11-10.)

Other defenders will also be sagging and converging to the ball, so the play should be stopped. Only a pressured shot or pass outside should be allowed. Preventing a lay up or open shot is the key to defending penetration. The post steps to the driver and slows his attack enough to allow the original defender to recover. The post defender must play two aginst one momentarily, but the objective is to buy time. If the lay-up shot is not easily allowed, a hustling defense will recover in time to stop any lay up at all.

Helping does not leave the post free of responsibility for his own man. As soon as the defense recovers to the ball, the helping defender must get back to his man. If a shot is attempted, the defensive post man should make every attempt to box out the opposing center.

Drawing the charge is a sometimes forgotten art among post players. They want to block lay ups and challenge the driver. The crowd's reaction to a rejection is very satisfying to the big man's ear. Unfortunately, too often the sharp shrill sound of the referee's whistle pierces the crowd's cheers. A foul results, two free throws are awarded, and the post man picks up a needless foul.

There are players who are fine shot blockers. Needless to say, most young and developing centers do not have the timing required to be consistent at rejecting. Drawing the charge can be done by any alert player who is sagging and eager to help stop penetration. Stepping into the path of a hard-charging opponent requires a certain amount of intestinal fortitude, but it is the type of courage I want all of my players to have. I drill my teams early in the season on drawing the charge. They are taught how to get position, how to receive contact, and how to fall without getting injured. The players take pride in their ability to get a charge, and I certainly voice my pleasure whenever they do it.

The alert post player who sees a potential lay up can jump into the lane quickly. The driver will often have his head down or be going too fast to change directions. The post man can draw the charge, and the opponent will still be wondering where he came from.

In drawing the offensive charge, the defender must establish position clearly before the opponent. If the shooter is already in the air, a defender cannot step in and draw contact. The offensive man is entitled to the path once he leaves his feet.

The feet should be firmly planted and the arms are held at the sides. This establishes a firm base and keeps the hands from reaching unnecessarily for a foul. The defender must stand still and take the contact in his chest. He should not turn sideways, duck down, back peddle, or fall early. All of these moves can be judged illegal and the charge will be nullified. Some will even lead to defensive fouls.

Having a team that enjoys drawing the charge is a plus for any coach. It establishes aggressive, inside defense and puts pride into team defensive play. Again, the post man is the key because he is always around the basket.

PLAYING IN FOUL TROUBLE

Aggressive defense will sometimes get basketball players into foul trouble. Whether inadvertent or not, fouls result in the coach having to make a decision. Should the player be allowed to continue in the game at the risk of disqualification? Can the team stay in the contest with the foul-plagued player on the bench? The decision and action of the coach can often spell the difference between victory and defeat.

Too often the player in early foul trouble is the post man. Whether he is the team's superstar, top rebounder, or defensive enforcer, the loss of a post man is serious business. When the team uses two centers and rotates them throughout the game, the problem is solved with a simple substitution. Unfortunately, most coaches have trouble finding one capable post player, let alone two. The team suffers if the center leaves, so the coach must make a decision that could decide the outcome of the game.

Knowing the players is the key to substitution. How do they handle foul trouble? Will the post man with two early fouls get mad and pick up a third right away? Or will he become timid and get lost out of fear of disqualification? In either case, the team suffers in the long run. Substitution would seem to be in order. Many times I have sat on the bench in amazement, as a substitute center turns the game in our favor through determination and hustle. The starting post man gets a rest and enters the game later to polish off a thoroughly worn-out opponent.

My personal philosophy calls for substitution for anyone who gets two fouls in the first half. If the team can maintain its position with the foul-plagued player on the bench, then I will save him until the second half. If the player is needed due to a shift in momentum, I will caution him and let him return to the action in the first half. No game is lost in the first half, but I certainly do not like to be blown out by half time.

If a player picks up a third foul in the first half, he is through for that half. I do not want him to have four fouls at half time. He would be virtually useless to the team in the second half.

A player who gets his fourth foul in the second half is in serious trouble. If the game is late, he must play hard and be very smart. If the clock shows more than five minutes, the coach should seriously consider pulling him for awhile. Again, knowing your personnel is the key. Some intelligent players can be cautioned and then avoid fouls for the rest of the game. Others will need a wind-down period to relax and get control of their emotions and actions.

You should always be thinking ahead and plan for foul trouble. Who will the back-up center be in case the starter fouls out? Will the foul-troubled player need rest or just caution? These questions should be answered before the game starts.

When the player in foul trouble is benched, he should immediately be praised for his hustle and contributions thus far. The foul situation must be related and assurance given that he will re-enter the contest. Now a rest break must take place, allowing the player to relax and recuperate. He will have a chance to assess his own performance and mentally prepare for the future adjustments. Later the coach can offer suggestions, corrections, or criticisms as needed. Defensive strategy may be changed or adjusted, and you can point out situations as the game continues.

Before sending the player back to the line up, caution him to be alert, play smart, and take no gambles. The player will be able to return feeling free to be aggressive but controlled.

Post men in foul trouble must avoid blocking shots, contesting for rebounds without proper position, and reaching to steal passes. They should limit themselves to fundamental basketball. That is, proper footwork, positioning, and heads-up play. Needless fouls must be avoided completely.

The extra tall post man can often play for long periods of time in foul trouble. If he can control himself, the big man can play passively and still be helpful to the team. His long arms and intimidating size will still make opponents think twice before shooting over him. This intimidation, along with rebounding abilities, makes the tall center valuable even though he cannot be aggressive.

When behind late in a game, the foul-troubled player must go all out.

He cannot hold back and allow the opponents to attack him successfully. When you are behind, you have to gamble. Make things happen! It makes no sense to save a player till the end of a losing contest.

During close finishes, the foul-plagued center must play smart basketball. He does not need to gamble unless the team falls behind in the closing minutes.

The foul situation of every player should be registered and followed. Make sure the players also know their fouls and how they should be adjusting. Communication lines must be kept open so both coach and players can work together. Again, do not be afraid to substitute. This is especially true early in the game, before the fourth quarter. The rest and chance for communication can be valuable towards finding the winning key for the late stages of a game.

DRILLS FOR IMPROVING POST MAN DEFENSE

Basketball players can often be encouraged to work on their offensive weaknesses during the off season. Getting them to train or improve their defense requires a different approach. Besides selling the importance of defense to the team, a coach must have drills and philosophies to give the players. The drills I use for post men are basically the same ones I use for all players; however, some areas receive extra attention during the practice time.

The team is usually broken into two groups—big men and guards. The head coach works with one group, using half of the court. The assistant coach takes the second group to the other end of the court. One or two defensive fundamentals are drilled and emphasized each day. A rotation of the drills keeps the team sharp and eliminates boredom.

Some of the defensive drills I use for post men are oulined below.

1. Distance Running

I have my players do a lot of distance work in the pre-practice season. The players with less stamina are encouraged to run all summer. The tall, slow developing, young post man is often in this category.

Distance running builds up the leg muscles, increases endurance, and prepares the player for the practice season. The distance should be one and a half miles up to five miles per day. I spend two to three weeks in September and October running the team for pre-season conditioning. The program is generally followed three days per week, every other day. When the first practice comes around, the players are ready to go full speed. There are less injuries, less sore muscles, and more time for practice.

2. Defensive Slides

When practice finally starts, the players are ready for defensive conditioning. Spread the team out over a quarter of the court and have them get in a *good* defensive stance. Check everyone's position to make sure the butt is low, knees bent, hands up, back straight, and weight on the balls of the feet. They should all hold position as you are checking. This conditions the mind as well as the legs.

After you are satisfied with their position, instruct the group to move "right," "left," "front," or "back." They should stay in a good defensive position, but quickly shift and move with the instructions. Ask for quick changes of direction, with short choppy steps, and hustle! I usually go for 30 seconds at a time the first day, increase to one minute sets the third day, and build toward five minutes straight. This drill should not consume more or less than five total minutes of practice time. It is a conditioning drill and is only used during pre-season practices.

Post men like to bend their backs, use long slides, and cruise through this drill. Encourage them to work for quickness and endurance.

3. Draw the Charge

If the post men are expected to stand in the key and take a charge, then they must drill on it periodically. This drill needs very little review, as the players get the idea quickly. Two lines are formed at mid court. Throw a ball to the man heading one line, and he becomes the driver. The head of the other line runs to the hoop and plants himself firmly in the path of the offensive man. The dribbler must go directly at the defender and attempt to score. The defender must take the charge squarely, fall to the floor, and bounce back up. (See Diagram 11-11.)

We sometimes add an extra requirement to the "Take the Charge Drill." After the charge is drawn, the coach or manager rolls a second ball onto the court. The defender gets up, dives on the loose ball, recovers and drives to the basket for three muscle shots. This is an excellent addition to the drill, which will help make your team aggressive.

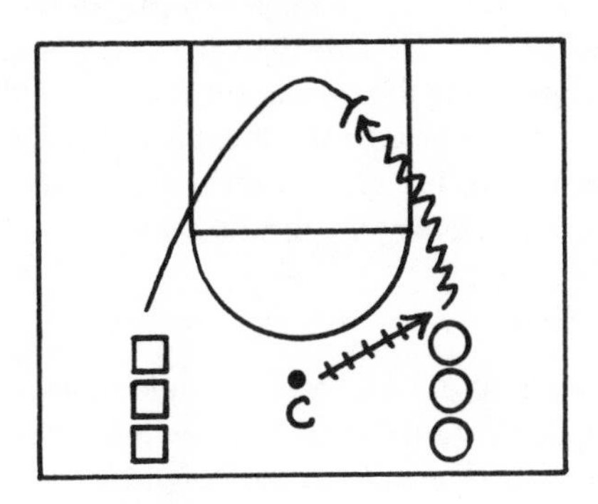

Diagram 11-11.
Taking the Charge

4. Reach-Back Drill

The players break into groups of three, five, or seven. One man is on defense, while the others try to pass the ball around him. The defender closes in and harasses the passer. When a pass is thrown, the defender practices the "Reach-Back Method" mentioned earlier in this chapter. If he gets a hand on the ball, the defender and passer exchange positions. The offensive men are required to wait until the defender is on them before passing.

5. One-on-One

I like to use this drill about twice a week in pre-season practices. The offensive man stands at the top of the key, the defense is on the bottom of the jump circle in the key. The defender starts with the ball, passes it to the offensive man, and closes out properly. The offensive man then performs three fakes slowly, allowing the defense to respond correctly. The moves are: a fake shot attempt, a fake drive to the right, and a fake drive to the left. The players can correct each other after they have learned proper defensive fundamentals. Following these three moves, the offensive man is allowed to go full speed and do any move he wants. When a shot is taken, the defender must block out and rebound the ball. The drill starts over again with the players switching positions.

I sometimes have the post men work from the free throw line or the low post areas. They go one-on-one starting with their backs to the basket. Post men must learn to cover opponents both facing the hoop and with their backs to it.

6. Two-on-One—Help and Recover

One of the primary jobs of the post man is to help teammates when the ball is moving to the basket. The two-on-one drill was designed to teach big men to help, while maintaining the responsibility of their own assigned man. The offense is represented by one man playing the low post and another driving from anywhere along the perimeter. The driver has only two options: (1) go for the lay up, or (2) pass to the low post. The defender must prevent the lay up, then recover to his man after the pass off is made. Preventing an open shot is considered victory for the defender.

7. Baseline Prevention

Since there is no help on the baseline, defenders of players at the wings must turn the dribbler toward the free throw line. The baseline prevention drill is a one-on-one drill that calls for the defender to turn the ball away from the baseline. A line of players starts at the wing position. The defender starts around the low post area with a ball. He passes to the first man in line and closes out on the baseline side. The offensive man must try to go quickly past the defender on the baseline. The defensive man must stop the penetration without fouling. If the drive to the baseline is successfully stopped, the offensive man can continue to drive in any direction that he feels is open. (See Diagram 11-12.)

When the shot is taken, the defensive man blocks out and rebounds. The offensive man becomes the new defender and the old defender goes to the end of the line. If at any time an offensive player gets by the defender on the baseline side, the drill is repeated. A defensive man must never be beaten on the baseline!

8. Flash Post Drill

A single line of players starts at the wing position. You are at the opposite wing with a ball. One defensive man is assigned to the first man in the line. He will be stationed in the key, so as to see the man and ball. (Flat triangle.) The offensive man pauses a few seconds, than tries to flash across the key for a pass. The defender must force the offensive man away from the baseline and up toward the free throw line.

The coach has many options to challenge the defensive man. He can drive and force the defender to "help and recover;" he may throw a cross-court pass to check the alertness of the defensive man; or he can shoot and check the blocking out tactics of the defender. In most cases, however, the coach should attempt to pass to the flashing post man. If the defender successfully knocks the ball away, the drill ends. If the pass is completed, the two players go "one-on-one." (See Diagram 11-13.)

9. Fronting Drill

This drill teaches post men how to contest passes to low post players. Three offensive men set up in a triangular formation: one at the low post, one in the corner, and one at the wing. The defensive man is required to use

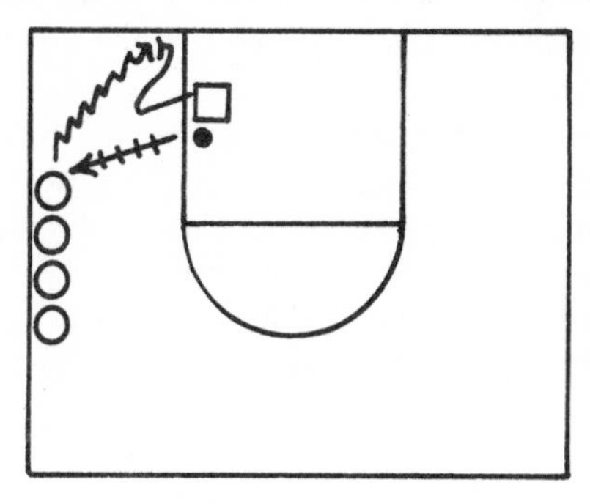

Diagram 11-12.
Baseline Prevention Drill

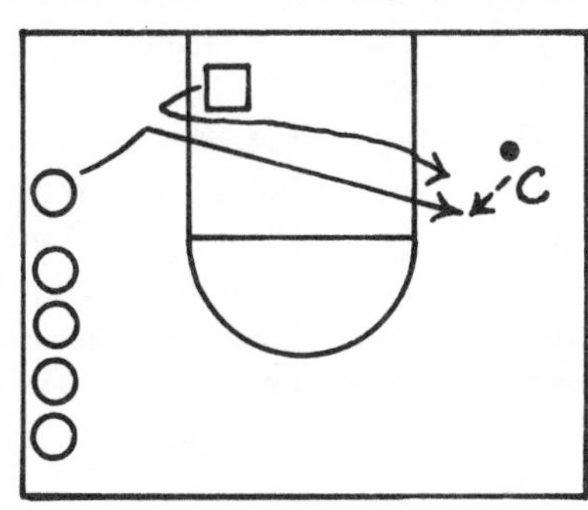

Diagram 11-13.
Flash Post Drill

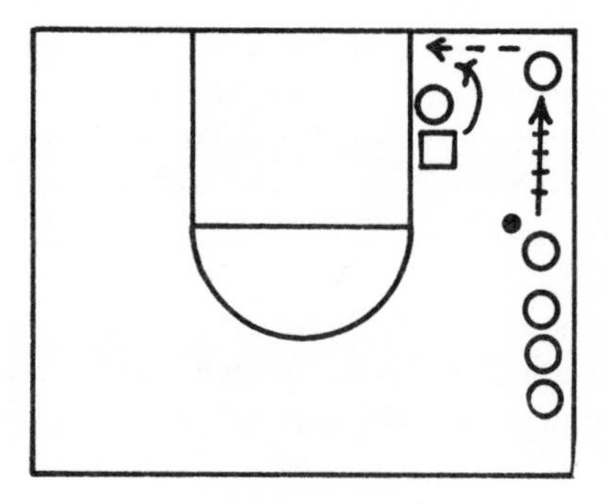

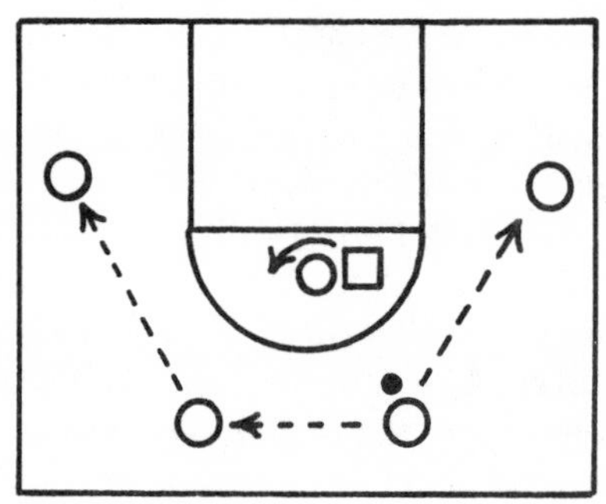

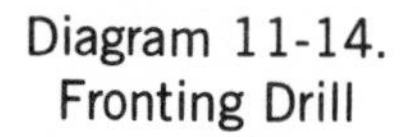

Diagram 11-14.
Fronting Drill

Diagram 11-15.
High Post Pass Prevention

proper fronting fundamentals as the ball is passed slowly from the wing to the corner. The feeders constantly look for an opening and try to feed the low post. The defensive man should follow the principles of fronting mentioned earlier in this chapter. (See Diagram 11-14.)

Watch for proper footwork and proper visual contact. The defender must move quickly and aggressively while maintaining eye contact with the ball. The near hand should always be raised and challenging the passing lane.

Sometimes the Fronting Drill and the Flash Post Drill can be combined into one drill. This should not be attempted until players have mastered the drills individually.

10. High Post Pass Prevent Drill

Four players are stationed around the perimeter of the court. (See Diagram 11-15.) A high post man and his defender are located somewhere around the free throw line. The ball is moved slowly around the perimeter, allowing the defender to move and challenge the passing lane. When proper footwork has been established, the offensive men may pass the ball quickly and try to get it to the post man.

The defensive man should follow the principles discussed earlier in this chapter. Those include: (1) no fronting of a high post player, (2) putting a hand in the passing lane, and (3) maintaining visual contact with the ball.

Later, the high post can be allowed to move to the low post. This calls for fronting tactics and places an extra challenge on the defender. Allow the high post to move once or twice. Constant motion will confuse the defender and ruin the learning situation.

11. Pass-Cut Defense

Sometimes the high post player will pass to a wing and cut to the low post. The defender must watch for this "give-and-go" play, or he may get

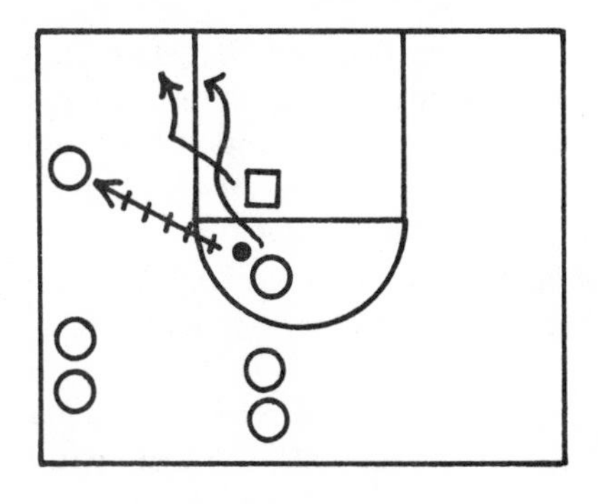

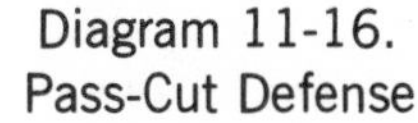

Diagram 11-16.
Pass-Cut Defense

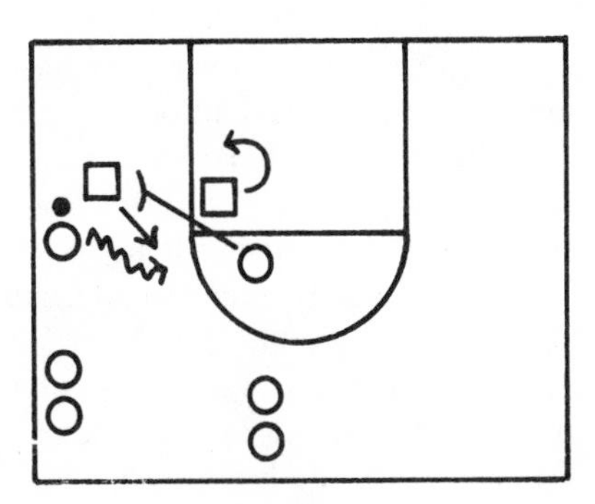

Diagram 11-17.
Help Off Screens

embarrassed. Diagram 11-16 illustrates this three-man drill which should be used for all players.

The defender must jump in the direction of any pass his man makes. The offensive man is then forced to cut away from the ball, and the defender can maintain a position between the ball and his man.

12. Help Off Screens

I generally use a form of two-on-two for this important drill. One offensive man sets a pick for the other and rolls to the basket. The post man defending the picker must call out the screen, then shift to a "containing" position. The defender must slow the dribbler until his teammate gets over the screen, then he retreats to the roll man.

The drill can be run in groups of four, or the entire team can form two lines and take turns. The team must be reminded that the drill is designed to help the defense, so they must go slowly on offense until everyone has learned the basics. (See Diagram 11-17.)

These are the basic breakdown drills I use for post men and all other players. Some drills require more emphasis for various positions, but basically I have all players review them. Once the fundamental drills of defense are learned, I try to teach team defense. My team runs a "four-on-four drill" for ten to twenty minutes each practice. In this drill, the players are expected to follow our rules and "breakdown defensive moves." If the coaches notice a mistake in defensive execution, we can point it out and refer to a "breakdown drill" as a corrective device.

The post men know, through our drills, exactly what is expected of them. They are never allowed to cruise through a "four-on-four drill."

To run a "four-on-four drill," four players are on offense, four on defense, and four watch and encourage. The offense keeps the ball until the defense gets five turnovers. Turnovers include: drawing the charge, rebounds, and steals or bad passes. After five turnovers, the offense becomes the defense; the defense goes to watch and encourage; and the previous watchers take over the ball. It is fast action and the players always go all out. Fouls by the defense result in an extra turn for the offense.

Post players are encouraged to mismatch themselves. Guards defend big men, and slow players guard quicker ones. This adds to the challenge and helps everyone improve defensively.

A post man needs to understand the importance of sound defensive play. If you can teach the big man good defensive fundamentals, the team will be anchored by a strong defender.

12

STOPPING OFFENSIVE POST MEN WITH YOUR PRESENT DEFENSE

As mentioned in earlier chapters, most offensive post men have not been developed to their fullest potential. They have limited moves, poor shot selection, or they are not used as scoring threats. Occasionally, your team will face an excellent post player. He may have a wide assortment of scoring moves, or he may be just too big to stop. This type of player can single-handedly defeat poor defensive clubs. Your team must know how to stop or at least limit the good post man, using your own basic defensive philosophy.

SCOUTING

It has been said that defense is a six-man game. The thought is that it takes five good defensive players and a knowledgable coach. The coach installs in his players a defensive philosophy, fundamental positioning, and conditioning of body and mind. Further preparation is possible when effective scouting methods are used.

Scouting is an important part of coaching quite often underrated. The value of scouting has been argued by coaches throughout the years. Some claim the emphasis should always be placed on your own team's style, with little regard for the opponent's attack. This is considered a positive approach to forcing your own game plan. Other coaches do not scout simply because of shortages in staff, time, and finances.

I try to scout every opponent as much as possible, because I want to know what to expect during upcoming games. Scouting aids your defense, provided you know what to look for. Watch for offensive tendencies, weak players, key scorers, opponents to sag off, and one-way drivers.

The following are questions I try to answer when scouting other teams:

1. What pattern or play do they favor in close situations?
2. Who is their key scorer, the one who can beat us?
3. What players can we give the outside shot?
4. Who are the best drivers?
5. Which players hit the offensive boards?
6. What will they do late in the game when the score is close?
7. Is the post man a legitimate scoring threat?
8. Which of our defenders can sag off and help stop other strong players?

When you have answered these questions, you are prepared to handle most situations that will occur during the game. The players can be schooled as to what they can expect. They will then be ready to stop the opponents.

Scouting is very important if you want to limit the opponent's post man. Since I fear the offensive attack of a good post man more than any other player, I watch him closely. If he is a legitimate scoring threat, I know my team will have to play a great defensive game to win. If the opposing pivot man is not a scorer, then my defensive center can play loose and help his teammates more. When my big man can free-lance on defense, the opponents will be getting poor percentage shots. We will force them to shoot under pressure inside, or back out to low percentage shot areas.

Once it has been determined that the opponent's post man is an offensive threat to be dealt with, the scout must next watch for particular tendencies. From what spot does the post make the majority of his baskets? From the low post? From outside? Off of the offensive boards?

If the big man is consistently scoring off of offensive rebounds, then your defensive post man must be instructed to block out tough on every shot attempt until your team secures the ball.

The post man who shoots well from the outside must be forced to put the ball on the floor. Find out which direction he favors and have your defender overplay tightly to that side. Other defenders should be reminded to converge in the key if the high post man dribbles.

The pivot man who scores from the low post presents the most problems to the defensive team. The alert scout watches for the move favored by the opponent's center. Does he always look to go baseline and take a muscle shot? Does he like to hook shoot? Does he see his teammates or will he shoot on every possession? Some big men will take poor percentage shots all night if the defense encourages it.

Consider and watch to see what the opponent's post man does against a fronting defense. Will the guards lob pass to him or will they panic and force passes? Will the post man clear out to the weak side or possibly get frustrated and confused?

Through effective scouting, the coach can find the best way to defend the post position. Since the post man is the key to most offensive attacks, defending that position is the key to team defense. Do not underestimate the value of scouting for defensive purposes. Limit your opponent's moves and you limit his scoring opportunities. This can be done through any defensive attack, whether it be man-to-man, zone, or full-court pressure. Look for weaknesses, then attack those areas with your best defense.

MAN-TO-MAN DEFENSES

I favor Man-to-Man Defense and generally use it in all situations. Chapter 11 dealt only with individual positioning for the post man in man-to-man defensive situations. Let us now consider some other alternatives you can use with these principles.

Good man-to-man defense involves more than a player stopping an assigned opponent from scoring. It requires each player to work with his teammates to deny any type of high percentage shot. Through effective scouting, you can instruct your team as to the type of shot you want them to give up. If the opposition has a great inside player, the defenders can sag and protect the internal zone. When an opponent has poor outside shooters, this is a most effective method of stopping the inside game. (See Diagram 12-1.)

The post man is blanketed and has no way to maneuver or get a pass. The defensive man -2- concedes the shot to -G- in hopes of confusing and rattling the shooter. For a poor outside shooter, a twenty footer is a very low percentage shot. Even the best shooters sometimes "swallow the olive" when left to shoot unmolested. The sagging strategy is a calculated gamble, hoping the opponents will not get hot from the outside. Your defense takes away the high percentage inside shot from the good post man. The scoring load falls onto perimeter players, who must now bear the unfamiliar pressure of carrying the offense.

The sagging technique works very well at the high school level because few teams have consistent outside shooters. Even good shooting high school and college teams have some weak outside shooters. By revising the sagging man-to-man defense slightly, you can designate certain defenders to sag. Their presence will be welcomed by the defensive post man.

Sagging from the weak side is another variation of man-to-man defense that can be used against good post players. The defensive post man fronts the offensive post man and attempts to stop all passing angles. The lob pass is the only available feed left, so a weak-side defender must move over and help out. (See Diagram 12-2.)

The weak-side help strategy works very well against teams that have good outside shooters, but a stagnate offense. If player -f- is inactive when the ball is on his opposite side, the defender -3- can actually two-time the low post -P-. Sometimes -f- may be determined to be a weak player whose offensive abilities are nonexistent. His defensive man -3- should be involved in helping on the post as much as possible.

When a lob pass is thrown over the post defender's head, the weak-side

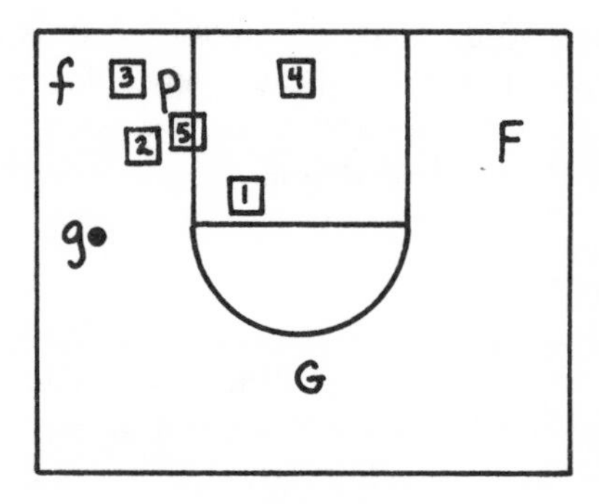

Diagram 12-1.
Sagging onto the Post

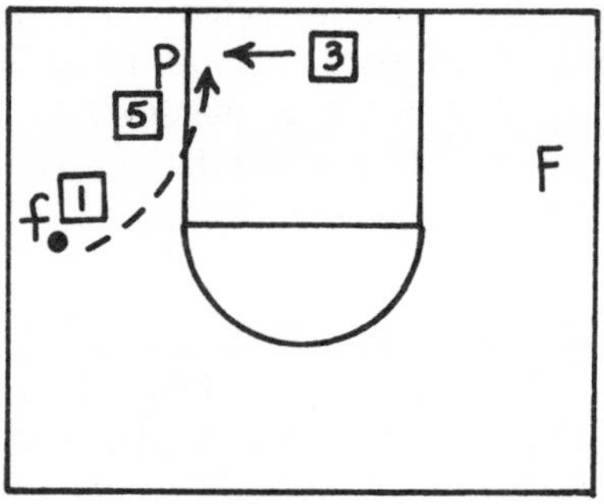

Diagram 12-2.
Weak Side Help and Fronting

helper should go for the ball, if possible. He has a good view of the ball and as much right as anyone to take the pass. Sometimes steals are possible, but deflections can be as valuable in this dangerous area.

If the weak-side helper has established position behind the post before the lob pass is attempted, he can elect to hold his ground and draw a charge. Since the offensive post man is focusing on the ball, he will be unaware of the defender behind him. As the offensive man moves to the hoop, he will often crash into the helping defender. This can be very beneficial to the defense in the long run. First, a foul is drawn on the big man, and it moves him closer to disqualification. Secondly, the offensive players involved will think twice before trying the lob pass again. When the opponents have to hesitate in their normal attacking methods, the defensive team moves a step closer to gaining control of the game.

Platoon Attack

Another method that can be used against the high-scoring post man is platoon attack. This involves substituting every few minutes, in an effort to force a fast pace and burn the opponents out. You can elect to substitute all five defenders, or just rotate post men.

In five-man platooning, all defenders harass their assigned man to the maximum. The ball is pressured constantly, all passing lanes are challenged, and the offense contested in every way possible. Over-committing will lead to some easy baskets, but the constant pressure should eventually wear the opponents out. One or two quick turnovers can sometimes destroy the stability of the opponents and eventually lead to victory for your team.

Substituting at the post position has been mentioned previously in this book. Two men alternate guarding the opponent's big superstar. Their job is to be as physical as possible and to play as hard as possible. Two players alternating can remain fresh and anxious to stop the assigned opponent. The defenders must not worry about being overaggressive, because they have ten fouls to use up between them. A very physical and hustling defensive job by two average post men can be most effective on one player. The opponent's big men will get worn out mentally and physically from the persistent pressure. Again, if the type of defense you use upsets the opponents, then your team has gained an edge on final victory.

ZONE DEFENSES

Zone defenses are very popular at the high school level and have also made their mark at the college level. Against poor outside shooting teams, the zone defense can be very effective. Some coaches employ zones as a change of pace during the game. They start with a pressuring man-to-man defense, then later slow the attack with a zone.

Zones can also be very effective against teams that rely on a good post man to score. The defenders key on the ball and shift with its movement. Three defensive players should be between the ball and the basket at all times. Because of this shifting and collapsing, it becomes virtually impossible to work the ball into the low post.

The 2-1-2 Zone Defense

Diagram 12-3 illustrates the basic 2-1-2 zone defensive alignment. Player -5- represents the best defensive big man. He must be mobile and intelligent, as well as tall. His basic responsibility is to front the opponent's star post man, thus preventing him from getting the ball inside the key.

The guards must be active as they play the two outside positions—-1- and -2-. One challenges the ball on the perimeter, while the other sags back into the key to help inside. The other front-line players, -3- and -4-, are responsible for rebound positioning and helping -5- stop internal attacks. Diagram 12-4 shows the positioning of all defenders with the ball at a wing position. Notice the three defenders -2-, -5-, and -3- between the ball and the basket.

The 1-3-1 Zone Defense

Another strong zone defense against a good post man is the 1-3-1 alignment. The best, big defender again plays the middle and attempts to stay between the ball and the post man. The other two front-line players play the wings and help on the post from the weak side. The guards fill the point and baseline spots. Their speed is used to cover much of the perimeter, while the big men concentrate on the opponent's pivot man.

As in the 2-1-2 zone, three players should be kept between the ball and the basket. The shifts of the 1-3-1 are very similar to the 2-1-2. Because the forwards do not have to cover the corners, they are more available for rebounding and jamming the internal zone. (See Diagram 12-5.)

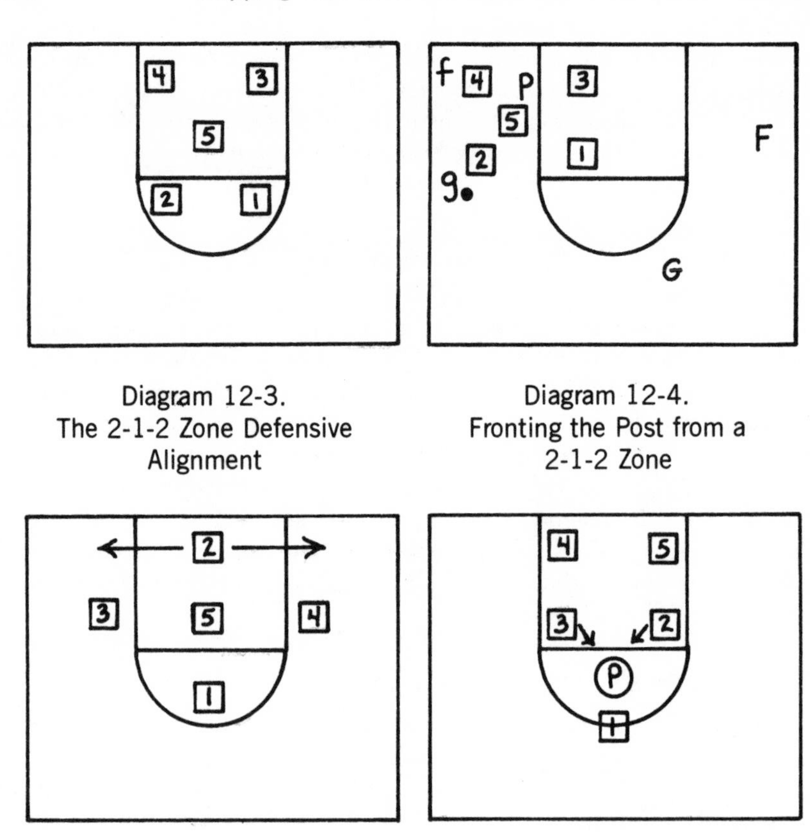

Diagram 12-3.
The 2-1-2 Zone Defensive Alignment

Diagram 12-4.
Fronting the Post from a 2-1-2 Zone

Diagram 12-5.
The 1-3-1 Zone

Diagram 12-6.
The 1-2-2 Zone

The 1-2-2 Zone Defense

Because no one defender can be assigned to stop the offensive post man, this defensive alignment is the weakest against a strong post man. The 1-2-2 relies on teamwork, quick shifting, and hustle. The defenders do not front the post man, but rather attempt to play close enough to deflect or steal passes to him. There are always two defenders near the offensive post man, one on either side. They must be alert for possible steals at all times. (See Diagram 12-6.)

If a pass is completed to the offensive post man, a minimum of three defenders should collapse on him. At the high post, the challengers would be -1-, -2-, and -3-.

When the ball goes to a corner, the low post area becomes a dangerous attacking zone. Diagram 12-7 illustrates the proper quick movements needed to stop this attack.

As the ball moves to the left corner, -4- defends against the perimeter

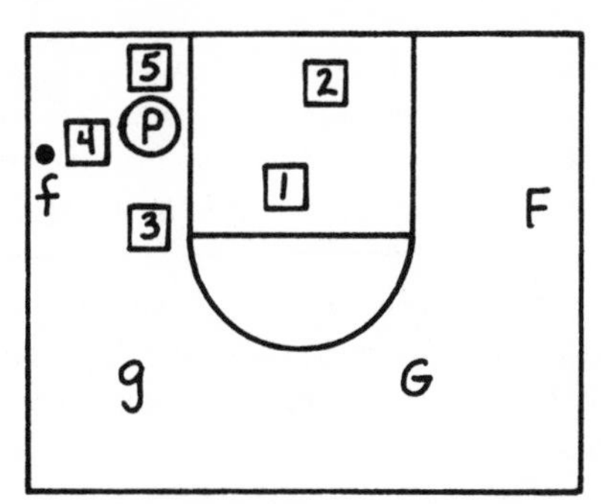

Diagram 12-7.
The 1-2-2 Versus a Low
Post Attack

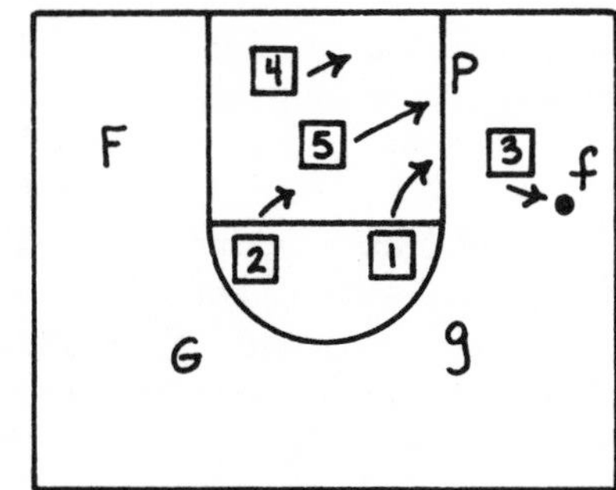

Diagram 12-8.
Match-Up Zone from 2-1-2
Alignment

shot. -5- tries to beat -P- to the low post and defends the baseline side. -2- sags in and looks for passes to -P- on the top side. -3- drops under the basket and takes the weak side rebound position.

The amount of movement required for this defense makes it advisable to use only with quick teams. The biggest players should man the -4- and -5- spots, so they can be in good rebounding positions. Because they must move from one corner to the opposite low post, it can easily be seen why quick and agile defenders are necessary. An intelligent and quick ball club can force many turnovers using a 1-2-2 zone defense. However, the 2-1-2 and 1-3-1 alignments offer more consistent one-on-one coverage of a superstar post player.

COMBINATION DEFENSES

Combination defenses include the Match-Up, Box-and-One, and Diamond-and-One Zones. The principles of man-to-man defense and zone defense are combined to form a tough team defense. These defenses are some of the most difficult to attack because offensive patterns are practically useless. By matching a tough, big defender on the opponent's post man, the defense can make it very hard for the offense to feed their big man.

The Match-Up Zone

Rules dictate the action of the defensive players in this zone. Basically, the match-up starts from a 1-3-1 or 2-1-2 alignment. The middle man is assigned to the offensive post player, and he plays him man-to-man. The other four defenders pick up opponents in their areas. They cover them man-to-man until the offensive player moves to a new area.

When a weak offensive player is in a defender's zone area, the defender can sag and help on the post man. In Diagram 12-8, offensive player -g- has been scouted and found to be no outside scoring threat. Defender -1- can leave his area and help on -P-, the offensive superstar.

The diagram illustrates -5- matching on the post -P-; weak-side defenders -4- and -2- sagging; and -3- pressuring the ball because it is in his area.

The match-up zone can have problems when two offensive players overload into one defender's area. Every match-up coach has his own set of rules to cover such occurrences. The main concern is to keep your best big man matched on their post player at all times. Make the opponents beat you from the outside with their lesser-talented players.

The Box-and-One

The box-and-one is a combination defense where four men play zone, and one player is assigned to stay with a particular opponent. This defense is commonly used against "one-man teams" that rely on an outside scorer to carry the offensive zone. It can also be used on an opponent that features a gifted post man. The defense basically follows the principles listed earlier for the 2-1-2 zone. The box-and-one does give some more freedom to the post defender, as he can now follow his man to the perimeter. If the opponent's center liked to go outside when congested in the key, the box-and-one can keep the pressure on him better than a 2-1-2 zone. Consider the box-and-one against a wandering post player.

In diagram 12-9, the post man -P- feels congested and wants the ball. As he moves to the wing, -5- stays with him and contests the pass. The other four defenders stay in their four-man zone defense—the box!

The Diamond-and-One

The diamond-and-one is similar to the box-and-one; only the initial alignment is different. (See Diagram 12-10.) The defense works like the 1-3-1 zone and basically follows its rules. Because of the point man on the align-

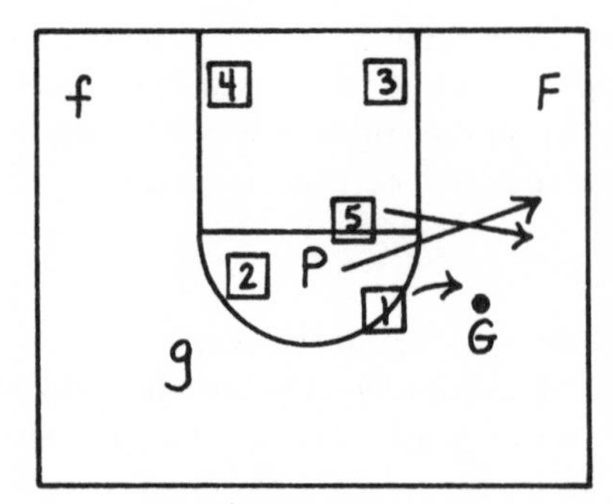

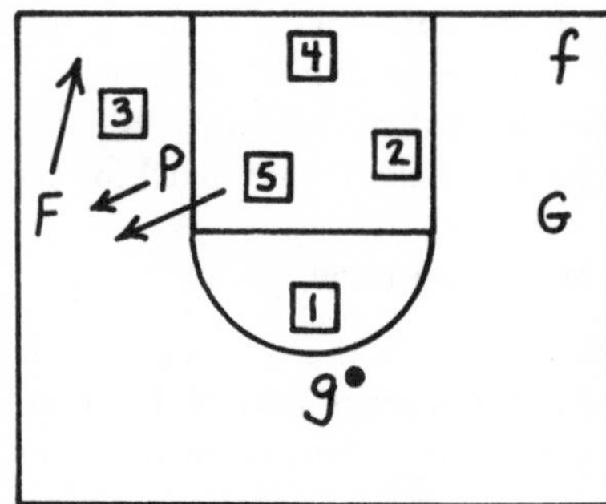

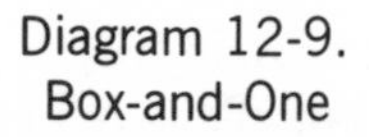
Diagram 12-9.
Box-and-One

Diagram 12-10.
Diamond-and-One

ment, the diamond-and-one works very well against one-guard attacks. Point man-1- can harass the opponent's guard, while -5- again chases the pivot player wherever he goes. The idea is to keep pressure on the ball and yet prevent the best player from getting it.

The box-and-one and diamond-and-one combination defenses can be very successful in preventing the ball going to the post. Even a weak defensive team can often confuse and defeat an opponent with a tall center, by using a combination defense.

Use the box-and-one versus two guard fronts, and the diamond-and-one versus one guard fronts.

PRESSING DEFENSES

Many basketball teams have adopted full court pressure defenses as part of their defensive philosophy. The press can be used for the entire game or periodically to change the pace.

The effect of full court pressure on the opponent's big man is usually positive for the defensive team. Listed below are some of these positive effects.

1. The tempo of the game picks up, thus wearing out the out-of-condition players. Fatigue makes the big man less effective.
2. Pressure forces the pace and disorganizes patterned teams. The big man may be left behind or out of position. By rushing the opponent's attack, players other than the post man will find reason to shoot. This gives the big man fewer shot opportunities.
3. More turnovers will result, thus giving your team extra shots at the hoop. The additional field goal attempts may be just what is needed to outscore a great post player.
4. The big man may have to move up-court as an inlet or safety valve. This gets him away from the basket and into a less effective area of the court. The post is usually a poor dribbler, so he could make some turnovers. This upsets his emotional state and swings momentum to your team.
5. Because the big man is forced to move to get the ball, he will often be off balance. Playing a moving position rather than a stationary one can lower the shooting percentage of the post man.

There are presses to fit any type of team. The slow team, tall team, or inexperienced team can utilize some pressing if the right attack is chosen. Again, as coach, you're responsible for finding a full court defense that fits the talents of your team.

For the teams who use full court pressure all year, only slight changes are needed to be effective against the superstar big man. It would be a big mistake to scrap the press for one game, just because you fear the opponent's post man. If your team has been winning with pressure and a fastbreak style, then it would be disaster to sag on defense and slow the offense. Your team will always play best when allowed to use their regular style. Have confidence in your style and stick with full court pressure versus the big man. Simple adjustments can make the press even more devastating against a team that relies on one man to carry the load.

Recalling my own last high school basketball game, pressure defense against a big man is well remembered. I was a member of the Rio Linda High School team which met Encina High School in the final game of the Sacramento Tournament of Champions. Encina had a very tall line-up featuring 6′11″ Jim Eakins. Eakins later went on to a fine career in the old American Basketball Association and the National Basketball Association. Our Rio Linda team started a 6′2″ center, and we went down from there. During that season, we had won a lot of games using the 2-2-1 full court zone press. With only one game left in the season and the tournament championship on the line, our fine coach Al McFadyen elected to stick with our pressing style. While coaches and fans alike were sure we would get destroyed. Rio Linda High School was on top going into the last quarter. Eakins had been held to a very low point total basically because our pressing kept him away from the basket.

It was one of the most exciting games in Sacramento basketball history; unfortunately, we lost three starters early in the fourth quarter. Eventually we lost the game too, as Eakins went on a rampage. The press deteriorated with the loss of key personnel, so Encina High School took the tempo away from us.

If we had dropped our press in favor of triple-teaming Eakins, we probably would have been bombed out early. Give the opponents your best shot, and it will pay off quite often.

There are three types of pressing defenses most commonly used in basketball today. They are: Man-to-Man Full Court, Zone Full Court, and Half Court Pressure. Whatever your team uses, simple adjustments can be utilized to control the opponent's big man.

Man-to-Man Press

This type of press is used in conjunction with man-to-man half court defense. All defenders extend their pressure to the full court, thus challenging the opponents during their entire possession.

The opponents will generally slow the pace of the game by letting one good dribbler beat the pressure. A good ball handler will hardly ever be forced into a rash of turnovers. Man-to-man pressure is successful against teams that have inexperienced guards or poor ball handlers. The guards will become so involved in getting the ball up-court that the big man will be forgotten.

Against good dribblers, the defense should gamble with occasional two-times. This forces the guard to pass off, and it picks up the pace of the game.

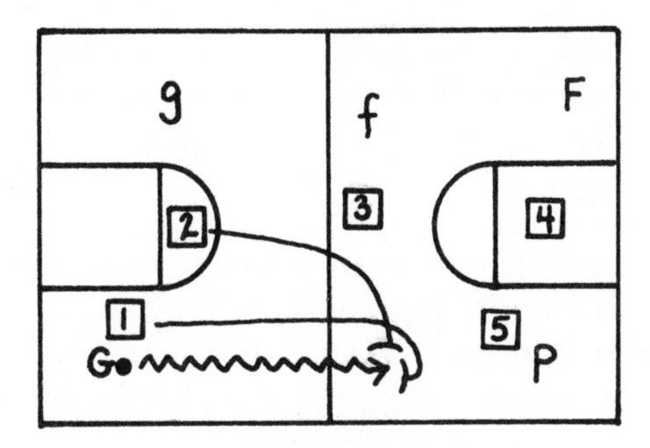

Diagram 12-11.
Man Press—Two-Time

By adding the two-time, confusion will develop in the opponents. The idea is to play fast, force turnovers, and keep the offense from getting too patterned. If the press is beaten, everyone recovers and picks up their assigned men.

Diagram 12-11 illustrates a two-time from a man-to-man press. Notice that the defensive post man is assigned to the opponent's big man. There is little chance of the big man getting free for an easy shot, because his defender does not get involved in the two-times.

Defender -1- runs the dribbler down the sideline to prevent formation of a fastbreak wave. Player -2- comes over to two-time from the blind side, leaving his man -g- momentarily free. Defender -5- stays with the post man and contests the passing lane. Players -3- and -4- loosen up and watch for lob passes. If ball handler -g- passes to the basket, all defenders must immediately retreat to within line of the ball. This is important as the extra bit of hustle required spells the difference between success and failure. When the ball nears the internal zone, all defenders must sag and jam the key. This help is needed to prevent easy baskets of streaking offensive players, and it slows the movement of the big man. When the offense sets up, all defenders find their assigned men and play tough half court defense.

Zone Presses

The zone presses force faster action because of the many two-times that are possible. Dribblers are immediately cut off and forced to give up the ball. The offensive big man is almost always required to move to the back court. Although he becomes a dangerous passing outlet, the post man is none-the-less in unfamiliar territory. The zone press forces all offensive men to help break the pressure, thus breaking up pattern play. Listed below are the three most popular zone presses. In each, the defensive big man should play the safety position. This will allow him to pick up the opponent's post man easier, once the press is broken.

1. **The 1-2-1-1 Press.** This press provides immediate pressure on the offense. The opponents have to work extra hard just to get the ball inbounds. The forecourt is protected only by the safety man, the defensive post man. All defenders must retreat quickly when the ball passes overhead.
2. **The 2-2-1 Press.** This press provides a little more protection around midcourt, while still allowing a lot of back-court pressure.
3. **The 2-1-2 Press.** This is a more conservative full court press that uses two big men well. Both big boys play the deep spots, with the weak-side man serving as the safety.

Because the full court zone press forces the offense to scatter over the court, the defensive post man does not need to worry about the opponent's big man right away. The safety should be totally involved in the press. He sees all the action in front of him, so he can advise his teammates of the opponent's movement. The safety must not be afraid to gamble if he sees a chance to steal a pass or pick up a loose ball. The offensive post will need time to set up, so his defensive man has plenty of time to recover. Diagram 12-12 illustrates the likely positions of players during a 1-2-1-1 press. Notice that -P- is stationed away from the basket to help out.

Conditioning and hustle are most important to teams that employ full court pressure. Any breakdown in retreating requirements can cause gaps in the defense. The opponents will get easy shots and demoralize the pressing team. Prepare your team in practice with tough conditioning drills. Any player who becomes too tired to retreat at full speed must be immediately replaced. There is no room for loafers in full court pressure.

Half Court Zone Press

Teams using a half court zone press can also defend the great post player quite well. The constant harassing and two-timing poses problems to perimeter players who want to feed the big man inside. Passes may be hurried, and thus thrown out of bounds or stolen. The post man may also have to leave his familiar low post area in order to relieve the pressure on the guards. As in full court pressure, the offense is forced to change its standard attack. Another plus for the defenders is that they have less court to cover. They use less energy and give up very few easy lay ups, as compared to full court pressure.

The most common setup for a half court press is the 1-3-1 alignment. (See Diagram 12-13.) Defender -5- is the best post defender, and he guards the opponent's big man. If the offensive post man leaves the low post area, -5- serves as safety and prevents any lay ups. Player -4- must be quick so he can cover the corners, while -1- takes the area above the free throw line. Players -2- and -3- two-time the right and left sides respectively.

Some teams like to drop into a regular 1-3-1 zone defense after the ball

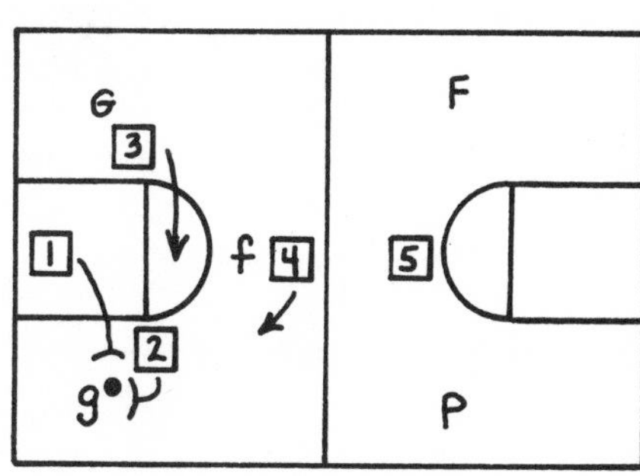

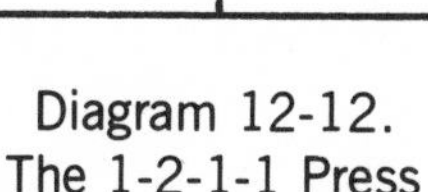
Diagram 12-12.
The 1-2-1-1 Press

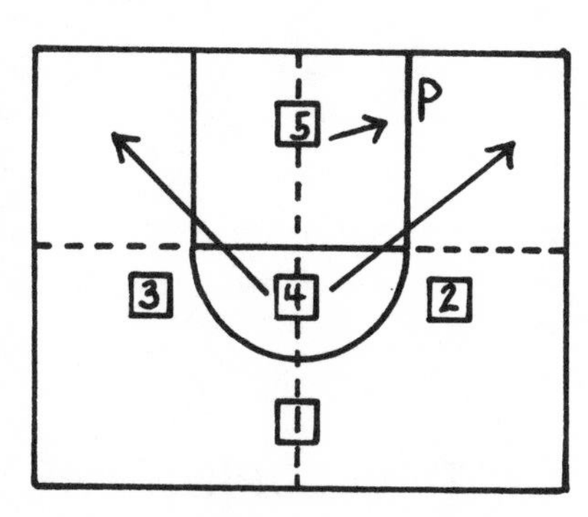

Diagram 12-13.
The 1-3-1 Half Court Press

passes the free throw line extended. When the ball goes to the corner, -4- and -5- switch areas and follow the rules of a 1-3-1 zone. This is a less risky attack that still applies some initial pressure on the perimeter players.

No matter what style of play your team employs, a few simple adjustments are all that is needed to slow a good post man. Granted, some post men seem impossible to stop, but the coach must do all he can to challenge the opponents. By making the opponent's post man work a little harder, you may wear him out enough to make the difference in the closing minutes of a game.

13

DEVELOPING THE EXTRA TALL PLAYER

A high school team with a 6′9″ center draws a lot of attention from the fans and press. As the extra tall player dominates game after game, an undercurrent of familiar basketball cries can be heard. "Anyone could win with that guy! Anybody can coach that team and win a championship."

People may make such rash judgments, but coaches know that winning with a big man is not all that easy. In his book, *They Call Me Coach*, U.C.L.A.'s John Wooden made an interesting comment to the news media after the graduation of superstar Lew Alcindor. He said, "It'll be nice to know that I'll again be doing my best to win rather than to keep from losing." The pressures of coaching "Big Lew," now known as Kareem Abdul Jabbar, were even a burden to college basketball's winningest coach.

Winning with the extra tall player is the coach's responsibility. If the big man becomes a superstar, credit is due to the coaches who develop him. When a tall player goes through a program and does not improve his skills, the coach can often be rightfully faulted.

Unless you are lucky enough to have a polished big man move into your high school district, you will never coach a great post man by sitting back and waiting. You will need to start at the lower levels, work through the off-seasons, and build with long range plans. This is also true at the college and university levels. Only a handful of college programs are capable of recruiting a superstar big man. The other 95 per cent of the college coaches will need to spend four years of hard work developing "diamonds in the rough."

When developing extra tall players, the important thing is to start early. Find them while they are young, encourage them to work on their skills, give them a chance to play, and be patient with their progress.

HOW TO SPOT POTENTIAL TALL PLAYERS

Height is relative to age and the quality of competition. A junior high coach will never run across a 6′9″ player, but a 5′11″ eighth grader could be the biggest player in his league. A 6′2″ freshman in high school usually towers over his competition. Small, country high schools will often appear awesome when they start a 6′5″ center. The coach must realize what is "extra tall" at his level of competition; otherwise, some potential big men may get lost in the shuffle.

It should also be noted that tall eighth graders may end up as short high school varsity players. In the same regard, a short freshman may grow to be a 6′8″ senior. Since I believe in starting the development of high school programs at the junior high level or lower, the following tips have been helpful to spot potential post men.

1. An eighth or ninth grader who is taller than his classmates will usually continue to be one of the tallest.
2. An average-sized player with proportionally long legs and arms will often grow into those limbs and become extra tall.
3. Younger brothers of former tall players can generally be counted on to grow to a similar height.
4. Check the heights of the players' fathers and mothers. If either is far above average, growth potential is almost assured.

DEVELOPING SKILLS AT THE LOWER LEVELS

A high school coach who has no control over the junior varsity or freshmen teams is facing a dead-end road. There has to be coordination and communication throughout the program before any long range success pattern will develop. The head coach should even try to maintain an influential relationship with the feeder schools in the area. Personalities being as they are, this is not always possible. By making himself available to the community, a varsity coach can develop friendships and rapport which will aid the entire program.

Most head coaches have control over the high school lower division teams. They get to know most of the students through physical education classes, or they can observe team tryouts. I always involve myself in the selection of the lower level squads. In fact, I try to involve the entire staff in the selection of all squads. We watch each other's early practices and meet often to discuss the future of every prospect. This method has two obvious advantages.

First, each boy is being evaluated by three or more coaches. This helps the head coach to avoid mistakes in judgment due to personality conflicts or just plain oversight. The youngsters who try out seem to accept the final choices much easier.

Secondly, the whole staff feels as though they are contributing to the program; and of course, they certainly are! If all members of the staff have input into the program, they will work better with the head coach. Communication opens up and the entire program benefits. With a staff that works together for the future of the program, schooling post men at the lower levels is an easier task. Thus, the coaches can seek out and develop the potential big men.

Just because a tall player may be lacking in skills, that is no reason to cut him from the squad. I have walked around many high school campuses where the tallest boys do not play basketball. While many have legitimate reasons for their lack of interest, I wonder how many could have become good players if they were encouraged at a younger age?

The coach's job is to develop skills, teach fundamentals, and improve the quality of play. Since post men are so important to the success of a basketball team, the coach must take time to develop them.

In my programs, we avoid cutting tall players at the freshman level. The only exception would be for attitude problems. Even then, we try our best to guide the ninth grader into a better development of character. Young teenagers are very impressionable and can often be successfully turned around.

By their sophomore year, the players know what we expect as far as character. Very seldom do we need to drop anyone for an attitude problem. Of course, that eventually makes the varsity team a very smooth-working unit.

Just keeping tall boys on the squad does nothing for the program if they are not developed. We start by getting our post men together and discussing their role on the team. They are told the importance of big man rebounding. Next, the internal offensive theory is explained. The tall man soon realizes he can be a very valuable member of the squad if he rebounds and develops his inside moves. Suddenly, his inability to keep up with the little dribbler or the ouside gunner is no longer a thorn in the side. By learning to do his job well inside, the big man can contribute to the success of the team.

Playing time is very important to the development of big men. They cannot learn to score or rebound by sitting on the bench. One ninth grade big man must start, even if he is not one of the five best players. All he needs to be is the *best big man.* This narrows the competition and lets all of the tall players know that they can play. The coach shows that the big man is important and that he will be given every chance to develop. Improvement in all post men will be amazing, as their confidence soars.

What good does it do the players or the coach to start and play five future guards at the freshman level? Why leave two 6′1″ ninth graders sitting on the bench, discouraged and wasting away? Play the big men and watch the improvement. Keep the little guys at guard and rotate them. It will allow them to learn their natural position and increase competition for the starting jobs. This method benefits both little men and tall players, but better yet, it benefits the future program.

I believe in using many players during the course of a game, as mentioned earlier. This goes double for the lower division teams. We expect to play at least ten players in the first half of every game. *No game is ever lost in the first half*, so why not get everyone into the action? When all players know they will get a chance to play, practice is never dull. Everyone is eager to listen and learn because they know they will be called on to perform.

This method not only allows one big man to play, but it also allows a second post man to gain game experience. After all, you never know which 6′0″ freshman will become a 6′8″ senior. Give them all a chance.

The lower division coaches must be concerned with development rather than won-loss records. The goal at the beginning of the season should be to have the best team at the end of the season. Games may be lost early; but as long as players are developed, the lower division coaches are winners.

The head coach should also follow the same guidelines. Give the big men a chance to play, especially in the nonleague season. Rest the starting center in the first half and give his back-up some playing time. The rest will keep the starting post man out of foul trouble and leave him refreshed and ready for the important second half. The back-up man gains experience and prepares himself for the future. You never know when sickness, injury, or foul trouble will eliminate the starting post man. His replacement can mean the difference between a league championship and disaster.

EMOTIONAL AND MENTAL DEVELOPMENT

The emotional development of teenagers is one of the most perplexing challenges in life. Dealing with the rapid changes of the body and the demands of society leaves many young people confused and withdrawn. Being six to ten inches taller than his peers presents an even greater burden on the extra tall young man.

Basketball is only a small part of a teenager's life. He still has to attend classes, go to social events, and deal with people in everyday situations. While being a basketball player may bring some notoriety and special praise, it can also bring extra pressure and over-exposure. The coach must recognize these problems and assist the big man in his mental and emotional development.

Rapid growth usually leaves a teenager lacking in physical development and coordination. His frame often appears to be only skin and bones because weight and bulk are hard to gain. The big man will sometimes be clumsy and awkward. While the rest of his body struggles to keep up with the rapid process of growth, his mind must be allowed to develop at a normal pace.

No one likes to be called a goon or freak! However, some people will call a tall teenager such degrading terms. Opponents, their fans, and even his own teammates will resort to such tactics during the most inopportune times. A concerned coach can help the extra tall player deal with these situations and make his life less of a struggle.

Encourage the big man often. Constant criticism will only cause him to be tight and unsure. Experience and time will bring about the true potential of a tall player. Reassure him that hard work and patience will pay dividends in the end.

Do not put the burden of winning on the young, big man. Basketball is a *team* game, where everyone has to do his part. Give the post man realistic goals, just as you would any other player. If the coach tells the big man he should score 20 points and get 15 rebounds when his present development would never allow such figures, then the big man will always feel frustrated. Ten points and ten rebounds might be a great contribution for some young post men. Let them experience success at one level before increasing the goals. The twenty points and fifteen rebounds night will come much faster to a confident player.

Do not baby the big man! He must work hard and play tough, or the coach should find a new post man. A potentially good post man is a competitor. He wants to be a good player and will work hard to reach his goal.

While the coach may be patient with the development of attitude in the lower programs, he must not accept poor behavior or laziness. The hardest-working big man can be rewarded with the starting game assignment, even when his talents may be lacking. This move will challenge the lazy man to work harder, or he will be left out. The hardest-working young big man will eventually end up being the best anyway.

PHYSICAL DEVELOPMENT AND COORDINATION

It has already been pointed out that an extra tall player usually lacks in physical development and coordination. While time will generally cure these deficiencies, the young basketball player does not always want to let nature run its course. Some of the best years of his playing career may be wasted if he does not correct his physical weaknesses early.

The coach's role should be one of encouraging but not pushing. The player must be willing to work extra, both after practice and in the off season. If he does not want to put in the time and effort, pushing and scolding will do no good. It might even turn the player off and cause him to dislike basketball altogether.

Occasional questioning about development, suggesting workouts, and offering praise for progress are the best forms of coach stimulation. Encouragement will keep the player motivated and anxious to continue the extra work.

Following are some ways to improve the big man's physical development, aggressiveness, and coordination.

1. Weight Training and Running

The off-season is a good time to build the body physically. I favor a weight program and distance running for the big men. My fall program is mandatory for all players, while the spring and summer plans are optional.

Distance running is an excellent form of exercise for the extra tall player. Since the big boys often lack stamina, running is a good way to condition the legs and lungs. We run one to three miles each day as a pre-season conditioning program. The off-season player is encouraged to jog two to five miles daily. The improvement in stamina and coordination is often amazing after six months of summer and fall work.

Adding bulk and weight to a thin post man can be accomplished through a vigorous weight program. Even in cases where the big boy still appears skinny after weight training, nevertheless, he will be solid and stronger. This is a distinct advantage to the thin and extra tall player.

Today, most schools have six station weight machines. They are simple to operate and can serve many athletes in a short time. Our workouts consist of three sets of ten repetitions on each of four stations. The first set is a warmup performed at an easy-to-work weight. The second set is done at about 80 per cent of the player's maximum effort. The third set is the maximum effort. When ten repetitions can be done at the maximum, the weight should be increased ten pounds. As the player becomes stronger, the work load will increase.

Any work with weights requires a day of rest between workouts. This allows the muscles a chance to stretch, retract, repair, and recover. My players usually lift on Monday, Wednesday, and Friday, allowing two days of rest on the weekend. When a running program is incorporated with the weight program, easy jogging takes place on lift days. Jogging serves to loosen the tightened muscles after a weight workout. It is also a relaxing way to end a day's work. Hard long distance running is done on the off days and on weekends.

2. Aggressiveness

Along with developing the physique, a coach should be concerned with developing an aggressive attitude. A tall player with no desire to mix it up inside will not help his team very much. He must be willing to get knocked around and do some knocking around of his own. Aggressiveness is a mental characteristic, with physical development an added enforcer.

While many people feel aggressiveness cannot be taught, I strongly disagree. Some players are aggressive by nature, but many others need to learn to assert themselves. You can provide the situations in which aggressiveness will develop. Again, encouragement is important to the young player. A tall, lanky post man needs the inspiration you can give.

Toughness drills are a must in practice. Players need to experience physical contact and should be complimented for their efforts. A dive on the floor for a loose ball, drawing a charge on a driving guard, or a solid block-out and rebound are all unique situations requiring your special praise. The comment will do a lot to inspire a player to continue his hustle, and it will also stimulate others to follow suit. Soon everyone on the team will compliment an aggressive play by a teammate, and eventually the whole squad will be hustling extra hard.

Besides words of encouragement, other forms of stimulating aggressiveness in big men are listed below.

1. The defensive players must call all fouls during off-season pick-up games. This helps to avoid petty calls by offensive players and cuts down on arguments. My players eventually get the attitude that it is below them to complain over contact. An aggressive style is nurtured.
2. The coaches call very few fouls during pre-season practice scrimmages. Only the obvious reaching violations are whistled, while bumping and colliding are ignored. Any player who complains or loses his cool is asked to rest for a while.
3. Aggressive training drills are used often in practice. Daily rebound block-outs are common to our practices. Intermittently we play "War" (Chapter 5), "Draw the Charge" (Chapter 11), and "Pressure on the Hoop" (Chapter 3).
4. Start the most aggressive players early in the season. Put a premium on toughness by showing the team how important aggressiveness is to the coach. This is a good way to motivate a top scorer who lacks a physical attitude.
5. Praise any player who is being aggressive in a game, even if he gets caught fouling a lot. He will soon learn what he can and cannot get away with in a game situation. Big men especially need to be complimented for physical play, even when it ends up in turnovers or fouls. The extra tall player may suffer physically for his aggressive efforts, but development will only come through practice.

3. Improving Coordination

To develop a player's skills, there is no substitute for playing time. The more an extra tall player works on his game, the better his coordination and confidence become. Besides game time, the big man can get a lot of work in the off season. Pick-up games, recreation leagues, and individual workouts are all ways an ambitious player may improve his skills.

Coaching in California for most of my career has been advantageous to my programs. Summer basketball camps, clinics, and leagues are common in most metropolitan areas. With two N.B.A. basketball teams and literally hundreds of colleges in the state, players have plenty of chances for exposure and motivation.

I try to have our gym open two or three nights a week during the spring, fall, and summer. The facility is available to anyone who wants to use the weights, work on fundamentals, or play basketball. Sometimes I limit the games to half court, but full court seems to be the players' favorite choice. Basketball is a fun game! You would be surprised how many players will show up to play in an open gym. Freshmen, sophomores, and varsity players mix it up and form balanced teams. The young players get to improve against the challenge of the experienced veterans, and the extra tall player gets to face different degrees of competition. Sometimes, my former players return from their colleges and supply added competition. Getting to work against better players does wonders for an inexperienced big man. Ideas are often exchanged between the players, and it is not uncommon to see the older players working with the younger ones after a game.

Summer leagues are great for stimulating basketball in the off season. They are actually informal games with scoreboard, officials, and uniforms, but no pressure from spectators or the press. The big man gets plenty of off-season work in game conditions.

Camps and clinics allow the big man to face other extra tall competition. While the post man may never have anyone as big as himself to go against in practice, summer camps offer the best players from all over the state. The challenge helps the big man, but the realization that he is not as great as he thinks may be the real lesson. I have seen many players return from camps with renewed enthusiasm for developing new skills.

Coordination of extra tall players also requires individual workouts and drills. Tipping, the Mikan Drill, rope jumping, and post moves were all mentioned earlier in this book. A big man who really wants to develop into a smooth player should spend some time on each drill daily.

Development of the big man can only be accomplished through hard work and desire on the part of the player. If the extra tall player wants to be a good post man, he will spend the time needed to meet his goals. The coach serves as a guide to off-season work, and he provides the encouragement that helps the player stick with his difficult task.

14

COACHING THE SUPERSTAR POST MAN

What happens after you develop a superstar post man? Either through the luck of a transfer, the hard work in years of developing potential big men, or great recruiting by college coaches, a coach may finally have a superstar big man on his team. Everything should be easy now, with victory after victory piling up, right? Well, not always. Quite often the work has only begun.

I recall my first year as a head coach. Having just finished college, I accepted the head job at Jesuit High School in Sacramento, California. The task of running a high school basketball program is difficult enough at any age, but I was only twenty-two years old. To further complicate my predicament, I inherited a winning team with a 6′10″ "Superstar."

Mark Wehrle was my "Superstar Post Man" during that initial year. Wehrle was mentioned in chapter 1, and readers will recall that the first season ended with a championship and happiness for all involved. But the season was not without its challenges, pressures, heartaches, and sleepless nights. I sometimes feel that the only reason I made it through without cracking was because I was too young and inexperienced to realize what was happening.

In working with a "Superstar Post Man," the coach has three basic areas of commitment.

1. To his own life and the members of his family.
2. To the team as a whole.
3. To the "Superstar" and his family.

Being able to keep these commitments in proper perspective and order is a most difficult challenge. The glory and publicity that goes with coaching a "Superstar" can be quite a boost to a coach's ego. When you are on top, those underneath can seem very far away. But it must be remembered that "every dog has his day," and yours may be around the corner. This year's champs can be next year's chumps! When the "Superstar" graduates, who will continue to make you a "great coach"?

After winning the area tournament in my first season as head coach, my personal goals certainly stepped up. It was easy! By age twenty-five I would be a head college coach, and at thirty I would be in the Pros. The El Dorado High School Cougars are hardly the Los Angeles Lakers, but thirty has come and gone. Nevertheless, I am happy and proud to be where I am today.

Do not get me wrong; goals are great to have. You cannot get anywhere in coaching without them. Keeping them in perspective and not letting them interfere with the three commitments mentioned earlier is the key. A coach should seek to advance himself when he is a winner, but not on the shirttail of his "Superstar." The team cannot be ignored just because one man seems to get all of the attention. And finally, the coach has a responsibility to the great player. The "Superstar" must be directed and advised in a conscientious manner during his time of glory.

Just as everyday people have different and unusual personalities, great basketball players also vary in their attitudes. Some tall superstars may shy away from the notoriety of their accomplishments, while others bask in the attention. Depending on the star's reaction to his success, the coach may have an enjoyable or trying experience.

I was fortunate to have coached a tremendous young man in Mark Wehrle. He was an outstanding student, popular with teammates and classmates, and a gentleman at all times. The faculty of Jesuit High School, his former coaches, and most notably his parents, were responsible for Wehrle's fine adjustment. Without their help, my job would not have been as easy.

KEEPING THE TALL SUPERSTAR OUT OF THE CLOUDS

A young player's coach can be a strong influence during the teenage years. Dealing with the young man for three hours a day and six to twelve months a year gives a basketball coach many opportunities to mold good or bad traits in the player. Through the agony of pre-season conditioning to the pressures of Friday night games, the coach will observe the player's attitude and reactions. Not even the young man's parents will get to see their son handle such demanding situations.

The "Superstar Post Man" is a special person, all right. But just how special should he be allowed to believe he is? Babying him, constantly letting him know how great he is, and ignoring the efforts of his teammates will only hurt the development of a young player. The coach has not helped his star player at all if the big boy does not realize he is the same as any other human being. He may be a great ball player, but life does not revolve around a basketball court. To use basketball fame as a rationale for being better than people around him will only cause problems in the "Star's" later life. The extra tall "Superstar" must believe in his abilities on the court in order to be successful. He must also be able to fit into the rest of the world when the games are over.

The conscientious coach will treat all of his players the same, from the "Superstar" down to the last man on the team. He will apply the same practice rules and training rules for everyone. If the big man misses practice, he should be reprimanded the same as a teammate would. Rules should be made for the TEAM, and the "Star" must always be aware that he is but one more member of the TEAM.

Dealing fairly and firmly with all members of the squad early in the season will generally make things run smoothly during the "dog days" of league. If your "Star" wants to test you, it is better to settle the issue right away. Let everyone, especially the "Star," know that you will treat the entire squad equally. They will all understand and appreciate your fairness.

It is smart coaching to develop your offense around a "Star" performer, especially an extra tall one. Balancing the attack somewhat is also advisable. The following points suggest why.

1. Some of the pressure to score is distributed throughout the squad.
2. Opponents cannot collapse their defenses on your ace.
3. Should the big man get injured or foul out, the offense will not falter.
4. All team members share in the thrill of making points.

Everyone wants to make baskets, but everyone wants to win too. When it gets down to the important moments in a game, a good team will gladly feed the ball to the "Star." Balancing the offense keeps all team members feeling like they really contribute, and it keeps the big man involved in team play.

While the "Superstar" may be drawing all of the publicity and attention, the rest of the team deserves recognition also. If the coach is quick to point this out, both publicly and at practice, the "Star" player cannot help but be influenced. He will realize that good passes enable him to score his points. Team defense and rebounding enable the team to win games. The "Superstar" may actually find that he is a lucky young man to be part of such a fine team. This, of course, is the goal in developing the great player.

Too often, points seem to be the measure of a superstar player. The coach should also encourage and comment on the rebounding, defense, and team play of his "Star." For a great high school player to become a good college performer, constant improvement in all areas is needed. The coach can help the "Star" correct any weaknesses in his game. There is always something that a player needs to work on. As the old saying goes, "If you do not improve, you deteriorate."

The coach should supply challenges for the "Star" to accept. It could be developing some advanced post moves, more strength, quickness, or maybe ball handling ability. By encouraging him to work on his weaknesses, the coach prevents the "Superstar" from becoming complacent. When there is always a challenge to be met, the big man will not rest on his laurels.

THE GLORY OF IT ALL

Earlier in the chapter I mentioned some of the wild thoughts that filled my head during Jesuit High School's great basketball season. It was fun winning game after game, reading the press clippings on our team, and being interviewed by television and radio sports announcers. The college recruiters came by or called daily to ask about our star, Mark Wehrle. We even had a second excellent college prospect in Larry Phayer, who eventually went on to play at the University of San Francisco. It was a banner year all right, but soon came the next year. No more Wehrle and no more Phayer, so the glory days ended as quickly as they came.

Even though the next season's Jesuit team won a league co-championship, the letdown for me was unbelievable. The newspapers, television, and radio people were no longer present at every game. The college coaches who were so friendly and took me to dinner occasionally, no longer came by the office or called.

The booster's club, parents, and even the administration questioned my coaching abilities. *Me*, the guy who one year earlier had been praised by everyone for doing such a great job! Reality set in. I finally came down to earth and saw what coaching was all about.

My situation is probably unique to most coaches, because I had a big winner my first year out. The point I want to make is that it could happen to anyone. A coach who struggles for years might be able to handle the personal side of winning much better than a first year man. He has experienced what it is like to be down while the opponents gain all the recognition. But it does not matter if a coach is in his first year or twenty-fifth year; he should try to prepare for the attention that comes with "Superstars" and winning.

Be the same gentleman in victory or defeat, winning seasons or losing ones. Be prepared for the demands on your time and personal life that go with coaching a "Superstar." Remember that next season you may be just another coach, like all the rest of us.

Dealing with the glory that goes to a star player is another serious aspect of coaching. The best method is to set a good example. If the coach does not get overly excited by the attention of outsiders, the "Superstar" will usually take the same approach. Placing minimal value on scoring records, point averages, and newspaper articles also helps players to keep the game in perspective.

Leaving a star player in the contest long after the final outcome has been decided is a sure way to lose friends and influence players improperly. To build up scores helps no one. It embarrasses the opponents, who will probably get even the next season anyway; it places your coaching values on points rather than on winning; and it limits your bench players' game time.

Some parents may argue that high scoring averages and scoring records are the only way their "Star" son will get recognition from the colleges. This is certainly false, because a good player will be noticed by the colleges, if indeed he is good enough.

Teach teamwork; develop teamwork; practice teamwork. This includes the coach as well as the "Superstar" and his teammates.

DEALING WITH RECRUITERS

Any decent high school basketball player over the height of 6′7″ will receive questionnaires and letters from colleges across the country. Recruiting services send lists to the colleges of all young men who may be potential college prospects. A follow-up information sheet is then sent by the college to all players on the list. Receiving a form letter from a college is not an offer of a basketball scholarship. It is merely the college coach's way of updating his files on prospects.

More than once I have heard a high school coach proclaim that a major college wants his 6′7″, gangly post man. Having seen the kid play a few times, I know from experience that State University could not use him for a manager, let alone a college player. But the kid's coach continues to boast of his star until March rolls around and State University has not been by. Suddenly, the player is faced with the reality that no one is going to give him a scholarship. His pride is hurt and he has trouble facing his friends. The young man may decide to go to State University on his own, to save face, or to prove a point. Maybe he just gives up basketball out of disgust.

All of the hurt and pain could have been avoided if the player's coach had done his job correctly. By not researching and counselling the young man properly, he has failed as a coach.

When a high school coach senses he may have a future college player, especially a "Superstar Post Man," he should make plans immediately to deal with recruiting. A meeting with the player and his parents is suggested. At this time, the coach can state his feelings concerning the potential of the player and gain some insight into the parents and player's viewpoint.

The coach who is inexperienced in judging college potential can ask for the opinions of other coaches. College coaches will give the best evaluations because they know what is needed at their level of play. Experienced high school coaches may also add some insight. The more research and opinions that can be gathered, the better chance a coach has of advising his "Superstar" properly.

It is important that the player be directed to a college that can use his talents. A challenge is important, but too much of a jump in competition can be damaging. The star player must realize that he can play college ball, but the key is picking a school that can use him. Basketball is an enjoyable game. It can be just as much fun playing for a small college as it is for a major university. The key is to find a school in which the player will have a reasonable chance to succeed.

When considering a college, the coach should attempt to get his player to answer the following questions:

1. What do you want to study in college besides basketball?
   Not everyone can make basketball their living. Youngsters sometimes forget that they will need a profession after their playing days have ended.
2. In what area do you want to go to college?
   Leaving home can be a trying experience for many young players. The adjustment may be too much for the young man, and his playing and grades will suffer. For others, a change in climate can open a new door to life. Will the player handle being away from home? This should be seriously considered.
3. What size of a college do you want to attend?
   The 30,000 student population of a State University may be hard for the small town country boy to handle. Would a small, private school be better?
4. Can you play with the competition of the college?
   The young man must realize he may end up on the bench or cut from the program if he does not fit in. He must be willing to face the competition and work extra hard to improve.

Having established the answers to the previous questions will help the coach to screen recruiters and recruiting letters. It will also help the college coaches, because the high school coach will be able to fill them in on the situation. Some colleges will be ruled out of the running; thus freeing the "Superstar," his team, and his coach from unneeded pressure.

Depending on the abilities of a player, the coach will need to establish recruiting rules for the outsiders. Some suggestions for the "Superstar caliber of prospect" are listed below.

1. All contacts should originate with the player's coach.
   The coach will know what the player's parents want and what is best for the young man. The recruiters can be discouraged if their school is not in the running, thus saving the player from an unwanted conversation.
2. The player's home should not be contacted during the season.
   A coach must keep his star player's mind on the upcoming games.

Constant phone calls at his home will make concentrating on the present quite difficult.

3. No recruiters will be allowed to visit practice sessions.
   Strangers present at practice make it hard on the "Star" and his teammates. They do not need distractions during their workouts. Besides, the recruiters can observe the player during a game if they want to evaluate properly.
4. Post game locker room visits should be kept to a minimum.
   The coach should have the final say on this touchy subject. Depending on the player's post game mental state, recruiters can be turned away or allowed to say "hello." Long recruiting pitches are forbidden, as this can be done after the season. A quick "Hello" and "Nice game" are enough on a game night. Most colleges are governed by rules which limit personal contacts, so this should not be a real problem.
5. No campus visits during the season.
   Again, the high school coach must be concerned about the present season. Allowing his star to fly around the country will only hurt the player and the team. There will be plenty of time for campus visits after the season finishes.

Once basketball season ends, the problems may just be starting. The choice of a college for the future education of a star player can be very tough. But if the player has followed the coach's suggestions and answered the questions listed earlier in the chapter, he will be able to narrow the number of choices down. A small figure like five or less is a good starting point for selecting finalists. All schools can be informed of the remaining choices. This will eliminate those not in contention from bothering the player and his family any further. The "Superstar" will then be able to concentrate on the finalists.

Visiting the campus of any potential choice is a must. The player should see where he will be spending the next four or five years. Hearing about how wonderful a campus is and seeing it for oneself may bring two entirely different pictures. Even when the college cannot pay for the visiting privileges, a player should find a way to visit the campus before committing himself. Spending a few dollars out of his own pocket is a lot cheaper than making a blind mistake.

The campus visit serves the future student-athlete in many ways.

1. He can see the campus and surrounding community.
2. He can look at the basketball facilities and field house.
3. He can check the dorms or living complexes.
4. He can meet the head coach and the basketball staff.
5. He can meet some of the players and ask their opinions.
6. He can visit professors in his desired field of study.

All of these give the student-athlete a big insight into his future at a college. Before the player makes his final selection, his coach can help by offering the following three questions.

1. Does the coach and his philosophy suit you?
   Why go to a school that plays patterned basketball if the "Superstar" wants to fastbreak? The player should be able to feel at ease with his new coach and system.
2. Does the college have room for a player like you?
   If the team already has a 6′10″ Superstar center who is only a freshman, where will that leave the recruit? Does he fit into their plans, or will he be just another body? A player needs to know where he stands in the future plans.
3. Are you satisfied with the financial picture?
   Some schools recruit players on "make it" systems. Should the player make the team, he would get a scholarship. This can make the financial picture quite shaky for a young man's parents. Find out how much it will cost you to go to college, including the scholarship package.

There is no guarantee that a player will be satisfied with his final selection, even when the best of plans is followed. However, if the coach can help his "Star" to look at the total picture, chances of success are much better.

So, how about you? Are you getting everything you can out of the post position? Look at your total picture and lay out some plans for developing your big men. Your chances of success will also be much better. PUT PRESSURE ON THE HOOP, and the pressure will be on the opponents.

INDEX